50 PEOPLE WHO F***ED UP SOUTH AFRICA

THE LOST DECADE

Alexander Parker
& Tim Richman
with cartoons from the archive of

ZAPIRO

50 PEOPLE WHO F***ED UP SOUTH AFRICA
THE LOST DECADE

Alexander Parker
& Tim Richman
with cartoons from the archive of
ZAPIRO

Published in South Africa by Mercury
an imprint of Burnet Media
info@burnetmedia.co.za
www.burnetmedia.co.za

First published in 2020
1 3 5 7 9 10 8 6 4 2

"Victoria Geoghegan" and "The Guptas" adapted from
50 People Who Stuffed Up The World, published in 2016

The cartoons and caricatures herein are replications or adaptations of works
by Zapiro that have appeared in a variety of publications over the years.
They are all products of the specific circumstances of the time,
though some have been altered for this publication.

ISBN: 9781990956096

Typeset in Minion Pro 11 pt on 14.5

Distributed by Jacana Media www.jacana.co.za
Printed by ABC Press www.abcpress.co.za

To our families at the end of a helluva year.

ABOUT THE CONTRIBUTORS

Alexander Parker, **Tim Richman** and **Zapiro** are the team behind the previous three bestselling *50 People* titles: *50 People Who Stuffed Up South Africa* (2010), *50 Flippen Brilliant South Africans* (2012) and *50 People Who Stuffed Up The World* (2016).

Parker and Richman have authored a number of books between them. Zapiro is South Africa's premier cartoonist. His latest annual anthology is *Do The Macorona* (2020).

Contents

Introduction

HAROLD WILSON'S OBSERVATION that a week is a long time in politics is borne out time and again. Wilson, a British Prime Minister in the 1960s, would have been surveying the Westminster landscape. For our purposes, however, perhaps Lenin's take is a little closer to the bone: "There are decades where nothing happens, and there are weeks where decades happen."

In South Africa, you can have three finance ministers over a long weekend and corruption trials that last 20 years. It is fast and slow. It is impossible to keep up with and yet exasperatingly unchanged. It can be an exhausting place to live.

In many ways, therefore, a decade in the politics and cultural life of a nation is an arbitrary stretch of time. Why ten years and not 12, or eight? In the case of this unacademic work, we choose the "lost decade" because November 2020 happens to mark the tenth anniversary of the publication of *50 People Who Stuffed Up South Africa*, and because President Ramaphosa spoke overtly of "nine lost years" of state capture under Jacob Zuma, which we are happy to parlay into a neat decade here. Conveniently, our timeline is bookended by the hope and success of the 2010 Soccer World Cup and the devastation of the pandemic year, 2020.

Thus constrained, it's necessary to explain the purpose of this book. The 50 people who reside here are responsible for neither the condition of this country in 2010, nor the fundamental social and cultural currents that have made so much of what they've done possible. Indeed, that is an offensive notion. Those bad bastards are in the other book, which quite rightly begins with Jan van Riebeeck's arrival at the Cape of Good Hope and – rather elegantly, we think – waltzes through the eras of the VOC, of Dutch, trekker, British and Zulu expansionism, imperialism and colonialism, through to the founding of this nation as we know it now, the early Afrikaner nationalists and the apartheid regime that ruled, lest we forget, from 1948 until 1994. It also includes some of the early post-democratic stuffer-uppers.

South Africa has been forged for centuries in the relentless fire of governments that considered black people sub-human. Its inequalities, contradictions and structural imbalances have been baked-in under a hot sun for 350 years. Expecting wholesale structural change in a quarter of a century is not a little like wondering why the Tankwa Karoo isn't a verdant jungle after a good rainy season. It is important to remember this when those of us so frustrated by the unmet potential of what could be wish for everyone to "just move on".

This is not to deny that some truly terrible people exist within these pages, but it is to say that things might have been different for many of them had they not inherited a country that has been so roundly stuffed up. There are, we would estimate, not a few who might have gone on to greatness in other circumstances, though we would prefer they go on to jail right now.

In many ways, South Africa is undergoing a reckoning in which it seems reasonable to ask whether this was all such a good idea. This country was invented in 1910 by Jan Smuts and Louis Botha – two polymaths that fate would throw together, and who managed, through sheer force of personality, to persuade an unsure Britain and an unwilling post-South African War Afrikaner populace that this merger of erstwhile Boer republics and British colonies was a decent plan. Such was their hubris that nobody considered asking the black folk who would make up the majority in this new country.

The ANC was founded in 1912, but black resistance to white domination here is as old as the hills, and has been expressed variously from the banks of the Liesbeek to the great plain at Isandlwana, at Ncome/Blood River, and for decades on the eastern fringes of British encroachment in the lands of the Xhosa people.

And so, then, here we are, in this place at this time. Much of what ails South Africa marches in step with international trends. Inequality is increasingly heightened. The urban/rural divide is only going to widen. The bankers and the lawyers and the corporations are getting stupid-rich. Crony capitalism is alive and well, and its policemen are rotten. Extreme opinions compounded in online bubbles are the order of the day. Black people are generally still poor. White people are generally better off.

The discourse is legitimately angrier and more impatient, and for enlightenment on these topics we humbly direct you to read Francis Fukuyama's *Identity* and Oliver Bullough's *Moneyland*. We are in the midst of extraordinary global change, and explanations for this lie elsewhere.

But there is a distressingly tumultuous South African amplification of all this fraught political upheaval. The 50 people in this book may not have been responsible for the state of the country in 2010, let alone in 1994, but they're still here for good reason. As in the original book, many of them are representatives of the particular crime they have committed, often one of very many in a contested space, and there are countless more who might have appeared here. Narrowing down the list was impossibly tricky, and you may well be disappointed by the absence of one of your pet peeves.

Either way, President Ramaphosa pretty much nailed it when he described the waste of the Zuma Years, his presence at the man's right hand through so much of it notwithstanding. In the dystopian, compassion-free wasteland that is social media, two things can never be true at once; in reality, as we try to make clear, that is so often the key to understanding. South Africa was saved by the ANC and South Africa is being destroyed by the ANC. Our economic salvation lies in the free enterprise of South Africans and yet too many businesses continue to behave appallingly. Taxpayers are justifiably livid at seeing their hard-earned contributions stolen, yet they are often loath to acknowledge their extraordinary good luck – what some might call their privilege – to be in a position to pay meaningful amounts of tax. Intergenerational wealth is just fine, but intergenerational poverty is not.

What's certain is that the people in this book have done great damage to a country that was already struggling. Their greatest collective crime is the squandering of hope and potential. This is an indignant book, as befits the times, because moving towards a better future is the foundation of civilisation and functional society. The lost decade was a decade of disappointment and disillusionment, to be sure, but we do discern light on the horizon.

It is too glib to simply claim the ongoing resilience of the average South African as a sturdiness unique to our people. It is infuriating, patronising and lazy – a classic trope of South African exceptionalism. People survive as best they can often in terrible circumstances, and they die too young.

It is the duty of the rest of us to make things better.

We are – just about – still a going concern. We are still a great-country-in-waiting. We are a ragtag assortment of disparate peoples from wildly diverse and varying backgrounds. It is our greatest strength and our greatest challenge. Most of us are good and decent. But, politics being what it is, the real bad buggers have found their way into power. South Africa can survive but things need to change – and while we can all agree that these 50 bastards are the first who need to go, that will be only the start. Let us understand what they've done. Let us call them out and call them names, where we must, because catharsis is necessary after times of darkness and abuse.

Afterwards, the rest is up to us.

Shaun Abrahams

b. March 1977

*National Director of Public Prosecutions (2015-2018); one
in a long line of politically compromised public prosecutors;
sheep in a wolf's job; wide-eyed, bushy-browed hand
of the state capturers*

*Dishonourable mentions: the Guptas, Nomgcobo Jiba,
Lawrence Mrwebi, Berning Ntlemeza, Jacob Zuma*

THE OLD-FASHIONED WAY OF STAGING a coup goes like this.

Arrest whichever president-for-life scumbag is currently residing
in the big house.
Seize control of the broadcasters.
Seize control of the airport and the borders.

Simple, really, in a time before social media. Then all you had to do was appear on Radio Failed State to assure the masses that this was a democratic revolution and elections could be expected sometime before the next ice age.

State capture is different in that there are fewer guns involved. It's a bloodless route to the same place, and it can be done, as South Africans have come to realise over the course of the last decade, even in a democracy with a complex economy such as ours. This way, instead of over-running the broadcaster with AK-wielding soldiers, it's more effective to just buy the guy who's running it. *(See Hlaudi Motsoeneng.)* There are, however, rather a few more institutions that need to be acquired for maximum effect. In a functioning democracy designed as carefully as South Africa's, the prospective capturers must ensure they have positioned all the right people in all the right places to be able to optimise their looting. It is a painstaking and costly process. Make one mistaken appointment in the constellation of corruption – Advocate Thuli Madonsela as Public Protector, for example – and it can set back the programme dramatically.

The junta of Jacob Zuma and his managers, the Guptas, didn't just take over the state broadcaster; they created their own broadcaster, along with a newspaper, and made friends with an entire media house. *(See The Guptas and Iqbal Survé.)* To pay the bills, it was important to get going on the looting early, and they made easy inroads into state-operated entities such as Eskom and SAA. *(See Brian Molefe and Dudu Myeni.)* Then, having stolen the money, it was obviously critical to avoid tax liabilities on the loot – so the revenue service was another expensive and necessary acquisition. *(See Tom Moyane.)* The demoralised and overwhelmed police force was relatively easy to handle, but a real challenge came with the prosecutors.

Prosecutors who did their job would have scuppered the state capture project, which could only go ahead if the law wasn't applied to the thieves. Thus, owning the National Prosecuting Authority (NPA) was a strategic priority. Those who did could look down their noses and imperiously say that they understood the division of powers in a democratic country, and that any complaints of corruption should be left to "the relevant authorities" – all along knowing that the relevant authorities were wholly owned entities of State Capture Pty Ltd.

The judiciary was far more difficult to own or influence *(see John Hlophe)*, but was perhaps not necessary. As much as Zuma may have understood that his actions with the NPA would eventually go through the commission-of-inquiry legal-challenge endless-appeals merry-go-round, there was an instinctive realisation that using state companies and departments to shovel enormous truckloads of swag into the Guptas' Dubai bank accounts is way faster than a legal process in South Africa.

And so we start proceedings here, in our potted review of the disastrous 2010s, with the battle for ownership of the NPA.

Readers may not remember much about Judge Christopher Nicholson, a once highly regarded jurist who had worked in small ways to undo some of apartheid's more abhorrent laws, and in smaller ways to undo its manifestations – he founded Natal's first non-racial cricket club, for example. But in the post-democratic era he dealt the country a blow that has wrought unfathomable damage. It was South Africa's misfortune that he was the man in the robes who dismissed Jacob Zuma's corruption charges in 2008 on procedural grounds. In his absolutely incendiary judgment, the consequences of which we are still reeling from today, he held that the prosecutors had experienced "baleful political influence".

Nicholson's judgment was eventually thrown out – ripped apart, in fact, by the Supreme Court of Appeal – but the damage had been done. Mbeki was out. Zuma was in. As columnist William Saunderson-Meyer observed, "Zuma and his populist cabal had parlayed the Nicholson ruling into a toxic presidency that would run for nine miserable years before ending in national ignominy and ruin." Quite so.

In the possibly uneducated view of these authors, it seems that both Nicholson and the Supreme Court were looking at the same quandary from different sides. They were both right in a way, but they were both also disastrously wrong. As Saunderson-Meyer wrote, "Does anyone seriously doubt that Mbeki – be it overtly or with a nudge and a wink

– influenced successive NPA heads to either prosecute or withhold prosecution, according to what best benefited him and the ANC?"

Either way, with Mbeki unceremoniously booted out, Zuma moonwalked with characteristic style from the High Court to Tuynhuis, and he was sworn in as President of South Africa in May 2009. Let us be perfectly clear: more evil thugs have inhabited those storied walls; nevertheless, this was the last damn thing South Africa needed, and after half a year's settling in the stage was set for the decade to come.

To be sure, then, Zuma's presidency started in an environment in which politics had for years very clearly shaped events at the NPA. Funny, for example, that when head prosecutor Vusi Pikoli wanted to execute a warrant of arrest against President Mbeki's catastrophically hopeless National Police Commissioner Jackie Selebi, it should suddenly be deemed that he had suffered an irretrievable breakdown of his relationship with the Minister of Justice, Brigitte Mabandla, and find himself out on his ear. So we shouldn't make the mistake of thinking that Zuma invented the idea of meddling with the NPA. The thing with Zuma was the shamelessness.

In the decade that concerns this book, the NPA has had four full-time national directors and three acting national directors to connect them. After a wrangle to get rid of Pikoli, there followed Zuma's appointment in 2009 of Menzi Simelane, who somehow staggered through three years before a court found his appointment to be invalid. It was clear to anyone who'd ever read a book that Simelane was a poor choice, but what followed really blew the mind. Next, Mxolisi Nxasana filled the role. This turned out to be a regrettable choice for Zuma, because in 2014 Nxasana dared to do his job and reinstate criminal charges against former crime intelligence boss Richard Mdluli. The Mdluli saga was one of those long-running ANC factional-fighting sub-plots that would eventually see the guy being sentenced to jail in 2020, all of 22 years after the fact. Back in 2014, though, he was Zuma's man, and reinstating criminal charges against him just wasn't on, so, in the way of any good spymaster, Zuma used the dirt he had on Nxasana to move him along. In this instance, he had undisclosed convictions for assault and was once acquitted, on the basis of self-defence, of murder. Not exactly NPA-leading material. Nxasana was paid R17 million to bugger off without too much hassle, and in June 2015, Zuma, to the surprise of even those most cynical about the perpetually politicised nature of the NPA, appointed one Shaun Abrahams to head the NPA.

Well, no mistakes this time.

Abrahams was a mid-level prosecutor with 17 years' experience. He was 39, he had the authority of a wet rag, and he was set to be the head clown of Zuma's tragic little circus.

Shaun the Sheep, as he came to be known, was complicit not only in the worst of state capture, but also in the gutting of the NPA, which shed committed and talented lawyers as they watched the institution collapse around them. The fact that there is only now, as we type these words in late 2020, any sign of a recovery at the NPA illustrates the severity of the harm that was done.

As head of the country's ultimate prosecuting authority, Abrahams was mandated to work closely with Berning Ntlemeza, head of the country's ultimate criminal investigation authority, the Hawks. Whereas Abrahams had flown under the radar, Ntlemeza was a walking controversy, closely connected to Mdluli, among others, and described by the Pretoria High Court as "biased and dishonest" and lacking "integrity and honour".

Together, they stood by and watched as the Guptas and the Zumas built a pathway paved with stolen South African gold, all the way to Dubai. This much was laid out in clearly actionable black-and-white glory as detailed analyses of the Gupta Leaks emails, from May 2017 onwards,

> "Prosecutors who stood for justice and who prosecuted without 'fear or favour' were systematically worked out and replaced by pliable prosecutors who acted towards political objectives and not in the interests of justice."
>
> *Former KZN Hawks head Johan Booysen, Zondo commission affidavit*

the work of a team of investigative journalists literally connecting the dots for any willing prosecutors.

Yet Abrahams and co did nothing as the state capturers destroyed SAA, ruined Transnet and utterly, completely trashed Eskom. And, as they say in the Verimark ads, that's not all! The standing aside was one thing, but charging a sitting finance minister with fraud was a new level even for the NPA...

In 2015, after the Nenegate debacle, South Africa found itself in the wholly embarrassing situation of having had three ministers of finance in five days. *(See Des van Rooyen.)* For Zuma, the ANC state capture crew and its running dogs, the EFF, the real nub of the problem was that the third one was Pravin Gordhan. This was not part of the plan. In his previous stint as finance minister, Gordhan had shown a disappointing reluctance to hand the keys to the treasury to the Gupta/Gucci mafia, and it wouldn't do to have him back there for long. Zuma must have been running short of ideas – until he realised he had a pet sheep at the NPA.

And that's how Shaun Abrahams ended up presiding over a prosecuting authority that charged a sitting finance minister with fraud in October 2016, just days before he was due to give his mid-term budget statement. And it was Abrahams who strode on as half a trillion rand of value was wiped off South African companies and the rand fell to historic lows against other currencies. It was Abrahams who bleated so terribly unconvincingly that he was operating absolutely independently and without any political interference whatsoever, as South Africa pitched inevitably toward the realm of junk status. It was Abrahams who put his signature on a charge sheet of politically motivated fantasy that told the outside world that this is not a serious country any more, so get your money out while you can.

And they did.

Elsewhere, Abrahams conspired with advocate Nomgcobo Jiba and others to implicate head of the Hawks in KwaZulu-Natal, Johan Booysen, along with his men, in tales of murder and police brutality in and around Durban. Their involvement was one element of the notorious

Cato Manor disinformation campaign, another exhausting saga that dragged out over much of the decade, initially in the *Sunday Times* and ultimately in the courts. Booysen had made the mistake of trying to do his job in Zuma family territory, but he was eventually vindicated in 2019 by the withdrawal of charges against him by Abrahams's successor Shamila Batohi.

By this stage, Abrahams had followed the lead of so many NPA heads before him: booted out of the job by a court. His appointment was found to be invalid due to the unconstitutional manner in which his predecessor had been winkled from the job, and in August 2018 he was despatched to pastures new. Jiba and fellow NPA prosecutor Lawrence Mrwebi, both steeped in disgrace and found to be unfit for the positions, followed suit.

For a sense of what might have motivated these highly qualified, lowly moralised individuals, consider that Jiba, who had been acting NDPP in 2012, was the wife of a man who had had his criminal record expunged, in 2010, by none other than Jacob Zuma. Quite what Zuma had on Shaun Abrahams, we don't know – but it must have been a whopper.

Batohi is on record as describing the rot that Abrahams had left as "much worse than I expected". We doubt she was expecting a picnic.

It's safe to say that Batohi is no Shaun the Sheep. But will she ever clean up the mess he left behind?

Adam Catzavelos

b. 28 December 1978

*Viral racist; not representative of the average
South African; just what we don't need*

WELL, THERE IT IS. Some Joburg non-entity with his Bedfordview accent telling us how much he loves the beach he's on because there's "not a k****r in sight", and then recording it at the ideal length for social media distribution. Like South Africa needs these grotesque distractions.

In August 2018, Adam Catzavelos filmed himself saying these words while on holiday in Greece:

"Let me give you a weather forecast here. Blue skies, beautiful day, amazing sea, and not one k***** in sight, fucken heaven on earth. You cannot beat this. You cannot beat this."

Then he pressed send.

The suppurating racism aside, what a very weird way to live. Something must be broken inside a person if he flies halfway around the world, walks onto a pristine beach and chooses to focus not on it being very lovely, not on it being very beautiful, but hey, look, there are no black people here!

Living with this level of racism must be so onerous. The cognitive cartwheels required to pile just about every damn thing, including a Greek beach, onto this particular hobby horse must be like some kind of debilitating mental illness.

But Adam Catzavelos isn't ill. He's just an intergalactic loser, the kind of moron who creates a click-fest spectacle on *TimesLive* and hands political race-baiters like Mbuyiseni Ndlozi and his friends at the EFF some more 95-unleaded for the flames.

Catzavelos would appear to have grown up in the security of a family business. He would appear to have never really struggled. And then he does this god-awful thing to his black compatriots, the overwhelming majority of whom struggle every day.

The Institute of Race Relations runs regular surveys that consistently show most South Africans to be reasonable and decent people. Most of us believe race relations have improved since 1994. Most of us want to live and let live. People like Adam Catzavelos, Vicki Momberg and Penny Sparrow, and their whites-hating equivalents, really do represent a sliver of society today. This lot, however, feel compelled to express to the world their prejudices, where they are amplified online and in the media by those who thrive on race-based controversy. In doing what they do, they directly affect our political discourse.

These days, the law rightly catches up with people like Catzavelos. In February 2020 he pleaded guilty to crimen injuria, and received a suspended sentence and R50,000 fine, on top of an earlier settlement agreement that saw him fined R150,000 and doing community service in Orlando, Soweto. Momberg, the notorious racist estate agent, got two years in the banger.

Perhaps, then, we should leave the final word to Nic Catzavelos, Adam's brother. In announcing that Adam's shares in the family business had been transferred to its staff, he said, "He made a video that is obscenely racist, which speaks for itself. There is no way the video could be taken out of context. You cannot wrap this up in cotton wool." And of the fury directed at the Catzavelos family and their business, he said, "Who wouldn't be angry? It's despicable, and given our country's history, it's completely understandable."

South Africa needs more Nic Catzaveloses and fewer Adam Catzaveloses. Still, all these years later, they are a poison in our society.

Adri Senekal de Wet

*Executive editor of Business Report; the polar opposite
of journalistic integrity; face of the critical media battle
between good and evil*

THESE DAYS IT DOESN'T TAKE TOO MANY CONVERSATIONS in the
Johannesburg northern suburbs or Cape Town southern suburbs to
work out that many South Africans who have the means are "looking for
opportunities overseas". Over the past few years the topic of emigration
has drifted from taboo to *de rigueur*, taking the dinner-party top spot
held by "why I bant/don't bant" earlier in the decade. In the first quarter
of 2019, the FNB Estate Agents Survey reported that 14.2% of all its
property sales were the result of families – and taxpayers – leaving the
country. In 2020, emigration specialists Henley & Partners reported a
near 50% increase in South Africans looking to move abroad in the first
half of the year. Numbers to give the bean counters at SARS more than
a few palpitations.

Many of those who have not yet emigrated but will do so in the coming years have "emotionally emigrated". They've stopped reading the news that doesn't immediately affect them; stopped worrying about the plight of the poor and the state of the country's finances. When something is broken beyond repair, you avert your gaze and look elsewhere.

But there are those among us made of sterner stuff. Those who continue to have hope. Those who continue to read the news…

Journalists are a strange breed. It's a calling, no doubt. The money is terrible; the Gucci-clad, AMG-driving ordure running the country will despise you; and the trolls, bots, racists, liars and conspiracy theorists will come for you in their digital droves. If you're a woman, you can expect some added misogyny from the EFF.

The fact that we can write a book such as this one is down to the best of this breed.

In the grander scheme, this book is hardly important, but the state of our democracy is, and the facts in this book are now free for dissemination for two reasons. First, because of the bravery of the old, long-dead liberation ANC that chucked media censorship in the bin three decades ago (worth remembering). And, second, because of the work of some relentlessly brave and unflaggingly dogged journalists. They are too many to mention, but where would we be without these modern heroes?

Adriaan Basson
Terry Bell
Jessica Bezuidenhout
Branko Brkic
Stefaans Brümmer
Susan Comrie
Vincent Cruywagen
Pieter Du Toit
Lionel Faull
Stephen Grootes
Ferial Haffajee
Ed Herbst

Andisiwe Makinana
Mondli Makhanya
Justice Malala
Sikonathi Mantshantsha
Karyn Maughan
Craig McKune
Pieter-Louis Myburgh
Bronwyn Nortje
Khadija Patel
Carol Paton
Richard Poplak
Micah Reddy
Sam Sole
Tabelo Timse
Marianne Thamm
Mandy Wiener
Dewald van Rensburg
Pauli Van Wyk
Songezo Zibi

Then, especially in the context of "the lost decade" of the Zuma Years, there is the granddaddy of reportage: Jacques Pauw, investigative journalist and author of *The President's Keepers*, a book that sold more than 200,000 copies and single-handedly shifted our political dial.

Most of those listed above worked on the game-changing Gupta Leaks. Some are brave analysts who say the things in public forums that need to be said. Together, they represent a broad ideological spectrum without extremities, which is as it should be. But they are hardly flawless. Between them, they have courted controversy, been accused of naivety *and* cynicism, faced justified criticism, held opinions that didn't stand the test of time, misjudged their marks and had to issue corrections, all while making questionable fashion decisions. Such is the path to tread of the committed journalist, but ultimately they are the truth tellers whose work has directly and positively influenced the unfolding of our recent history.

At the other end of the scale, however, the media has played its part in our parlous state as well.

In his recent book *So, For The Record*, media veteran Anton Harber describes the Guptas' New Age Media, Iqbal Survé's Sekunjalo Independent Media and the SABC as "direct examples of the growing phenomenon of media capture, where the media lost their autonomy and their ability to act with a will of their own, and their primary function of informing the public became secondary to servicing vested interests". This is a polite way of saying that these three institutions – one dead, one dying, one now possibly resurrected – have been stuffed to hell and back by the megalomaniacs who run them. We'll get to the key actors in all three in the pages to come.

Elsewhere, the major media houses have battled to adapt in a decade in which every hand clutching a smartphone has become its own publisher, often on multiple platforms. Mass-readership news websites here have fallen, as they have around the world, for the Google Ads-driven spiral of doom, chasing clicks for cash. Hence underpaid junior editors read something on their Twitter, believe it to be "news", rehash it as "Mzansi reacts to [insert Twitter outrage *du jour*]", tweet it out and watch the merry-go-round. If that fails, give Julius Malema some more publicity.

Kudos, then, to the likes of *Daily Maverick* for pioneering a subscription model that's generating reader trust, global acclaim and actual revenue, and even to *News24* for daring to partially go behind a paywall in 2020.

Our media houses have faced a real battle during the state capture years – from the online tech onslaught, from the state capturers and, in some ways most disappointingly, from journalists who have fallen prey to the disinformation game and becomes its disseminators.

Some of the most prominent cock-ups have occurred at the *Sunday Times* which, because of its power and reach, found itself particularly vulnerable to the efforts of ANC factions to discredit each other. Top reporters should be savvy enough to avoid the traps, however, and the *Sunday Times* has published some really damaging drivel, notably about the SARS "rogue unit" (air cover designed to protect the looters at SARS), the "Cato Manor death squad" (nonsense designed to protect Zuma and friends from difficult SAPS investigations) and, weirdly, a front-page splash about the sea around Cape Town being sold to China (just nonsense). All hugely damaging, and there are journalists whose good names will never recover from this.

But by far the worst thing to come out of media in the past decade is the phenomenon known as Adri Senekal de Wet. Journalists are, as we've seen, as flawed as everyone else. They can be corrupt and they can be naive. Altogether too many are activists masquerading as analysts. They quite naturally bring their own anger and guilt and bias and prejudice to their work. They're human. Adri Senekal de Wet, however, is like nothing our world of journalism has seen before.

De Wet was once Sekunjalo Investment Holdings' "stakeholder relations executive". That is, she was Iqbal Survé's spin doctor, which made her an obvious choice to take over as "executive editor" of *Business Report*, the business and finance daily distributed with Independent titles, including *The Star*, *Cape Times*, *The Mercury* and *Pretoria News*.

Business Report used to matter. It may have played second fiddle to *Business Day*, but its reach and sheer circulation made it an important publication for those watching the traditional economy and the political economy. While continuing to retain good reporters who were, privately, aghast and horrified at what was going on around them, De Wet set about to be chief arse-kisser of her boss, his companies and their various creative adventures in corporate finance.

Anybody who's spent any time in a real newsroom will tell you that at the absolute best there is little respect for the paper's owners. It's why good newspapers work, and the business owners and managers generally steer clear of the newsroom as you would a nest of cobras. Independent Media no longer produces good newspapers. Under Survé, it has come to resemble a cult. Those who could see it for what it is were fired or ran for the hills. Those who fell for it, fell hard – like De Wet and fellow Independent editors Gasant Abarder and Aneez Salie.

De Wet refers in bizarre glowing terms to her leader as "Doc", and appears to have pitched for her *Business Report* position with a 3,500-

word "open letter" she wrote to him, supposedly out of the blue, in 2016.

"My only link with you today is that I am one of your 5,000 FB friends," she wrote, in case anyone might dare to think this was a paid-for PR spiel. "I think if FB did not have a 5,000 limit you would have a million friends by now?"

Then: "Dr Survé, when I read the latest articles about you, I have to ask myself, why aren't you reacting? This is ridiculous! How can ANYBODY question YOU?"

The letter goes on and on – you can almost smell the brown-nosing through the screen; she barely comes up for air – but that, in a nutshell, appears to be the editorial approach she has subsequently adopted for *Business Report*. (If it was a job application, she nailed it!)

De Wet sealed her fate as the anti-journalist with an incoherent attack on veteran investigative reporter Sam Sole after he exposed Survé's laughable attempt to extract billions out of investors with the public offering of his hollow entity Sagarmatha Technologies. Despite De Wet's hare-brained attempts to spin the offering as an "African unicorn" and

---

Dear Adri Senekal de Wet,

I do realise that, as editor of *Business Report*, one of Independent's stable of publications, you have to sing for your supper and that is why you so often leap with alacrity to the defence of your boss, Dr Iqbal Survé.

I also realise that – given the one-sided way you and your publications have covered (and continue to cover) the issue of government pensioners' money being channelled to Survé and his companies in circumstances best described as questionable – you would not recognise real journalism if it bit you in the bum…

You, Adri, will end up on the wrong side of history. You may not realise this, but karma is not a brand of margarine.

Brendan Seery, 2019

> "South Africa, we have a problem. There is a move afoot in the country that is potentially far more dangerous than the Guptas' attempted takeover of the country, and that is media manipulation and unethical reporting designed to prevent broader economic participation."
>
> *Independent Media editorial, apparently written by Adri Senekal de Wet as she battled the irony gods, April 2018*

her boss as the next Jeff Bezos, Sagarmatha collapsed under the weight of its own internal vacuum.

Unique as she may be, Adri Senekal de Wet represents the dark temptations our journalists face and often can't resist. No doubt she will continue to heap praise onto her boss on the single-ply known as *Business Report*. Follow the incentive, and say a prayer for the real journalists still out there.

Wouldn't it be lovely if the likes of Adri emigrated?

See Jack Dorsey, The Guptas, Hlaudi Motsoeneng, Iqbal Survé.

Bathabile Dlamini

b. 10 September 1962

Minister of Social Development (2010-2018); Minister of Women in the Presidency (2018-2019); Leader of the ANC Women's League (still!); gormless face of government indifference; giver-away of the government game

LUMKA OLIPHANT, SPOKESPERSON FOR BATHABILE DLAMINI, went beyond the usual polite rejoinders to criticism of her principal when she suggested in January 2017 that upbraiding Dlamini for her politics was fine, but that otherwise people shouldn't "talk shit about her".

This was in response to claims that Dlamini, erstwhile social development minister, was drunk on the job once again. She has since claimed to suffer from epilepsy, and that her medication had recently been changed.

Drunk or not, there's enough video evidence of the minister appearing to be "unsteady on her feet", as they say. Either way, Bathabile Dlamini's real crimes are not her alleged drunkenness or even the scale of her corruption. To use her own phrase, given the magnitude of the looting going on around her, her contribution was "smallanyana" stuff. A couple of hundred grand pilfered so she could holiday on the public purse. A million bucks or thereabouts of South African Social Security Agency (Sassa) money blown on her children's security detail. A billion or so of irregular expenditure by the agency itself.

One of the remarkable things about Bathabile Dlamini is that she is a senior member of the ANC who has actually been prosecuted for graft. We can only assume somebody buggered up there – they didn't even lose the docket! – because she was forced to plead guilty to fraud involving R254,000 in 2006. She was sentenced to a R120,000 fine or five years' imprisonment with an additional five-year suspended sentence – this was as part of the Travelgate scandal for the now quaint-sounding crime of using parliamentary vouchers intended for air travel to pay for extras like hotel accommodation and whatnot. Just a cheeky little holiday on us, you see.

Still, small beer. Entry-level stuff for the Zuma era. Nothing to frighten the horses at treasury. She's on our list for something else, then.

As social development minister, Dlamini was supposed to oversee one of the most critical of day-to-day functions of the government. It's not a function that gets too much mileage at middle-class dinner parties and it doesn't keep the economists up all night. But concerned South Africans were extremely worried that when tasked with transferring the job of paying out social grants from Cash Paymaster Services to the state, she appeared to be too busy being unsteady on her feet at the One & Only hotel in Cape Town to bother to get it done.

Some facts are required here. First, we're not going to whinge about taxpayers' money as if taxpayers are the primary victims of the theft of state funds. It is money supplied by taxpayers, but the victims are the poorest of the poor. Dlamini's stays at hotels between June 2009 and August 2011 cost the most vulnerable people in our country three quarters of a million rand.

Oliphant would haughtily claim that this was necessary as "the very nature of the minister's work is working with the poor, who are in very rural areas of the country and which require her to be constantly out of the office together with her staff".

Okay, fair's fair. As much as you might hold Dlamini in disdain for her unsteadiness of foot, she surely deserves reasonable accommodation as she ranges across the land executing her solemn duty. As when she visited the impoverished communities in the remote rural hinterland that is Green Point, Cape Town without suitable accommodation. Teeming as it is with herds of untamed German tourists and hardened gangs of Bantry Bay teenagers armed with fully-automatic gelatos, it explains, we feel, 53 nights (as in fifty-three nights, nearly eight straight weeks) in the Radisson Blu Hotel, 26 nights in the Westin Grand Arabella Quays, and the five nights where she was really forced to slum it with the rurals at the One & Only.

As the minister contemplated her pillow menu, too exhausted to traipse the distance to her ministerial Cape Town accommodation literally several kilometres away, one wonders if her assertion in 2016 that R753 a month was enough for a person to live off created a little dissonance. Or did the unsteady feet ensure such difficult thoughts didn't keep the minister up at night? We will probably never know.

In any case, the quantum of the cash isn't why Dlamini is here. If this book was graded on the simple basis of how much money people stole – or, if you prefer, spent irregularly – Dlamini probably wouldn't have made the top 500. She is here for being a particularly good example of the odd mixture of incompetence, greed and that most egregious of political crimes, indifference.

It's the not-giving-a-damn that sticks in the craw. Imagine being put in a position to do something that will fundamentally improve the lives of 45% of South African households. A position in which the decisions you make can really help 17 million people. Those of us who do ordinary jobs take some solace in the idea that we contribute to society with charitable work and donations, and through our limited economic activity and the taxes we pay. But to literally be the minister of Social Development, the individual whose work it is to pay our poor compatriots the money they need to feed themselves? It's hard, in all honesty, to imagine a greater privilege and a weightier task.

The scale and power of the multiplier effect would weigh on the average Joe; the idea that a small incremental improvement in a process, or a buck or two saved here and there, might have profoundly positive consequences across societies, communities and families. Study after study shows that the poor, most especially poor women, are prodigiously efficient with limited resources; that they more than anyone know how to stretch a rand.

The libertarian podcast boets like to pooh-pooh this kind of thing. But social grants mean people are able to function in society, and are able to care adequately for their children, who may, in turn, not end up as costly wards of the state. They can care for themselves to a level where, given an opportunity, it is at least possible for them to contribute – to get to work clothed, fed and housed.

Social grants are the thread upon which the lives of so many of our citizens depend. And Dlamini was indifferent to the point of caricature. It was Dlamini's job to ensure the handover of Sassa payments was done by 31 March 2017. Let's leave the commentary to the Constitutional Court, which was forced to rule on a matter brought by the Black Sash NGO – note, please, not through any government process – a matter of weeks ahead of the catastrophe that would have befallen millions of South Africans. Criticising Dlamini's "extraordinary conduct" with regard to a previous order that she get her Sassa ducks in a row, the court said that there was "no indication on the papers that [the minister] showed any interest in Sassa's progress before October last year".

"Since April 2016 the responsible functionaries of Sassa have been aware that it could not comply with the undertaking to the Court that it would be able to pay social grants from 1 April 2017. The

Minister was apparently informed of this only in October 2016. There is no indication on the papers that she showed any interest in Sassa's progress in that regard before that. Despite warnings from counsel and CPS, neither Sassa nor the Minister took any steps to inform the Court of the problems they were experiencing. Nor did they see fit to approach the Court for authorisation to regularise or ameliorate the situation. When, eventually, Sassa brought an application on 28 February 2017 for authorisation, the Minister intervened and ordered Sassa to withdraw the application. On 3 March 2017, the Minister and Sassa filed a supplementary progress report, without any acknowledgement that they were under any legal obligation to do so."

In the end, despite Dlamini's worst efforts, the crisis was averted. But it had been officially established that she didn't give a damn. As explained by constitutional legal whizz Pierre de Vos, "The people of South Africa (and the court) could not trust the South African Social Security Agency and Dlamini to do their job to ensure the delivery of social grants as required by the Constitution." She "could not be trusted not to mislead the Constitutional Court in future". In 2018, that's exactly what the court would find.

Throughout this sorry saga, Dlamini neglected her duty to such an extent that she has earned the ironic reputation as an enabler of what some might call white monopoly capital. In this instance, the company that benefited by repeated extensions to its contract was Cash Paymaster Services, which earned more than a billion rand's profits in the five years to 2017. The fellow who ran it in that time, Serge Belamant, survived various allegations that the company had used Black Economic Empowerment fronting to secure the original contract, and he received an estimated R263 million payout for his efforts on his resignation that year.

This should all be humiliating, career-ending stuff for the minister involved, right? Surprise! Of course not. Dlamini knew her real job was not the feeding of 12 million children; it was the backing of uBaba, her homie Jacob Zuma, at the upcoming ANC elective congress. Which, as

"The office which she occupied demands a greater commitment to ethical behaviour and requires a high commitment to public service. The Department of Social Development is as much responsible for the realisation of rights outlined in the Constitution as this court, and she used her position as minister of the department to place herself between constitutionally enshrined rights and those entitled to them...

"It has been a sorry saga, and it is proper that Minister Dlamini must, in her personal capacity, bear a portion of the costs. It would account for her degree of culpability in misleading the court, conduct which is deserving of censure by this court as a mark of displeasure, more so since she held a position of responsibility as a member of the Executive. Her conduct is inimical to the values underpinning the Constitution that she undertook to uphold when she took up office."

Constitutional Court ruling finding that Bathabile Dlamini had misled the court, September 2018

leader of the ANC Women's League, she did by bravely supporting JZ's anointed candidate, Nkosazana Dlamini-Zuma. Ultimately it was *that* that was her undoing. When Cyril Ramaphosa, no doubt to her surprise, won the presidency instead, she was removed, within two weeks, from the Social Development ministry and tucked away for safekeeping as the Minister of Women in the Presidency.

It was a necessary demotion, before her outright ejection from Cabinet in 2019, and yet there was some pathos in her relocation to a ministry that ostensibly oversees the wellbeing of South Africa's women. In a country that recorded 450,000 rape complaints in the decade to September 2019, and yet where the overwhelming majority of rapes go unreported, one cannot imagine a worse candidate to address yet another awful facet of South African life – not merely an indifferent placeholder, but someone who, as head cheerleader at the ANCWL, saw fit to stand firmly behind such an antediluvian symbol of philandering and sexist patriarchy as Jacob Zuma for so many years.

Bathabile Dlamini has few redeeming qualities. She is short on struggle history compared to others here, and there's no real contribution to anything other than the coffers of the Radisson Blu and the cellars of KWV. No innovation, no accomplishment that earns her a mitigating paragraph in our quest for fairness and balance, no small intervention that made something just a little bit better for millions in desperate need of the dignity that is their right.

Well, there is one thing.

She did manage to capture, in one short sentence, the depraved logic that has underpinned so much governmental wrongdoing throughout our lost decade. Her profound insight, the brief Eureka moment on which she rose as an Archimedean ringer of truth, her single instance of competence, was a phrase that explained how the edifice of Zuma Years state capture was not merely built on a foundation of quicksand, but that buried within were the skeletons of all who now walked the corridors of power and ran deals in its side rooms. And that uBaba knew precisely where they all lay.

"All of us there in the NEC," she said, speaking about the ANC's National Executive Committee, in an interview with the SABC in 2016, "have our smallanyana skeletons, and we don't want to take out all the skeletons because all hell will break loose."

And there you have it. Thank you, minister.

Before and since, however, nothing.

May her contribution to the misery of South Africa's poor, and her astounding indifference to them, never be forgotten.

Nkosazana Dlamini-Zuma

b. 27 January 1949

Minister of Cooperative Governance and Traditional Affairs; Minister in the Presidency (2018-2019); Minister of Home Affairs (2009-2012); Minister of Foreign Affairs (1999-2009); Minister of Health (1994-1999); Chairperson of the African Union Commission (2012-2017); JZ's ex; authoritarian vision of the hellscape alternative future we missed out on

IF THE COVID-19 LOCKDOWN CRISIS DID ANYTHING, it gave us a view of what life would have been like under President Nkosazana Dlamini-Zuma. In full cognisance of President Ramaphosa's twilight nightmare that he calls the "new dawn", we gained some real understanding of the calibre of the bullet we have dodged. Because for a while there she was pretty much our prime minister.

Despite her colourful attire and jaunty abbreviation, NDZ presents herself like the embodiment of Soviet architecture. Concrete, technocratic and unsmiling, she serves the coffee cold.

Dlamini-Zuma has been a permanent feature of our politics since democracy. Entire human beings have been born, educated and despatched into adult life during her tenure in high office. They turn 30 in three years. So experience on the job certainly isn't the issue here, although her track record is, despite what the strategically placed publicists will have had you believe over the years, a patchwork of mediocrity, fleeting competence and occasional disaster.

The traumatic flashbacks to her greatest hits were brought on by her overseeing, as head of Cooperative Governance, the handling of the Covid crisis. It was a nasty little hospital pass from Ramaphosa that would have been difficult to handle for the nimblest of political operators. And nimble NDZ is not, so it just brought out her authoritarian worst. Whatever faint vestiges of fun and lightness of being the global pandemic had allowed to remain by that point were systematically eradicated under her watchful eye. There would be no alcohol, no tobacco, certainly no zolling, and apparently no laughter or human warmth if she could help it.

In our quest to allocate praise where it is due, however, we must acknowledge Dlamini-Zuma's many years in exile. Also, she rescued Home Affairs from the bedlam that preceded her reign there from 2009. If you can remember a time when there was a competent Home Affairs department, then you remember the impact of Dlamini-Zuma.

Older readers, however, will further remember the scandal and nepotism that marked her initial role in Cabinet as Minister of Health going back to the Mandela presidency – a time in which the battle against Aids was marked by Virodene quackery and the *Sarafina II* "educational play" embarrassment (in hindsight, such a little cutie of a jobs-for-pals affair). And who can forget her tenure as foreign minister, around the turn of the century, when she looked on approvingly as Robert Mugabe turned the wonderful and functioning democracy north of our border to ruin? Presumably Minister Lindiwe Zulu, who in 2019 lamented the "millions of Zimbabweans living in South Africa" before exhorting them to get "involved in the resolution of the conflict in Zimbabwe". To remind her, they are here as a direct result of Dlamini-Zuma's "quiet diplomacy", which applauded Mugabe's narrow racial retribution at all costs while also happening to trash South Africa's newly earned moral standing in the international community.

And so to more recent times.

Jacob Zuma – NDZ's ex, if you hadn't worked it out, and much discussed elsewhere in this book – is forever mischaracterised. He is a traditional rural man of limited education. He doesn't understand money or business or economics or finance. That's all white monopoly capital to him. And yet he is notoriously charming and funny and, more than anything, is a genuinely gifted securocrat and ruthless politician. That's why, when it started to occur to him that he would not be president for life and that his successors, and their prosecutors, might have opinions on his laissez-faire attitude to the keys to our treasury, he set in motion a plan for his succession. To avoid the bad smell of local politics and ANC factionalism, he sent Nkosazana off to another exile, this time in Addis Ababa. There, amid some pushback, she managed to get herself elected as chair of the African Union. The initial difficulty was that it broke the unwritten rule that the larger economies do not put up candidates for the position, and the machinations required to

"A recent study by a reputable research institute compared the number of times [Nkosazana Dlamini-Zuma] smiled with the number of times former ANC spokesperson Carl Niehaus told the truth. The research, soon to be published in an academic journal, found that Niehaus told the truth more often than Dlamini-Zuma smiled."

Mondli Makhanya, May 2020

get her into it cemented South Africa's reputation on the continent as a bunch of arrogant wankers. But to hell with that, because for Zuma this was actually important – for his future freedom, he would need to parachute in a (relatively) untainted puppet candidate for election to the ANC presidency when his time was up.

And how very, very nearly it worked. *(See David Mabuza.)*

It is testament to the amount of damage inflicted on Zuma's watch that, three years after his failure to install his ex-wife and proxy candidate, we're in a hole as deep and dire as we are.

And as for Nkosazana Dlamini-Zuma, she was, we can only assume, happy to play the puppet and keep on digging. No smiley face for her.

Jack Dorsey

b. 19 November 1976

*Founder and CEO of Twitter; founder and CEO of Square;
righteous startup billionaire who thinks he can do
two things at once, but is doing such a bad job of
the first thing that it's actually ruining the world,
South Africa in particular*

Dishonourable mention: Mark Zuckerberg

IT'S TAKEN RATHER A WHILE, but the world is finally waking up to the realisation that social media isn't the fun little friend-making pastime it was made out to be way back in the mid-2000s, when it all seemed so new and exciting. Back then Tiger Woods was just a good golfer, Charlie Sheen was still on *Two And A Half Men*, and MySpace and its fresh competition, Facebook, were pioneering the Web 2.0. What could possibly go wrong?

Well, if you were MySpace, you could be consigned to the dustbin of internet history* by a brilliant young sociopath from Harvard; and if you were the human race, you could be duped into believing that nice progressive tech people in Silicon Valley were happy to give everyone in the world some harmless fun for free. Turns out they weren't. They were lining us up to sell our souls for filthy lucre.

Since those innocent newsfeed-free, likes-free, teenage-suicide-free days, social media has revealed itself for what it is: a modern psychology experiment being performed on billions of people around the world, based on the worst principles of growth-for-growth's-sake profiteering. And with the experiment results now coming in thick and fast, we're realising what's been foisted upon us. Social media makes us sad, envious and depressed; encourages bullying, victimisation and shaming; distracts us from doing meaningful things like working, relaxing or interacting with three-dimensional people face to face; reduces our ability to empathise with others; compartmentalises us and entrenches our biases; foments polarisation, intolerance and societal division; casts doubt on simple truth; and ultimately has a material effect on politics, elections and thus the healthy functioning of society.

If this is news to you, we suggest you put this book down right now and go watch *The Social Dilemma*. Not that people haven't been pointing this stuff out for years, but when the guy who co-invented the "like" button tells you it has the same effect on your dopamine levels as nicotine or crack cocaine, and the guy who "monetised" Facebook tells you his children are not allowed screen time, let alone social media time, it feels that much more real.

In short, they couldn't have invented a narcotic to do more damage than social media, which by now should really be called anti-society media. To do what they've done they had to create a digital drug, and then employ the world's finest Ivy League-trained engineers and most sophisticated AI to continuously refine it, year in and year out, to be

---

* Technically MySpace is still a thing.

more and more "habit-forming". As the historian Yuval Noah Harari has been warning for some time, the algorithms that control your social media feeds are designed to get to know you better than you know yourself. Why? So they can hack you.

They do this by using every super-refined psychological trick in the book to keep you "engaged" – that is, online on their platform, continually clicking, scrolling, watching – and then gathering as much data about you as possible in the process. What articles you read, what videos you watch, what links you chase, what posts you like, the number of milliseconds your mouse hovers over a particular image.

All this effort is so they can sell you to advertisers for targeted marketing, which they do in spades. This is the essence of "surveillance capitalism", and in itself it isn't necessarily the end of the world. Most of us don't actually mind good, relevant advertising, and it's possibly one of the reasons why people struggle to see the enormous net negative that social media presents to society. If we're now seeing ads that are more relevant to us – fewer Tampax ads if that's not your thing, fewer *Call of Duty* ads if you're not a gamer – then isn't that a good idea?

The problem comes in the collateral damage of keeping us engaged. And, if we haven't made it clear enough, the damage is monstrous. It is cluster bombs over the very fabric of civilised society and depleted uranium left in the water that irrigates our daily conversation. When sensible political commentators such as Douglas Murray and Richard Kreitner speak of "the possible dissolution of the United States" or even the threat of a second civil war, this is only because anti-social media has made this possible.

In the US, Mark Zuckerberg is rightly the prime target for opprobrium when this topic is raised. There are many reasons why he has in recent years been called to defend Facebook before Congress, and why he's the first name on the list when MSNBC host Joe Scarborough writes, "Mark, Sheryl and Jack, you have revealed yourselves to be vapid vulgarians who put at risk Americans' health, racial justice, fair elections and basic truths."

One is that Facebook's own research found, in 2018, that their "algorithms exploit the human brain's attraction to divisiveness" and

> "What these companies have done is created a business model where the most incendiary, upsetting, controversial, and oftentimes false and damaging things get more oxygen than they deserve because we are a tribal species and when people say things that are upsetting we tend to engage. Engagement equals enrichment. The more rage equals the more clicks equals the more Nissan ads."
>
> *Scott Galloway, author of The Four*

that, without intervention, they would feed users "more and more divisive content in an effort to gain user attention and increase time on the platform". (Facebook shelved the report.) Another is that foreign influence over Facebook groups had a material effect on the US elections in 2016.

Facebook is the world's biggest social media platform, with around 2.7 billion unique monthly users; it owns the third-, fourth- and sixth-biggest social networks*; and Zuckerberg isn't just CEO, he's the majority shareholder. What he says goes, which makes him quite probably the most influential individual in the world. All of which makes his ongoing refusal to act decisively against the damage his platforms are doing to societies everywhere that much more unforgivable.

If US antitrust hearings don't result in Facebook being broken up, the US really is doomed. But as much as we have argued that Zuckerberg is the modern world's Antichrist *(see 50 People Who Stuffed Up The World)*, his influence in South Africa is outdone by another smug punch-me-in-the-face tech geek who refuses to make the connection between the destructive results of his particular social network and how he runs it.

This is hipster-bearded Jack Dorsey, the third of Scarborough's vulgarians (the other being Sheryl Sandberg of Facebook), and co-

---

* Respectively, WhatsApp (about two billion unique users), Facebook Messenger (1.3 billion) and Instagram (1.1 billion).

founder and current CEO of Twitter. Though Twitter has a reported ad reach of 2.3 million users in South Africa compared to 20 million on Facebook, it is the social network that has powered much of our racialised online rage and declining journalistic standards over the last decade. Not just that; it made a specific and material contribution to the Guptas' state capture operation that caused so much harm to our politics, economy and society. *(See Victoria Geoghegan.)* For allowing this damage, Dorsey gets our big thumbs down ahead of the Zuck.

In South Africa, our elections are not (yet) targeted for manipulation via Facebook sites. Rather, our entire political landscape is targeted for manipulation by Twitter bots, trolls, sock puppets and bad actors. And Twitter is used as a bullhorn to initiate real physical and economic damage, as when Julius Malema tweeted, on 6 September 2020: "@Clicks_SA see you tomorrow. Fellow fighters and ground forces; ATTACK!!!" This was in response to a thoughtless Clicks advertisement for TRESemmé shampoo, which the ever-alert Malema used to generate headlines and relevance for his party. The following day, 7 September, several Clicks stores were vandalised by EFF members and dozens forced to close. On 8 September, Clicks chose to shutter 400 stores to avert further mayhem. Thousands of mostly black staff were affected.

With a single tweet Malema had managed to mobilise an army of chaos and amplify a racially insensitive incident into a racial war. The most telling vignette caught on camera was a white "granny" pulling a gun on black EFF supporters outside a Clicks store at the Walmer Park Shopping Centre in Port Elizabeth. The woman and several EFF members were arrested.

Thus we see the cause-and-effect processes of Twitter. Emotions triggered. Biases entrenched. Rage and conflict exploding online and ultimately in reality. This would be terrible in any society, but in one with such a history of division as ours it is devastating. South Africa is a society desperate for healing, for bridging the gaps between races and classes; and this requires human interaction and empathy – both of which are entirely eliminated on Twitter because of its complete lack of shared reality. Instead, we have egomaniacs and narcissists, who

> "For the good of their profession, their mental health, and indeed wider society, they [journalists] should all get off Twitter now. And they should never, ever come back."
>
> *Thomas Moller-Nielsen*

in no way represent the average South African, supposedly leading the national narrative, aided and abetted by lowlife politicians who know the value of race-war distractions, and an underfunded and poorly led media.

Which brings us to the next point: how our journalists have fallen so hard for it.

A quarter of Twitter's authenticated worldwide users are journalists or media organisations, but as philosopher Thomas Moller-Nielsen explains it, if you were to design a platform to actively reduce journalistic standards at global scale, you would be hard-pressed to do better than inventing Twitter. While offering "a veneer of journalistic utility", it remains "strictly at odds with the aims of the journalism profession". As a social network, one of its inherent abilities is to customise its user experience and so keep people in their echo chambers, isolated from an objective view of the world. And Twitter, specifically, is a killer of objective truth – a 2018 MIT study showed that fake news on Twitter spreads six times faster than real news. It is also entirely unrepresentative of the public at large. Twitter fights and toxic meltdowns are the equivalent of deranged soapbox evangelists going at each other after a bender, and really do not merit being turned into supposed news articles.

If the inability to disseminate objective and meaningful truth to the public is the death of journalism, here's the nail in the coffin: Twitter (along with Facebook) steals the precious advertising revenue that might otherwise have gone to actual media companies so desperate for it.

When does journalistic self-awareness alight on the realisation that spending more time on Twitter than doing actual journalism is self-defeating and ruinous? Perhaps that time is nigh.

Twitter came into being in 2006, but its rise in South Africa matches remarkably closely the period covered in this book. We might, for practical purposes, say that Twitter has had a valid political presence here since Mandy Wiener and colleagues started live-tweeting the Jackie Selebi corruption trial in April 2010. It's been downhill ever since.

In July 2020 the editor of *News24*, Adriaan Basson, who had tweeted alongside Wiener at the trial, announced he was stepping back from Twitter. "Almost exactly ten years ago, I was one of the first South African journalists to join Twitter," he wrote. "The biggest mistake the media made was to think Twitter is representative of the reading population or the public at large; that journalists should go to Twitter to know what South Africans say and think."

Well, yes. And what a pity so few journalists have done likewise.

How is it that supposedly savvy newsroom editors and online media operators have been so blind to the damage it causes? Do they really not see it, or are they so desperate for the clicks to pay the bills that they feel it's the moral price they have to pay to do real journalism?

What a slippery ethical slope that is – not too far removed from the practices of the dodgy politicians and businessmen that those real journalists investigate.

Social media platforms in their current format epitomise broken capitalism. They prioritise shareholders with absolute disregard for the commonwealth. They promote hatred, division and radicalisation, and Twitter – with far fewer users than Facebook, YouTube, Instagram or even TikTok – is optimised for this in particular. But Dorsey appears to have no idea of the damage it does. If he did, he wouldn't spend half his time working at another company; he is CEO of both Twitter and the financial payments company Square. He wouldn't announce he was going to spend a year swanning about Africa rather than knuckling down at HQ to resolve real issues that affect hundreds of millions of real people. (His plans were put on hold by Covid-19.) He wouldn't claim that Twitter's "purpose is to serve the public conversation", which is quite evidently the polar opposite of what it does.

If we were to summarise him in a couple of tweets, Dorsey is an

> "We're creating a culture that's not compatible with basic sanity. We're amplifying incommensurable delusions everywhere all at once."
>
> *Sam Harris, on social media*

ice-bathing, silent-retreating, righteous asshole who on one hand can preach about "social justice reform" and donate $10 million to Ibram X Kendi's Center for Antiracist Research to promote "equity and justice for all", and on the other hand lacks the self-awareness to realise that the company he leads is actively sickening the world, not healing it. Or, perhaps, he "just, simply put, doesn't give a shit", in the words of tech commentator Scott Galloway, and is also a member of the Silicon Valley sociopath club.

Either way, there is a raft of rather easy fixes for Twitter: first one, get a new CEO.

One of the devil's greatest tricks, as Keyser Söze knew so well, was to make you think he doesn't exist. In that sense Twitter is the darkest of angels. Its hundreds of millions of users clearly have no idea how it's addling their minds; our news editors and journalists are only now catching on to the damage it causes; and its part-time CEO Jack Dorsey appears to be, like Del Amitri, the last to know.

Rage may be its speciality, but rage isn't exclusive to Twitter: #screwyoujack.

See Adri Senekal de Wet.

Jessie Duarte &
Gwede Mantashe

Duarte: b. 19 September 1953
Mantashe: b. 21 June 1955

Deputy Secretary General (since 2012) and Secretary General (2007-2017) of the ANC; high priests of the broad church of ANC contradiction; defenders of the ANC faith and enablers of its unaccountability

LET US BEGIN THIS FIRST OF SEVERAL ENTRIES in the book on the structural problems that define the ruling party of South Africa with a "who said it?" humdinger. Which of these quotes is from George Orwell and which is from an ANC elder and ex-president of South Africa?

"The leaders will now enjoy the champagne, and of course they do so on your behalf through their lips."

"Day and night we are watching over your welfare. It is for *your* sake that we drink that milk and eat those apples."

The apples and milk do rather give the game away – that's from *Animal Farm*, of course, published in 1945. But how is that first quote *not* Orwell? How is it not an unlikely parody of the worst of authoritarian propaganda?

Tragically, it isn't. It is from the mouth of Kgalema Motlanthe, no less, delivered in earnest at the ANC's 100-year celebration to a crowd of restive proletariat in the Free State Stadium in Bloemfontein in January 2012.

It was Orwell's genius to reveal the machinations of totalitarian corruption to the world in allegory form that even children could understand; more so that he's still getting it right so many decades later. And to see just how right, let's play out the full milk and apple quote, uttered in the book by the fat little pig known as Squealer.

"Day and night we are watching over your welfare. It is for *your* sake that we drink that milk and eat those apples. Do you know what would happen if we pigs failed in our duty? Jones would come back! Yes, Jones would come back! Surely, comrades, surely there is no-one among you who wants to see Jones come back?"

There it is: the Orwellian insight into how a senior ANC official might get away with a line of such callous disregard with barely a raised eyebrow, and indeed how the ANC has survived so long in power despite doing such a disastrous job of governing the country. The fear of "Jones" is an essential tenet of ANC dogma.

In the book, Squealer is second in command on Manor Farm and head of propaganda, a position largely paralleled in our little comparison here with that of Secretary-General of the ANC, effectively the party CEO, who throughout the Zuma Years was Gwede Mantashe.

The problem of who is in charge at the ANC has been, since the party's national conference at Nasrec in December 2017, pronounced, to say the least. It is the focus of the party's factionalism, and to many it is the very battle of good versus evil in modern South Africa. We will come, in future pages, to how Ace Magashule came to occupy the position of SG of the ANC, and the uncertainty and damage he causes there. But before we get there we must give space to his forerunner, Gwede Mantashe, and his (and Ace's) deputy, Jessie Duarte. Because, make no mistake, when Mantashe was SG of the ANC, he was in charge. So much so that he was generally accepted to be the second-most-powerful person in the country. He was Zuma's enforcer – and Duarte became the enforcer's enforcer.

It has become a useful cliché to describe the ANC as "a broad church". It really is filled with capitalists and communists, free marketeers and statists, BEE fat cats and Marxist trade unionists, real struggle veterans and less real struggle veterans – "a strange combination of highly acquisitive behaviour and socialist ideology", as one commentator put it. And it is the ongoing role of the SG and his deputy to serve the varied congregation faithfully so that they might be at peace with their individual places in the universe.

Mantashe and Duarte showed constant devotion to the cause under Zuma, even as its contradictions were rattling its foundations. They were the ones who stood in front of the cameras – now with an SACP cap on (Mantashe was its chair for six years), now wearing Cartier shades – fighting the good fight, declaring miracles, banishing unholy thoughts.

The fundamental contradiction for them to square was how the party of the people could allow so many of its members to become obscenely wealthy – both legally, through economic policies that exacerbate inequality, and illegally, through gross corruption – at the cost of those who are poor. How it could "ensure that South Africa does belong to all who live in it", in Duarte's own words, but sell it out to a family of swindlers from abroad. One imagines them spending hours praying hard over that last one, especially around 2016, as the Gupta house of cards started to collapse.

Back then, Mantashe and Duarte had spearheaded a move by the ANC and its Cabinet members to bring pressure to bear on the big four South African banks for being part of "white monopoly capital oppressing black-owned businesses". Why? Because they had dared to close the accounts of Oakbay Investments, the Gupta family's holding company, through which it ran the bulk of its state capture operation. The ANC approach followed a direct request from Oakbay.

In 2018 (as deputy to Magashule), Duarte went on record to defend the party's decision to appoint Tony Yengeni to chair its crime and corruption committee. Yengeni, famously, is the only politician who has served prison time for Arms Deal corruption, having failed to declare a discount he had received on a Mercedes-Benz. "The conviction of comrade Tony Yengeni worries many in the ANC," said Duarte. "What are we saying? If you negotiate a vehicle in this country you dare not negotiate a discount because that's corruption?"

It's important to understand that both Mantashe and Duarte are intelligent and streetwise. Whereas it can serve the party's purposes to allow a few dummies in Cabinet – to say thank you for their service to the cause, or because it's useful to have a few pliable morons in positions of power – smarts are an absolute requirement for the SG positions. Mantashe honed his skills over many years at the National Union of Mineworkers and as a Boksburg councillor. Duarte, in turn, learnt at the foot of Mandela himself, first as his assistant, and later as the spokeswoman for the ANC. These are not positions for the weak of spirit or mind.

"In recent years, especially since the infamous Polokwane conference, we have observed so much ill-discipline from ANC members, and yet few remedial or corrective actions are taken. This is not only worrisome but blatantly disgusting, because it presupposes that no-one in the ANC sees anything wrong with the conduct of certain members."

Oscar van Heerden, author and ANC member

Yet it appears that even the sharpest minds can fall victim to the self-deception of faith and thus enable truly abominable behaviour. Author Michael Shermer might have been speaking of Duarte and Mantashe when he noted that, "Smart people believe weird things because they are skilled at defending beliefs they arrived at for non-smart reasons."

Mantashe was the man who orchestrated Zuma's rise to the top at Polokwane, came to form a partnership with him of unprecedented power, and then for so long offered his wiles and savvy in the defence of a man who was so clearly doing structural and reputational damage to South Africa. In the same way, Duarte became the apostolic guard who defended every bridge a cadre might walk over to deliver his or her gift of patronage. You could even be a convicted criminal, as with Yengeni, and she would defend you just as long as you wore an ANC T-shirt.

The contradictions at the heart of the battle between party and state were well illustrated in Mantashe's attitude to Public Protector Thuli Madonsela, once she began, in 2012, to investigate the misuse of state funds for upgrades to Zuma's Nkandla homestead in KwaZulu-Natal. In response, Mantashe was at the forefront of an aggressive and personal ANC response that would come to symbolise the party's wretched willingness to defend the indefensible.

Yet at the farewell dinner to honour her departure from office in 2016, Mantashe then said, "I agree with Premier David Makhura when he said you saved us from ourselves. You did and we never acknowledged that. You leave the ANC wiser as you go."

So which is it? Was she "playing tactics", "protecting the interests of a particular section of society", consistently trying to "discredit the ANC and its leadership in government"? Or was she saving it?

Existential questions for the high priests of the ANC, you might think. Except no. Because even today, with Zuma gone, you suspect that Mantashe and Duarte adhere to neither side of that particular dilemma. They were just doing what needed to be done at the time, because the real dogma for them – the unwritten scripture that defined their roles – was simply that the party must be protected, in the moment, at all costs. Never mind what happened yesterday or what may happen tomorrow.

> "How long will you defend the unjust and show partiality to the wicked?
>
> Defend the cause of the weak and fatherless, maintain the rights of the poor and oppressed.
>
> Rescue the weak and needy, deliver them from the hand of the wicked.
>
> They know nothing, they understand nothing.
>
> They walk about in darkness; all the foundations of the earth are shaken."
>
> *Psalm 82*

Remember that while Mantashe supported him, Zuma remained in power. Without Mantashe, Zuma could not survive. They say the turning point was Nenegate. *(See Des van Rooyen.)* Wherever it may have been, it raises the question: did Mantashe eventually abandon Zuma because finally, after all these years, his eyes were suddenly opened to the destruction of the state capture project undertaken on his watch? Or was he simply following his faith? A faith in the ANC above all else that is unshakeable across so much of the party, and thus explains so much of the tragedy of the last decade?

See David Mabuza, Ace Magashule, Supra Mahumapelo, Baleka Mbete, Gavin Watson.

The fund manager

Not particularly effective investor of money; always incomprehensible, often unnecessary drain on the pockets and pensions of many South Africans

A POINT WORTH MAKING IN THESE ORWELLIAN TIMES is that, despite the familiar Siberian chill of expropriative glee that gusts through the commentary of the comfortable, wealth is no crime.

Equally, setting out to impoverish those who have attained it does nothing to advance and dignify those who have not. This is not some verisimilar idea, but is as true and as immovable as the koppies of the Great Karoo.

In fact, persistent and endemic poverty is of far greater concern than the far lower incidence of prodigious wealth. It should be what exercises us and tugs at our conscience more than anything. It is regrettably easy to simply blame the rich, and so it remains a dispiritingly successful and long-lived deceit that poverty is created by the wealthy.

In any case, if for the purposes of this entry we can agree that wealth is not a crime in itself, then it must be something else that catapults our poor fund manager onto our list. We know that he, unlike so many others between these covers, probably did not steal a cent, and indeed that he didn't need to bother.

The fund manager finds himself here because he is a talisman for an industry that has given customers sub-inflation returns and consistently underperformed the indices during this miserable last decade. In this time of political chaos, when some financial stability might have helped us sleep a smidgen better at night, he delivered worse-than-mediocre work while he and his brethren continued to remunerate themselves stratospherically and, in another unforgivable crime, build vast swathes of Higgovale while they were at it.

South African fund managers, also known as asset managers (same difference, if you didn't know), tend to live in different cities to our wanker bankers, though they traverse similar ethical terrain. The former congregate on the mountain slopes of Cape Town, while the latter can be found cruising around Westcliff and Saxonwold in Johannesburg. The former, as a rule of thumb, wangle their money from the financially illiterate; the latter do their wangling from the financially literate. If you need an example, a fund manager might, via his army of financial advisers, convince a working-class stiff to invest his pension in a money-sink the workings of which he cannot comprehend, while a wanker banker might convince a corporate CEO to buy a down-and-out retailer in Australia that then loses said corporate billions over the next five years and costs the CEO his job.

With the definitions established, let us get past another notion here. Whingeing about wanker bankers might be a game for the wealthy, but complaining about fund managers absolutely is not. What they do affects anyone with a pension, whether they mop the floor or own the company. Getting it right really matters, especially in South Africa, where people don't save enough for retirement and are cast onto the mortuary slab of state services or become a burden to their family once they stop working.

And so let us deal with a remarkable statistic. Over the years 2014-2019 three out of four South African fund managers underperformed the market, according to the S&P Indices versus Active (SPIVA) South Africa scorecard. Instead they fiddled, using their enormously expensive insight to actively manage portfolios of investments, with the end result being that the people whose money they were playing with were made poorer in real terms, and sometimes even in actual terms. For this service they charged a whopping 3%, which they spent on plastering Higgovale with festering carbuncles and hindering the movement of the productive workforce on their R200,000 bicycles. This is why, if you speak to any vaguely competent financial advisers, they will laugh – a-ha-ha-ha – at the positively hilarious industry understanding that the bulk of fund managers are likely to lose you money.

One riposte from the managers' camp is that it's unfair to judge them in a bull market, and that their clients will be grateful when the markets start tanking. But when exactly that happened in early 2020, with great big piles of Covid poo in extreme motion, it turned out they were too busy improving their PBs for the Cycle Tour to notice.

The failure of the fund-management industry presents a difficult challenge. It obviously cannot be regulated by the state (let's not give the comrades any bright ideas), but it also seems incapable of self-regulating, of finding a way to align how it remunerates itself with the returns it gives its customers.

"[A]ctive managers who aim to beat the market by picking winning stocks have long predicted that demand for their expertise would return if conditions become more volatile, and the time for that revelation would seem to be upon us. Global stocks crashed as the Covid-19 pandemic ripped around the world, and the most common measure of volatility, the VIX, reached a historic peak. But the active managers' supposed return to glory was underwhelming at best."

Ruan Jooste, April 2020

For most clients, fund managers have become destroyers of wealth, an active drain on prosperity – and the opacity of what these people do is key to the mugging-in-motion they represent. The industry's language is clannish and exclusionary. The "product portfolios" the firms offer are as baffling to decode as an Enigma machine or your Vodacom contract. Nobody has time for it and we just let the professionals get on with it. It is an industry that thrives on its own clients' confusion and intimidation, the fact that we're all too embarrassed to say to some slimeball in ostentatious Italian shoes that "I have no clue what all this means, and it is a legal requirement that falls on you, not me, to get me to understand it, so start speaking in plain English, pal..."

One day you'll need your pension, either way. And if you were to work out where your money's gone, the chances are more than likely that you'll discover that the fees you've paid to your fund-management firm are eye-wateringly close to equalling the gains you've made on your portfolio, which, as we've mentioned, will be worse than the broader index in three out of four cases.

It's at this point you may ask, "Where the hell is my money?" The answer is made of carbon fibre and resides between your fund manager's sweaty balls, a toy that he parks in the fifth garage at *Maison Travertine* in Higgovale. And yes, you paid for that too, along with the Porsche Cayenne that the trophy wife uses to take Hugo to Bishops every morning.

To steal a Wall Street anecdote and ham-fistedly mash it onto Cape Town, is it not reasonable to ask where the bulk of the clients' houses are? They're in Goodwood and Pimville and Mamelodi and Melville and Durban North, that's where. These are the neighbourhoods where people who create wealth and add value to the economy live.

When did you last speak to the people looking after your pension? Perhaps consider doing just that, finding out how much you've paid them, and how much value they've delivered for that fee. The chances are it'll blow your socks off.

The fund manager is a tick on the ballsack of the working South African. It's time he explained – in English – what the hell it is he actually does for us.

Victoria Geoghegan

b. 27 June 1983

Mind polluter; Gupta reputation launderer; architect of the destructive, racially divisive campaign to sustain state capture; cause of Bell Pottinger's self-destruction; poster girl for amoral psycho-corporate public relations that sees no qualms in the destabilisation of entire countries

Dishonourable mentions: Timothy Bell, the Guptas, James Henderson, Mzwanele Manyi, Andile Mngxitama

ONCE UPON A TIME, VICTORIA GEOGHEGAN was an ambitious upper-level executive on a straight-line trajectory to the top of the public-relations universe. Now she is the face of the dramatic implosion of one of the world's most recognisable and influential PR companies, and an unholy symbol of the public's almost complete mistrust in the industry she represents. Also, everyone in South Africa hates her.

The PR company that Geoghegan once worked for, and once existed, was Bell Pottinger, a UK-based operation with a reputation for embracing the seediest of well-paying clients, from Oscar Pistorius and Rolf Harris to the Pinochet Foundation and the wife of Bashar al-Assad. Its confidential client list was, one imagines, a stolen photocopy of the Devil's Rolodex.

In 2016, Bell Pottinger took on one client too many, however: the Gupta brothers, friends of President Zuma of South Africa and his immediate family. The full extent of that relationship was being incrementally revealed in the South African and international press at the time, with undesirable results for the brothers and their businesses. They were being painted as criminals and corrupters who influenced the highest political decisions in the land, plundered the South African treasury and economy at will, and really belonged in jail. The court of public opinion was becoming increasingly hostile, equating Zuma and the Guptas with the new concept of state capture, and important banks and financial institutions were refusing to do business with them. The "Zuptas" needed a PR makeover – or, at least, something to distract their critics from their shameless appropriation of state resources.

Enter Bell Pottinger, apparently introduced to the Guptas by two men intimately involved in the global arms trade: Fana Hlongwane, notorious for his role in South Africa's corrupt and wasteful Arms Deal, and Christopher Geoghegan, former COO of BAE Systems, which was one of the chief beneficiaries of said deal and also a Bell Pottinger client. Fast-forward through the relevant meetings and strategy discussions and a fee agreement of £100,000 per month plus expenses, and Geoghegan's daughter Victoria found herself heading up the account of Oakbay Investments, the Guptas' holding company. All very cosy to this point.

Having joined Bell Pottinger at age 21, Victoria Geoghegan apparently had no qualms about dealing with the odd ropey client – with her father happy to sell overpriced fighter trainers to the South African government, sleeping peacefully after a hard day's unconscionable work presumably runs in the family. Rather, she took a fast route up the career ladder, and under her guidance Bell Pottinger orchestrated the dissemination of a new narrative for the South African public to consume: the hoodoo of "white monopoly capital".

Essentially a childlike no-*you*-are! response to the criticisms of state capture, claims of white monopoly capital dumped the blame for South Africa's increasingly dire economic situation into the laps of white-owned businesses that were supposedly still running the country and reaping the spoils of apartheid. The briefest moment of lucid thought on the matter would reveal what bunk this idea was, but the ambitious and apparently amoral Geoghegan knew, as any vaguely competent PR minion does, that it's hearts, not minds, that matter in such campaigns. Led by an army of fake Twitter accounts – Twitterbots – the message went out: *It's all about race.* This is a powerful method of distraction just about anywhere in the world these days, but in South Africa, a country defined by its history of racial division, this was as cynical and reprehensible a move as could be imagined. It was a campaign that would later be described by the UK's Public Relations and Communications Association (PRCA), the largest PR association in Europe, as "by any reasonable standard of judgment likely to inflame racial discord", "beyond the pale" and "the most serious breach of our code of conduct in the history of the organisation".

In this instance, however, it was also a campaign that was quite easily identified. The Twitterbots gave themselves away with a predilection for transmitting Gupta propaganda at exactly the same time, geolocators that revealed they were created in India, and laughably unlikely spreadsheet-generated names such as Bongi Vorster, Dlamini Louw and Iminathi Junior. There was a sense of shamelessness to it all that might fly in South Africa, where the Zuptas were so used to doing what they want and getting away with it, but once the UK press picked up on the story, Geoghegan, her campaign and Bell Pottinger itself were doomed. Major clients departed almost overnight, and the (non-Twitterbot) social-media response was vehement and determined. Geoghegan had committed the fatal PR crime of becoming the story and, with flaming irony, social-media rage would ensure she was fired for her efforts.

In December 2016, at the age of just 33, Victoria Geoghegan had been appointed MD of Bell Pottinger's financial and corporate division, reward for her work on the Gupta account. In July 2017, she was forced to resign, along with others who had worked with her. Two months later, Bell Pottinger was expelled from the PRCA for five years for inciting racial hatred, acting against the public interest and generally bringing the industry into disrepute. A week after that, the company went into administration.

It is worth pointing out that the destruction of Bell Pottinger was a rare instance in which mass social-media rage became a force for good. For those who might be tempted to overstate the case, however, let's not forget how it all began in the first place. Geoghegan had harnessed the destructive powers of social media, and her weapon of choice eventually backfired and sunk her.

No-one who knows the story is likely to take her for a good, decent human being. Over the course of a year or so, she became the demon in the average South African's ear, a disseminator of social poison who cared nought for the damage she was wreaking on an entire country – someone who proudly displayed her charitable credentials as a supporter of schoolchildren in Nigeria, while being intimately involved in undermining the future of schoolchildren in South Africa.

It must be acknowledged, though, that she was hardly acting in isolation, and two of the great modern PR sharks deserve special

"[The Guptas] looked at where we are fragile as a society. The first point where we are the most soft, the most fragile, is race relations... The easiest thing they've done is to resuscitate some of the terms that were there. Concepts such as 'white monopoly capital', 'radical economic transformation' – those terms were meant just to divide."

Ralph Mathekga, interviewed in the documentary Influence

mention whenever her name crops up. They are Timothy Bell and James Henderson.

As Margaret Thatcher's top spin doctor and then the founder of Bell Pottinger itself, the late Baron Bell was essentially British PR aristocracy, which may sound rather fancy but should not, we'd suggest, be considered an aspirational status unless being a self-inflated arse of dubious morality correlates with your vision of greatness. For an immediate sense of the man, we recommend watching the award-winning 2020 documentary *Influence*, of which he is the unapologetically frank focal point. Bell was intimately involved in, and excited by, the early negotiations with his company's new clients, the Guptas, but with the self-preservation instincts of a gutter weasel on garbage day, he soon spotted the impending disaster and skittered into disaffected and condescending exile in August 2016. When Tim Bell doesn't want your business, you know you're bad news.

Henderson, meanwhile, the CEO of Bell Pottinger with the oleaginous sheen of an otter in an oil slick, lacked such foresight. After pushing the *how-should-I-know-what-my-employees-were-up-to?* defence as far as it could go, he was forced to take a fall just days before the PRCA ruling in September 2017 – but his resignation proved futile. His fiancée Heather Kerzner, the socialite ex-wife of Sol Kerzner, had invested millions of pounds in Bell Pottinger only months before the Gupta scandal started playing out, and together the two owned 37% of the company, a share that quickly became worthless. A few days after Henderson's resignation, the Henderson-Kerzner wedding was put on indefinite hold. There's only so much schadenfreude to be extracted in the circumstances, but South African observers took what they could.

Bell, who died in 2019, and Henderson were industry heavyweights who had built up Bell Pottinger into an enormously effective multinational that employed hundreds of people and influenced millions in countries across the world, from Chile to Iraq. This was hardly a case in isolation, so it says rather a lot that what they allowed to happen in South Africa was so loathsome that it sunk their business.

"Well, they said, 'We want to run a campaign [saying] that all the money is stuck with the white people and there's nothing left for you.' And we said, 'Look, I'm sure we can manage something. We can organise marches in the streets, demonstrations.'"

Tim Bell, interviewed in Influence

Anyone with the vaguest understanding of human nature knows that deep in the heart of all people – less deep in some than in others – lie the calcified seams of our worst terrors and instincts: racism, bigotry, fear of the other. It's taken thousands of years of civilisation to temper these embers of potential destruction with mutual respect and understanding, and codified laws, so that we might get along and build societies together, and in so doing lift up all within them.

South Africa, with its particular past, will always be prone to those looking to stoke the embers to their own advantage, and mostly the attempts are raw, instinctive and inherently political. Mzwanele "Jimmy" Manyi – putting it out there, as Director-General of Labour in 2010, that there were too many coloureds in the Western Cape. The white genocide crowd – always gunning for its own purified and independent homeland. The EFF – practically founded on this way of being. Andile Mngxitama of Black First Land First – a guy so toxic even the EFF expelled him, and yet so incoherent in his thinking that he was happy to work with "capital" Bell Pottinger and consider them "friends".

But righteous, indignant and even understandable race-baiting, as destructive as it is, is somehow less repugnant than the weaponised, monetised programme of influence that Victoria Geoghegan put her name to on behalf of Bell Pottinger. She did her bit to tear apart a country without, it would appear, the merest scruple on her face, only the monthly retainer and her career trajectory in mind.

There are, sadly, rather a lot of Victoria Geoghegans in the PR industry, but she just happened to be the one who ignored every *single* moral fibre in her body. The one who seems to have done whatever her clients, the godawful Guptas, wanted done, even if it meant gilding the enormous turd they had dumped on South Africa and its people.

As of September 2020, Geoghegan and Henderson, along with a colleague named Nick Lambert, had been targeted for formal directorship disqualification by the Insolvency Service in the UK. The bare minimum, we'd say. Jail sentences would be more appropriate.

Malusi Gigaba

b. 30 August 1971

*Former minister of Public Enterprises, Home Affairs
and (can you believe it?!) Finance; once promising young
political gun; Zupta bagman; victim of his own ego
and vanity – and Zuma's sharp eye*

Dishonourable mentions: the Guptas, Jacob Zuma

SOUTH AFRICA'S MOST FAMOUS PENIS belongs to Malusi Gigaba. It was just a short video clip in the trainwreck-in-perpetuity that is Gigaba's personal life, but in suggesting that the viewer "imagine this was in your mouth" it struck a certain chord.

To be sure, it was a hard no from us, thanks – but then again, Gigaba was at pains to stress that the video was private and intended for his wife

Norma, not Pornhub, which is where it trended, and that he was aware that his phone was hacked on a regular basis and woe is he. Which raises the question: if you're a high-profile political figure and you know your phone is vulnerable, why on earth would you send dick pics?

This little vignette regarding Gigaba's inability to successfully manage his home affairs might in a sensible country have given his seniors pause for thought. Because it was hardly the first time Gigaba had let his vanity get the better of him. But here, where the president can be a philandering kleptocrat with the single-minded purpose to enable the sacking of public finances and institutions, "appropriate" means something completely different.

And so it came to pass that Malusi Gigaba became one of the Zuptas' go-to guys. This after it had all begun with so much promise.

Knowledge Malusi Nkanyezi Gigaba took a well-worn political journey from apartheid schooling in his native Zululand to university at Durban-Westville and then on to the Communist Party and the ANC. His obvious talents saw him elected Youth League president three times in a row. He seemed diligent and serious, and Thabo Mbeki saw enough in the man to appoint him to the position of deputy minister of Home Affairs in 2004 at the age of 32.

The defenestration of Mbeki by Zuma's thugs at the ANC National Conference in Polokwane in 2007 was a moment of moral inflection in our country, when those walking a certain path might be tempted to turn down another. When apparently good people might start doing noticeably bad things. When Zuma, the ultimate securocrat, might look to identify those he regarded as pliable, just as his managers, the Gupta brothers, had identified him.

People who run spies will tell you that they are less like Fleming's James Bond and more like Le Carré's George Smiley. They are not inevitable forces of nature; rather, their handlers have something on them. Or, as Bathabile Dlamini showed us in her lone moment of public insight, there are smallanyana skeletons to be used as leverage. But the leverage is not always dirt from the past. In some cases it is a vulnerability in the present, and there is no vulnerability in modern South Africa quite like, as Hansie Cronje once explained it, an "unfortunate love of money". So it would seem that the trappings of high office and obscene wealth appealed to Malusi Gigaba's sense of self-importance.

Once Zuma ascended to the presidency in 2009, it didn't take too long. He needed a bag boy at the department of Public Enterprises to allow the Guptas to get going with the looting of their choice of state-owned enterprises (SOEs), so in 2010 he fired the impeccably qualified lifelong ANC lefty Barbara Hogan, and appointed Gigaba. His principal qualification appeared to be averting his gaze.

Towards the end of his catastrophic reign at Public Enterprises, when the wrecking ball of state capture was bashing at the pillars of SAA, Transnet and Eskom, Gigaba appeared at the State of the Nation Address in an SAA pilot's uniform. To say this is inappropriate doesn't begin to express it. A340 and 747 captains need huge experience, and those who have flown for our national carrier are highly regarded. As SAA has now all but collapsed, its captains have become hot property on the global aviation market, and that very South African stab of pride-rage no doubt awaits us in the near future as we hear our Emirates Captain Willem van der Merwe welcome us on flight EK-what-what to Dubai. Which is to say that Gigaba doesn't have the right to appropriate the uniform of a cartoon character, let alone a South African Airways captain.

It would seem Gigaba's ongoing problem is "reading the room". The opening of Parliament is a grotesque circus in which our corrupt government officials flaunt what they've bought with the money they've stolen from us. It is not a nine-year-old's fancy-dress party.

Moving on to Home Affairs later in 2014, Gigaba became the poster boy for the destruction of tourism by implementing, doubling down on, changing and then giving up on the most absurd visa regulations in the world. They required that children coming into the country carry with them an unabridged birth certificate and a letter of consent from any non-present parent, and they proved enormously frustrating for tourists wanting to come and spend foreign currency in our country. How this benefited the Zupta cabal is not clear, and it's possible that it may have simply been to hurt the Western Cape which, with actual strategic intent, was successfully growing inbound tourist numbers year-on-year, but had a nasty habit of voting for the wrong people. Whatever the reason, it seems Gigaba's fragile ego played a part.

When Redi Tlhabi, respected author and radio personality, suggested on Twitter that the entire visa shambles and the tens of thousands of jobs lost because of it was because his ex-wife allowed her cousin to take Gigaba's daughter to Cuba to see her, Gigaba gave Tlhabi a very public ultimatum to retract and apologise or face the full wrath of his attorneys.

Tlhabi declined and Gigaba did nothing. But, as the long-suffering public would discover, Gigaba was developing a habit of using state institutions to fight his petty little domestic battles.

Anyway, Gigaba's unmatched ability to act as enabler-in-chief as the Zuptas destroyed our electricity generation system, national airline, railways and ports meant that by 2017 he was destined to attain greater heights. By this time, Zuma was emboldened enough to remove Pravin Gordhan as finance minister, and in his place, the nation was asked to imagine instead that this prick was in our finance ministry… And that, folks, is state capture in action.

There are many contenders for the date that marked the exact nadir of the Zuma administration, but the appointment of Gigaba to head the treasury on 31 March 2017 is a hard one to look past. This was the year that both Standards & Poor's and Fitch downgraded South Africa to sub-investment grade junk status, and Gigaba's permanent visage during his 11 months as finance minister was one of deer-in-the-headlights how-did-I-get-myself-into-this mute horror. He did, however, manage to massage the financial situation as wisely as he could, getting government to okay accumulated travel bills of R870,000+ for his second wife, Norma, as she accompanied him on global roadshows to try to prevent imminent junking of the economy.

Norma was the well- if not long-matched Instagram primping preener who developed a habit of posting pictures of herself spending her taxpayer-funded R16,000 daily allowance in all kinds of bog-ordinary locations that would only ever impress those who've never left Pretoria. It's a fun game, actually, to compare Norma's mortifyingly vain fashion-crime insta-pose nonsense with the ordinary Manhattanites going about their business around her. She looks more of a puffed-up imbecile there than she does here, which is quite a feat.

Malusi and Norma didn't work out, though. Their relationship fell apart not too long after he was forced out of Cabinet (can you believe it). Having been shifted by Cyril Ramaphosa from the finance ministry, in one of the first official moves to try to fix the steaming mess that Zuma had left behind, he was put in charge of Home Affairs once more, but the state capture years of dodgy personal filmography and lying under oath were fast catching up to him. Only weeks after the viral willy wafting emerged, the killer blow was delivered by the Constitutional Court, which denied his bid to overturn an earlier finding that he had told porkies under oath. In that instance, it was in an attempt to allow the Guptas to muscle in on action at OR Tambo after he, as minister of Home Affairs in 2016, had initially approved the Oppenheimer family's private Fireblade terminal. In trying to reverse that decision he found himself up against Nicky Oppenheimer on a hiding to nothing that would eventually see him moved on from Cabinet. That it was one of the richest people in the country who brought about his fall from grace, salary and influence would no doubt have devastated the strutting Gigaba all the more.

"[Gigaba's arguments were] disingenuous, spurious and fundamentally flawed, laboured and meritless, bad in law, astonishing, palpably untrue, untenable and not sustained by objective evidence, uncreditworthy and nonsensical... A court does not readily make findings that a minister's version is untenable and palpably untrue. In this matter it had to be done."

*Judge Sulet Potterill of the Pretoria High Court,
ruling against Gigaba in the Fireblade case*

The story with Norma still had a little way to run, though. In July 2020 she found herself arrested by the Hawks and thrown in jail overnight for keying a Mercedes-Benz G63. The car in question, with a price tag of around R3.2 million, absolutely didn't belong to Malusi Gigaba, though he was fortunate enough to have friends who lent it to him. And friends who, it seems, could arrange for his wife to be locked up on a Friday afternoon.

One wonders what happens to a man like Gigaba, reduced to bitterly calling in favours from the cops to teach his wife a lesson, as she put it, in yet another public/domestic embarrassment, and arguing in Parliament about penis size with the EFF.

Gigaba is a cautionary tale about integrity and what might have been in more moral times. Swept up with the business-class tickets and the ministerial perks, he forgot that power is fleeting. Now his longer-term fate lies in that of the ANC. If the Zuma/Magashule gangsters prevail, he'll be fine.

If not, we bet he looks great in orange.

See Brian Molefe.

Guan Jiang Guang

Massage parlour owner; mates with a minister; rhino horn trafficker; symbol of the decimation of South Africa's rhino

Dishonourable mention: David Mahlobo

IT MAY BE A POINT WE MAKE TOO OFTEN IN THIS BOOK, but what the hell. The cognitive biases, ideological bubbles and false dichotomies heaped upon the world by the big social media networks in their drive for more monetisable rage are a problem.

Exhibit A would be an internet meme (to use the word correctly, for a change) that did the rounds on the South African internet in the early 20-teens. It was a classic false dichotomy: who cares about a rhinoceros when other really bad shit happens in South Africa?!

How the savants mocked people who put those red rhino horns on the front of their cars. As one smug commentator put it, "When the state gunned down 34 miners in Marikana for asking for a living wage, they were silent." (Also: "the plastic rhino horns look like dildos".)

You could have fun with this wearisome posturing, in a *reductio-ad-absurdum* kind of way. When battery hens were being mistreated, they were silent. When the Chinese continued to occupy Tibet, they were silent. When I was served a dissatisfying Caesar salad at the News Café in Sandton, they were silent. When the French government changed regulations that allowed cheese manufacturers to use the name "Camembert" when the cheese has been made with pasteurised milk, instead of raw milk, they were silent.

"When a terrible thing happened and I needed to clamber over the dead at Marikana to proclaim my virtue, they were silent," seems to be a fairer analysis of this very online, very boring line of argument. Because most adults are actually able to hold two (or more!) unrelated and objectively true facts in their heads at the same time.

You *can* care about both. It's only Twitter's algorithms that don't like it.

And so to the rhinos. They matter a great deal. They are a relic, dinosaurs in a modern world, and they are, for one thing, important to tourism. Far more importantly, though, rhinos are beautiful and, to steal from the philosopher Roger Scruton, "beauty is vanishing from our world because we live as though it did not matter".

It's worth remembering that the first and most devastating rhino poachers were the European settlers. According to veteran wildlife reporter Mic Smith, it is estimated that in East Africa, "170,000 black rhinos were killed for the trade in their horn between 1849 and 1895 to supply 11,000kg/year to Asia". And in South Africa, "the white hunters and their guests shot South Africa almost out of elephant and rhino except for in a few areas, by 1860".

So, before we get too excited about the market for rhino horn as some kind of crude form of Viagra for priapically unimpressive Asian men, let's first get some facts straight. Rhino populations were obliterated by uncontrolled trophy hunting during the colonial era, and the tenuous state of our rhino populations has a lot less to do with Eastern erections, much as some people may like the salaciousness of the idea.

That established, we can surely agree that the shooting and killing of African rhinos for their horns was, and remains, a tragedy for South Africa's natural heritage, whatever the reasons. Those reasons include the buddy-buddy relationship between Jacob Zuma's disastrous Minister of State Security David Mahlobo and a Chinese national by the name of Guan Jiang Guang, who was a known rhino horn smuggler. Known, that is, to everyone except David Mahlobo, which is quite something since Mahlobo was our security minister at the time and Guan was a bona fide self-confessed criminal. But then Mahlobo also claimed he thought he was going to Guan's "spa" which was code for "massage parlour" which was code for brothel. Of course, Guan vanished in a puff of smoke the minute their cosy relationship emerged.

That was all in 2016, with rhino poaching in South Africa at its awful peak, and serpentine syndicates of businessmen, veterinarians and poaching grunts running amok. Between 2013 and 2017 more than a thousand rhinos, out of a population of approximately 20,000, were killed and butchered for their horns each year in the country.

The good news is that, by the end of the decade, it appeared that the tide had turned and we were beginning to win the war against the poachers, with killings declining for a fifth consecutive year. The departure of Mahlobo from Cabinet in 2018 may or may not have been relevant. What absolutely was relevant was the coordinated human effort it took to marshal the forces required to take on the gangsters and smugglers, like Guan, who care nothing for the natural world. It's a response that echoes the efforts of conservation pioneers like Ian Player and Magqubu Ntombela many decades ago, who rescued the white rhino, in particular, from the verge of extinction. Given that South Africa is home to around 80% of the world's rhinos, this is worth celebrating.

Still, far too many rhinos are dying and the war on poaching is far from over. It has distracted SANParks from the difficult business of running our precious national parks, it has brought violent and dangerous people into our natural places, and it has caused harm to our tourism.

"Beauty is an ultimate value – something that we pursue for its own sake, and for the pursuit of which no further reason need be given. Beauty should therefore be compared to truth and goodness, one member of a trio of ultimate values which justify our rational inclinations."

Roger Scruton

But apart from anything else, it's just brutal and inhuman to mow down a rhinoceros with an AK-47 and hack off its horn while it lies there, dying. Surely, even in the post-truth era, we can all agree on that?

The Guptas

b. in a time when countries were colonised by other countries, not families (c. the late 1960s)

Modern familial colonists; three-headed embodiment of South African state capture; Zuma's puppeteers

Dishonourable mentions: Malusi Gigaba, Des van Rooyen, Duduzane Zuma, Jacob Zuma, Mosebenzi Zwane et al

ALEKSANDR SOLZHENITSYN OBSERVED that you only need a mouthful of seawater to know the taste of the ocean. With that in mind, consider the story that shot the Gupta brothers to infamy in South Africa.

In 2013, the niece of Ajay, Atul and Rajesh Gupta was getting married, and the brothers Gupta wanted to put on a show for their friends and family and business associates to remember. They wanted glitz and glamour and excess at the classiest joint they could think of, Sun City, and, perhaps unfortunately for other less-resourceful brothers, they didn't want to pay for it. So they arranged for the South African taxpayer to do so instead; which is to say, they stole money via a government department and assigned portions of that money to cover the wedding costs. They then booked out Sun City for four days, chartered an Airbus to fly in the family from India, and got permission from their friend Jacob Zuma, the President of South Africa, to land it at Waterkloof Air Force Base, a national key point that was conveniently close to their chosen party destination. Illegal blue-light escorts chaperoned them on their last leg of the journey, before they enjoyed "the event of the millennium" with a suitably impressed guest list of ministers, businessmen and peddlers of influence. As a noteworthy aside, the Guptas demanded that the event organisers provide only white waiters, which appears to validate widespread claims that they are anti-black racists.

The amount of money involved in this little heist is hardly eye-watering by state capture standards: a round R30 million. Really not worth getting your panties in a twist about compared to some of the quantities acquired without warrant, blatantly thieved or simply blown out of existence in many other pages of this book. But the Gupta wedding was a revealing event, a garishly wonderful peek into the way the brothers do business. In the words of journalist Richard Poplak, it "was a political event designed to make a political statement: *We own this country*." In hindsight, though, it proved more than even that.

For one, it was the gig that placed the Guptas squarely in the public's eye. Before the wedding, from around 2010, investigative journalists had been probing their questionable relationship with Zuma; they weren't unknown in South Africa, but they weren't really dinner-time conversation either. Afterwards, they certainly were, and eventually they would be "the most hated family in South Africa". The wedding was the link between the two estimations, their debutante ball. Notably, this wasn't for the thievery of the R30 million, details of which would only be revealed much later; it was for the flaunting of their relationship with Zuma, the famous "Number One", who could arrange the use of the country's premier air force base if he sat ever-so-comfortably in your pocket.

Second, the wedding was a who's who of almost all the paid-off, ethically compromised players who had been drawn into the Gupta orbit, and who would in the following years reveal themselves as complicit in the looting of the country. The draft guest list, laughably misspelt as it was, offered some raw insight into the family's ambition. Just about every politician with an inkling of power was spreadsheeted, from the president through the Cabinet to all the premiers, along with dozens of SOE executives, heads of the major banks and the most prominent white monopoly capitalists in the country, Johann Rupert, Jonathan Oppenheimer and Koos Bekker. (Bell Pottinger hadn't been paid to spread the WMC poison just yet, so this wasn't a problem.) They even earmarked spots for well-known journalists "Ferel" Haffajee, "Philisia" Oppelt and Peter Bruce so that, one presumes, the masses might learn of this splendid affair. (In the end, they got a PR company to send out media updates.)

When the time came, discretion got the better of most of those targeted for acquisition, but many prominent figures succumbed to temptation: the dupe they wanted as finance minister (see Des van Rooyen); the dupe they eventually got as finance minister (see Malusi Gigaba); the dupes who would audit for them (see below).

Following the outcry over the Waterkloof landing, Jacob Zuma himself withdrew his RSVP at the last moment, but there were various other Zumas in his stead. The most conspicuous was his slick but pliable son Duduzane, who had been appointed as director of Mabengela Investments, a Gupta company, in 2008. He was only 25 at the time, with no qualifications to speak of bar one: his father had recently become president of the ANC. By 2013 Duduzane was in the process of amassing a fortune in business with the Guptas, and would come to be seen as a greasy nexus between the families; the point of contact between the man with power and the men with money. He appears to have served as inspiration for other children of politicians, not least the Magashule boys, to head down the slippery slope to where business meets political influence.

Which leads us to the Gupta wedding's third insight: the mechanics of the job. In this instance, the basics required were a morally flexible contact in the department of agriculture of a friendly province, a bogus dairy project, a few front companies to launder the money, and an amenable transnational auditor – really, not much more than that.

The Guptas' key man here was one Mosebenzi Zwane, another wedding attendee, who was MEC for Agriculture and Rural Development for one of Zuma's key men, Premier of the Free State Ace Magashule. Zwane helped set up a dairy project near his home town of Vrede and award the contract, worth R114 million, to Estina (Pty) Ltd, a company wholly unqualified for the job. The project would, however, never get going: a plot of land was leased, the poor locals were sold some promises of a better life, and that was about it. Instead, the bulk of the money was transferred to a Gupta-run shell company in Dubai and then laundered back into South Africa via several more Gupta shells.

One company in particular, Linkway Trading, ended up receiving exactly R30 million from another company, Accurate Investments Limited. The invoice in question described the payment for "V&A Function", which happened to be the initials of Vega and Aakash, the bride and groom at the wedding in question. All that was left to do was for the Guptas' auditors, KPMG, to look the other way as they signed

"No airplane in the world can land without permission."

Atul Gupta, telling the truth and giving the game away in an interview with the SABC shortly after the Sun City wedding

off, which they did by pretending that Accurate and Linkway were unrelated parties. They no doubt considered this a fair trade for their wedding invites.

And, lo, the deed was done.

The brazenness of it all defines the process. Just as they set up a newspaper and news channel – *The New Age* and ANN7 – that were quite clearly their propaganda outlets from day one, so the Vrede-dairy-farm-as-wedding-fund was exactly what it looked like. They felt no need to set up a rudimentary dairy project as cover. They couldn't be bothered to come up with a less crackable reference than "V&A Function". The auditors even wrote off the whole thing as a business expense: no taxes paid on the stolen tax money – now that's tax optimisation, boys! For the Guptas, by now ensconced as the family behind the people who ran South Africa, repercussions were the merest hypothetical.

And hey, wasn't it a cracking party? Invoices that formed part of the Gupta Leaks revealed that very nearly half a million bucks went on booze alone. It does raise the question: if you steal money, does it by some poorly understood course of nature mean that you must be *completely* tasteless? Had the Guptas actually earned the R30 million they blew on this wedding, one wonders whether it might have been an iota less nauseating. Might they have looked at the cost of the harpists, for example, or the scale of the fireworks display (invoiced cost: R300,000) and thought, you know, let's turn this down a bit? Maybe this is just ever so slightly disgusting?

Now, drink up that seawater and imagine this vignette played out again and again and again. Imagine that the Guptas hadn't merely "captured" a provincial farming project, but an entire country, its senior politicians and its treasury; that the R30 million wedding really is a mouthful of pilfering compared to the ocean of thievery in which the Gupta brothers swim. Well, no need to imagine; just page through any number of entries in this book.

By some estimates, these émigrés – apparently despatched by their father from India in the early 1990s to "take advantage" of the opportunities that might arise in the country's new political era – have acquired somewhere in the region of a hundred billion rand in their rigging of tenders, plundering of state apparatus and effective insider-trading as a result of their relationship with the president of the country. But "a hundred billion rand" is one of those thumbsuck guesstimates that does no justice to the enormity of the damage they've wrought. For they haven't stolen mere money from the South African people; they've stolen years from its economic trajectory and even the lives of its citizens. They've destabilised the entire country, torn its ruling party to pieces, sewn noxious racial discord among its people (as we saw a couple of entries ago), rendered ineffective whole ministries and SOEs. They've thrown a generation of mainly black South Africans under the bus and, when it all came to a head and they began to reap the whirlwind of public then journalistic then finally political retribution, they skipped abroad with their loot piled high in the private jet. That was April 2016.

The Guptas left wholesale destruction in their wake – those who had presumed a Zuma presidency would be corrupt and disastrous way back in 2009 could not have imagined this. But the moment they left was also the moment a pinprick of hope revealed itself to the country. And it was the moment Zuma was suddenly no longer untouchable.

Today, with a new NPA in place, we would very much like to encourage the Guptas to return.

John Hlophe

b. 19 May 1959

Judge President of the Western Cape; South Africa's most controversial judge; embodiment of the Stalingrad legal defence; judicial credibility killer; victim player; the lower standard

Dishonourable mentions: Michael Hulley, Jacob Zuma

INNOCENT UNTIL PROVEN GUILTY.

Right?

We live in an age when this fundamental tenet of the liberal justice system is seen to be at risk in so many spheres of life, in particular those described and amplified on social media. Modern-day witch-hunts by Twitter require the merest suggestion of improper behaviour or impure thought for the accused to be harangued, bullied or targeted for cancellation by self-imposed enforcers of moral virtue.

There was early Twitter-mob victim Justine Sacco, a South African working in New York who, while on a flight from London to Cape Town in 2013, was denounced by the social media hive mind, which then created a hashtag dedicated to having her fired before her plane landed. She had told a bad joke.*

There was the philosopher Roger Scruton (referenced a few pages back), who was sacked from a UK government advisory position in 2019 in response to a social media uproar because of remarks he had made that were deemed intolerant. His quotes had been deliberately taken out of context by a journalist, and he later received an apology from government and was reinstated.

More recently and famously, there is JK Rowling, who has been designated a TERF (trans-exclusionary radical feminist), denounced by many of the actors whose careers she helped launch, and sent dozens of death threats. This, most notably, after she had objected to the term "people who menstruate" in a tweet.

In South Africa, the accusations of Salem are most pronounced when the charge has anything to with race. If you're H&M or Clicks, for instance, and you don't quality-control your advertisements, you may find your stores trashed by EFF trolls the next day – which happened in January 2018 to the former and September 2020 to the latter. Accused, tried and sentenced with just one tweet from above. No mitigating circumstances here.

Though the real-world effects are dramatic and life-affecting in these cases and others like them, notice, please, that none of this is actual judicial justice. Thankfully, the notion of innocent until proven guilty is something we still adhere to in our liberal democracy, a tenet that

---

* Sacco was fired shortly after landing, and spent a year trying to get her career back on track. Her offending tweet, sent from Heathrow Airport, read, "Going to Africa. Hope I don't get Aids. Just kidding. I'm white!"

underscores the very fabric of modern civilisation. Without it you may as well live in a Kafka novel.

So we'll draw our line in the sand here. John Hlophe is innocent of any crime until proven guilty. But we have to say, it's not looking good for him.

* * * *

In a microcosm of modern existence, the court of popular justice and the court of actual justice swing from one extreme to the other. On social and even mainstream media: instant, often wildly misguided mob verdicts. In South African courts of law: painfully drawn-out and politicised legal wrangles seemingly without any verdicts.

In recent years we've acquired a dedicated term for the latter phenomenon – the Stalingrad defence, in which a defendant's vast legal team obfuscates, prevaricates, procrastinates and discombobulates, using all the legal tricks of the trade to kick a case's can down the road. *Ab initio, inter alia*, they object to matters of procedure and personnel, apply for stays of prosecution, change legal representatives, encourage "extraneous litigation", call in sick, appeal all verdicts, delay and postpone, postpone and delay, *bovis stercus ad infinitum*. Basically, it's professional ducking and diving to ensure your client never has his day in court. Ideally for the proponent, it goes on until someone somewhere gets the case thrown out. And it's given that much more room to play out in South Africa because of the sorry state of the NPA which, even when it isn't being actively influenced from above, is under so much operational pressure that regular delays from its side are inevitable.

The most prominent proponent of the Stalingrad defence is, of course, Jacob Zuma, who used it, under the guidance of his legal field marshal Michael Hulley, with such effect that it bridged his entire presidency. He could be president of a country of 50 million people with grave charges of fraud and money laundering hanging over his head because innocent until proven guilty, your honour. Charges of corruption relating to the Arms Deal were first brought against Zuma in 2005, the same year that Schabir Shaik was convicted in a separate trial and sent to prison for being in a corrupt relationship with him. The logic of it all seemed fairly watertight: Schabir Shaik was guilty of being in a corrupt relationship with Jacob Zuma, therefore Jacob Zuma was... Fast-forward 15 years and we still don't have an official answer.

For some insight into the practicalities of these things, consider more recent events in the case. In May 2019, a stay of prosecution application by Zuma and his co-accused, the French arms manufacturer Thales, was heard in the KwaZulu-Natal High Court. It took until October of that year for the full bench of three judges to reach and declare its verdict, which was that the application should be dismissed and the corruption trial should continue. With the actual trial of Zuma due to commence within days of the announcement, political commentators optimistically wondered whether the Stalingrad strategy had finally been defeated. But, as if by magic, a year slid on by, and by the following September there had been no meaningful progress, to the point that the Jacob Zuma Foundation could issue a statement claiming that inadequacies at the NPA were unfairly delaying the hearing of the case. (One of the clearest indicators that the Stalingrad strategy is being deployed is when the suspect boldly makes it known that he wants his day in court, a proposition that is entirely at odds with all other evidence.)

So we see that Zuma, still innocent after all these years, has proved to be something of a contemporary legal pioneer. Today we see his strategy reflected across many political cases, notably in the way ANC Secretary-General Ace Magashule merrily defends party officials who face accusations of corruption but have yet to face the sticky end of a trial. Recent examples include ANC Limpopo treasurer Danny Msiza and deputy chairperson Florence Radzilani, both implicated in the VBS Mutual Bank scandal – and in defending them, he is effectively defending himself. Remember, innocent until proven blah blah... Now let us all get back to work on the taxpayer's dime.

Ace and the cadres have been shown the magic trick and they'll keep using it, because a precedent has been set and there is evidently no viable counter-strategy.

* * * *

The Stalingrad defence isn't just at play on the political battlefield. We see it in business, in our local homeowners' association disputes and, perhaps most worryingly, in our precious judiciary. One of our finest proponents of the strategy is also one of the most senior legal figures in the land: Judge President of the Western Cape Division of the High Court of South Africa, John Hlophe. In a sense, much of Hlophe's career has been a Stalingrad defence, with accusations of all sorts going back nearly two decades.

Appointed Judge President in 2000, Hlophe was considered an especially bright young star of the South African judiciary. His background was truly something. Born at the height of apartheid in Madundube, a rural backwater in northern KwaZulu-Natal, the story goes that he was identified by the local farmer's wife as the brightest kid in the area and sent off to Prospect Farm Primary School. It was a vanishingly rare opportunity for the child of a traditional healer and a sugar-cane cutter to make something of himself, and it was the first step that ultimately saw him becoming a Cambridge scholarship winner and a potential future Chief Justice of South Africa. A helluva tale.

But about four years into his role as Judge President, the epic trajectory he was following seems to have veered off course, and he has been served the full breakfast buffet of allegations since: misconduct, corruption, defamation, nepotism, racism, playing the race card, disparaging colleagues, creating a "climate of fear and intimidation", assault, abuse, aggression, sexual impropriety and essentially being an incorrigible asshole. In late 2020 he even faced the surely ludicrous accusation of being involved in a plot to assassinate his deputy, Patricia Goliath. Then again, the list of other high-profile judges he has publicly and often splenetically butted heads with include Dikgang Moseneke, Johann Kriegler, Jeanette Traverso, Edwin King, Pius Langa and Mogoeng Mogoeng – the latter two while they were Chief Justices.

Hlophe is the most senior judge in the Western Cape, and should be a rock of calm, authority and morality, above reproach. And yet his life and career reads, as *Business Day* reporter Karyn Maughan puts it, "like a long-running soap opera: sensational, interminable and even repetitive".

Of Hlophe's many notable controversies, the most public and potentially ruinous, both to him and the reputation of our courts, is the 2008 allegation that he attempted to influence two judges, Bess Nkabinde and Chris Jaftha, to ensure a Constitutional Court ruling went in favour of Jacob Zuma. As a result, he has faced impeachment on the matter for all of 12 years and counting, interminably delayed by ongoing legal challenges, and mixed in with other scandal, including an obscure dispute between Environment Minister Barbara Creecy and Hlophe's attorney Barnabas Xulu.

Unsurprisingly, Hlophe categorically denies it all, and again he has followed Zuma's lead, playing the persecution card on a regular basis. He's not the bad guy, folks, he's the victim. Innocent until blah.

Here's the thing. Whether he is innocent or guilty, victim or villain, is now well besides the point. For people in position of great authority, there is critical need for a culture of "higher standard" to apply. If your reputation is brought into disrepute, you should stand down while you defend your name, and in so doing protect the integrity of the institution you represent.

Sadly, our lost decade offers perilously few examples of high-profile public figures who have done the right thing and stood down for causing controversy and impugning the reputation of a state institution. We count one: Nhlanhla Nene, who resigned from the position of minister of finance in October 2018, when he admitted to having meetings with the Guptas that he had previously denied. These weren't criminal offences in themselves, but he did the decent thing – unlike Hlophe, Zuma, Magashule and the cadres who take their cues from above.

> "'Innocent until proven guilty' indeed appears to mean 'innocent until the last avenue of appeal has been exhausted'. While that could be a good working requirement for mafia bosses, surely that should not be a standard that the aspirant leaders of our society should adhere to?"
>
> Stephen Grootes, September 2020

> "The impropriety of the judge president's insistence on occupying the office while accused of such a serious charge is all the greater. The suspicion alone disqualifies him. The judge president has no more right to continue in judicial office than a suspected paedophile has to continue running a nursery school."
>
> *Justice Johann Kriegler, writing in February 2009*

> "Prompt and transparent action is needed to dissipate the toxic atmosphere on the Western Cape Bench. Manifestly the starting point – and hopefully the solution – is the urgent removal of the judge president... The problem created by Judge Hlophe has to be confronted once and for all. Every day of inaction that passes further erodes public faith and optimism."
>
> *Justice Johann Kriegler, writing in February 2020 about exactly the same case*

This book is about the opportunities forgone in our "lost" last decade. If ever it needed a metaphor, it is the ongoing principal legal cases against Zuma and Hlophe – both started before the decade began and both will end, if they ever end, well after it has finished. Judge Hlophe, in particular, ultimately comes to epitomise the legal maxim that "justice delayed is justice denied". In his case, the justice is to the South African public, who have watched the integrity of the country's courts shudder and strain in crisis as the system struggles to hold itself accountable. "Teflon John", as he has come to be known, remains technically clean after all these years, but has proved to be a deep smear on our judiciary to the detriment of us all.

There is, however, a glimmer of hope. As effective as it is, South Africans recently discovered that the Stalingrad defence is not entirely impervious to the steady assault of process over time. After 21 years of stalling and evasion, one of the ropiest fellows of our post-democratic history, former spy chief Richard Mdluli, was finally convicted for kidnapping and assault in September 2020. It wasn't the murder conviction it might have been, given that the man he assaulted in 1999 later ended up shot dead, and he was yet to be cheered into prison by an ANC send-off party by the time this book went to print, but a fortress of injustice had finally been penetrated.

Zuma, Hlophe and their fellow strategists would, we hope, have read the news in their foxholes with some concern.

Trevor Hoole
& friends

*Disgraced ex-employees of KPMG; usually nameless
suits who enabled massive corporate and political fraud;
representatives of the failure of Big Four auditing*

Dishonourable mentions: Sipho Malaba, Jacques Wessels

IN ITS EXCELLENT REPORT "THE AUDITORS", Open Secrets unleashed this little gem onto the world:

> "In 2016, in South Africa, 25% of the JSE's top 40 companies appointed individuals who were previously employed by their external auditors as chairperson of their audit committees."

Indeed, this convenient cosiness between corporations and their supposedly independent auditors is a structural problem faced by the global economy, a problem that might relatively easily be fixed if anyone had the appetite for it.

As much as one may bring an auditor's "professional scepticism" to the lefty capitalism-is-evil tone of "The Auditors", the fact is that Deloitte had audited Murray & Roberts, the building giant, for 117 years prior to the regulator enforcing mandatory rotation. Deloitte had also looked after Tongaat Hulett for 82 years.

It requires not an iota of anti-capitalist sentiment to see the problem here. If you've been with somebody for 117 years, or even a mere 82, it's gone beyond a transactional relationship. You're a couple, co-dependent, joined at the hip. There are no secrets between you and you see past each other's flaws. In elderly humans this is all rather sweet, but on the JSE – where the pensions of real elderly people reside – it's problematic, to say the least.

Well, they don't seem bothered at the gleaming head office of Giganticorp, Sandton. The incredibly slick annual-results presentations with messages sharply honed by the best communications experts in the country, the interim reports, the quarterly sales figures, the balance sheets and the cash positions – all are signed off by their "independent" auditor, with whom they've been sharing pillow talk since early last century. And all are used in good faith by asset managers and pension fund administrators to help them decide where to store the meagre wealth earned in a lifetime of hard work by nurses, cops and street sweepers.

When Murray & Roberts was fined more than R370 million by the Competition Commission for sector collusion relating to construction projects for the 2010 Soccer World Cup, one would hope that the auditors were genuinely not to blame – but might they have kept a sharper lookout without a century's relationship to obscure the view? And how do we explain Tongaat Hulett overstating its assets by more than R10 billion without mentioning the bean counters?

The authors of the "The Auditors" adopt a legitimately furious tone, and are quick to ensure the reader understands that the cosy arrangements between the Big Four accounting firms – Deloitte, KPMG, EY and PwC – and their clients are enormously dangerous, and have already caused significant economic harm. After all, if strict processes are muddied with personal relationships and institutional intimacy, it takes just one bad apple and the whole barrel can be poisoned.

Before we get into that, "one bad apple" is best written as "one bad auditing apple", because, as has been observed elsewhere, it takes two to tango. JSE regulations and auditing requirements exist because there is a regulatory presumption that businesspeople will – if you'll excuse some straight talking – take the piss, cut corners and generally make themselves look better than they are. We know that people like Markus Jooste exist and invariably find their way to the top of the corporate tree, and that's why we don't let them count their own beans.

Anybody who's ever experienced a proper corporate audit will adopt the Border War 1,000-yard stare and tell you how tough it is. Real auditors are simply relentless. They miss nothing. Loose auditing, though, is like corruption. Once you've let one thing slide, they've got you. Until the day you die, *you will have let that one thing slide*, and it will forever be something those who benefited from this act of laissez-faire auditing can use against you as leverage for future auditing largesse.

It's thin-edge-of-the-wedge stuff. Because soon enough, loose auditing *is* corruption. One "Let's carry that small cost into the next fiscal because then I'll make target and get an additional 50% bonus" can, with the same auditor, quickly unravel into something like, "How about we pay you R23 million for a report that says what we tell you to say?" We can't say for sure that that's how Tom Moyane's relationship with KPMG started out, but that's certainly where it ended up when the auditor delivered its fabricated report on the SARS "rogue unit".

With the Big Four making up more than 99% of accounting services for the top 500 companies on the Nasdaq, and 100% in the FTSE top 100, this risk is, as the analysts say, almost baked in. There has been scandal after scandal, but South Africa, where graft is the only operating system the government understands, where inequality is stark, where the grey area between those who survive and those who starve is a populous locale, and where the lifeline that measly pensions offer is so critical, there was perhaps a perfect vacuum of vulnerability.

The crime of the auditors is that they are the Great Enablers. The supposedly upstanding pillars of Castle Capital's very existence are supposed to ensure the protection of the smallest shareholders from the depredations of the Sandton charlatans in their Hugo Boss suits, BMW M-what-whats and other accoutrements of New Money. Instead, the auditors burned their clipboards and asked for the tailor's contact details.

The sense that grand-scale corruption is the purlieu of the government and the state's businesses is troublesome. This untrue idea serves as grist to the anti-black racists' mill. It serves those who hate the ANC for other reasons. Equally, it creates space for white white-collar criminals to operate with even more impunity than their black state-employed brethren. And, finally, it allows the state capturers to ask (with reason) why the hell Markus Jooste is not in jail. Regrettably, it allows them to conclude (without reason) that it is because he is white. Twitter sock puppets and bots paid for by the gangsters are only too happy to amplify this nonsense.

> "It is hard to accept that an alert external auditor, using proper standards of professional scepticism and common sense, and with insight into all of Steinhoff's accounts, should not have raised red flags earlier."
> *Open Secrets, on Deloitte's failure to detect Steinhoff's R106 billion fraud*

There is no space here to go into the many scandals and failures of the Big Four around the world, from Enron to Lehman Brothers. They have jointly signed off on the most appalling theft and destruction of value, and there is some succour to be had in knowing we have not been specifically neglected in South Africa. But neglected we have been, most notably in recent years. Deloitte didn't spot R106 billion worth of fraud committed over many years at Steinhoff. PwC missed numerous problems at SAA. KPMG signed off on the SARS "rogue unit" report, the Gupta wedding at Sun City as financed by the Vrede/Estina dairy project, and the looting of funds at VBS Mutual Bank.

That first one was a biggie, which is why we have an entry dedicated to Markus Jooste. In short, if you have a pension scheme, chances are you were a Steinhoff shareholder. Nearly a thousand schemes held stock. The value of that particular investment has plummeted 98% and has cost state workers alone – that's the nurses and cops and street sweepers – a cool R21 billion.

But it isn't always easy for the average observer to make sense of the accounting shenanigans that see unfathomable sums of money vanishing into the ether. They are derelictions of duty, and occasionally crimes, that seem to exist in another dimension; the interactions of nameless, faceless suits behind gleaming glass edifices in Sandton or Midrand. Somewhere along the line a fine of many millions may be paid but then it seems to be business/accounting as usual.

So let's put a few names to them. Let's call out some of the individuals involved, the bad apples. Let's talk about Trevor, Jacques and Sipho, and their colleagues Steven, Ahmed, Mike, Muhammad, Herman, Johan and Mickey, all former employees at KPMG.

There is something vomit-inducing about the way state capture and old-fashioned robbery was enabled, to put it mildly, by Trevor Hoole, Jacques Wessels and Sipho Malaba. In the first case, Hoole was the CEO of KPMG South Africa who evaded the tough questions as it became increasingly evident that the SARS "rogue unit" report that his company had put together was more than a little mistaken. It was, in fact, a sham that was composed, almost word for word in places, of what Jacob Zuma's lieutenant Tom Moyane wanted it to be composed of. To protect Zuma and his cronies, it would lead to the unjustified firing of 50 SARS officials, and cause incalculable damage to the state's ability to collect taxes. When KPMG finally acknowledged its complicity and retracted its findings in September 2017, Hoole was forced to resign, along with seven others, who we'll name here just in case you ever happen to find yourself attending a dinner party in their presence. They were COO Steven Louw, chairman of the board Ahmed Jaffer, and senior

> "KPMG South Africa CEO Trevor Hoole is at best a man who has looked the other way as his associates undertake work that enriches and empowers the Zupta clique, transforming South Africa into a kleptocracy. The KPMG name has popped up with increasing frequency wherever there is the smell of state capture and corruption."
>
> *Thulisizwe Sithole, 2017*

executives Mike Oddy, Muhammad Saloojee, Herman de Beer, Johan Geel and Mickey Bove.

Jacques Wessels, meanwhile, was the grease that lubricated the wheels of the Gupta family's looting of the Vrede/Estina dairy project so that one of their daughters might have a glamorous wedding. It's a sorry affair we covered two entries back. For his efforts, Wessels cracked the nod to the wedding in 2013 and was barred from practising as an auditor in 2019.

Finally, to Sipho Malaba, the auditor arrested in connection with the looting of more than R2 billion from VBS Mutual Bank, a bank created specifically to cater to the poorest of poor South Africans. It has been widely reported that Malaba received more than R30 million of the savings cash and illegally deposited municipal funds that the VBS thieves enlisted him to sanitise with a KPMG sign-off. You'd think a salary of more than R2.5 million would be enough to compensate you for the work of protecting the poor, but evidently Malaba had a pressing need to have a Range Rover, Land Rover *and* Mercedes-Benzes in his Fourways driveway.

In Malaba's case, it appears that a trainee auditor at KPMG first sounded the alarm that the numbers weren't adding up, which would suggest that some of the nameless, faceless suits at the auditors are still good apples. Best we do what we can to look after them and weed out the rotten ones.

See The Guptas, Markus Jooste, Tom Moyane, Dudu Myeni, Floyd Shivambu.

Thamsanqa Jantjie

b. 1979

Dabbler in necklacing and mob justice; frequenter of mental health facilities; sign-language interpreter unable to do sign-language interpreting; victim of South African state incompetence

IN 2003, AN INFURIATED COMMUNITY caught two men with stolen televisions and, in that South African way, they took it upon themselves to necklace them.

"It was a community thing, what you call mob justice, and I was also there," Thamsanqa Jantjie told the *Sunday Times*. Jantjie would never face trial for the murders, as others did, as he was apparently not considered mentally fit to stand trial. He was instead institutionalised for a year.

Jump ahead to 10 December 2013, and South Africa was at the epicentre of a rare and poignant global moment. Nelson Mandela, the icon, had died, and the world's attention was focused on Soccer City in Johannesburg for the most important state memorial service in our country's history.

South Africa had been readying for some time for the passing of its first democratic president and the colossus of modern world history. The newspapers had been prepared, the columns written, the pictures chosen, the analysis done and dusted. The details of his funeral, his lying in state, and the accompanying events, had been hashed out years in advance, with the input of Mandela himself. Preparations had been made for the arrival of more than a hundred heads of state and 50 former heads of state; of kings, queens, princes and princesses.

This was our moment. We had this.

So quite how a mentally unwell mob-murder participant was called only the day before to handle the sign-language interpretation, we can only imagine. This was, it turns out, a man who had recently suffered a relapse, but who delayed a scheduled admission to the Sterkfontein Psychiatric Hospital when the opportunity arose to attend the service. For a man in a fragile state of mind, it's hard to imagine a more intimidating request. And yet there was Thamsanqa Jantjie, standing but a metre from US President Barack Obama, UN Secretary-General Ban Ki-moon and an array of world leaders as they delivered their eulogies, flailing his arms about in an utterly incomprehensible last-guy-on-the-dance-floor-at-3am manner while, as he would explain it, hallucinating about angels flying about the stadium.

"I don't remember any of this at all," he said to the Associated Press when shown footage of himself on stage.

The deaf community was understandably appalled, as the eulogies were rendered meaningless by Jantjie's nonsensical signing. The Americans were flabbergasted – formally they were "upset" – that a man with Jantjie's history and who admits to suffering from bouts of violence had managed to get anywhere near Obama. Somehow, South Africa had fluffed its lines on the grandest stage imaginable.

Nobody can be held accountable for their own illness, but Jantjie was the worst possible guy in the wrong place at a critical moment. In time, an apology from government was forthcoming, though it was couched, not unexpectedly, in begrudging indifference and evasion. "When somebody provides a service of a sign-language interpreter," said Deputy Disability Minister Hendrietta Bogopane-Zulu, "I don't think… somebody would say: 'Is your head okay? Do you have any mental disability?' I think the focus was on: 'Are you able to sign? Can you provide the services?'"

Except that he wasn't able to sign, was he?

Bogopane-Zulu apologised to the deaf community but said there was no reason for the country to be embarrassed.

Of course not. Nothing to see here. Just par for the course.

Markus Jooste

b. 22 January 1961

*CEO of Steinhoff International (2000-2017);
Stellenbosch mafioso; irregular accountant; insider trader;
swarthy face of corporate malfeasance; most loathed
businessman in South Africa?*

IF ENTITLEMENT IS OUR GREAT DISEASE, then that can only leave Marcus Jooste as some kind of national super-spreader. Jooste was, until 2017, the CEO of Steinhoff International, and we believe he is a very bad man indeed. For what it's worth, he is also sensationally unlikeable.

Spokesman for the National Prosecuting Authority (NPA) Sipho Ngwema promises that Jooste will get his day in court one day, but in the meantime we are left to ponder the startling injustice of that day not coming sooner than it will. Indeed, why it hasn't come already. This is yet another consequence of the damage inflicted upon South Africa through the NPA's capture by the Zupta ghouls, as outlined in the first entry in the book. *(See Shaun Abrahams.)*

Steal a loaf of bread from Pick n Pay and the police will come and you will go to court and you'll be sentenced in a month. Steal hundreds of millions of rands or destroy the wealth of many people at an astonishing scale, and there just isn't the capacity at the NPA to handle the complexities of the case. Three years after the collapse of Steinhoff due to "accounting irregularities", Jooste still roams the streets of Stellenbosch and Hermanus without having faced a prosecutor.

It's important to understand that the NPA's dearth of prosecutors with the skills to take on the Steinhoff case, and Jooste's enduring freedom, are not some kind of indicator of the lack of severity of the crime. Let us not make this mistake. If state capture and government corruption is deplorable because public funds are supposed to work to our collective benefit, then those directors of listed companies hold in their hands private money that is even harder-earned than it might have been. Any kind of corporate fraud or negligence on top of the already existing government fraud or negligence thus becomes a double whammy. It is the decimation of the scant funds that people are able to save *after* paying tax, and *after* paying for the consequences of their tax being stolen.

So, once you've paid your income tax, your VAT, your rates and your development levies, and your sin taxes (as you drink to forget the trauma of trying to make ends meet in this country); once you've settled your eye-watering transfer duty and made provisions for the death tax you will pay when you die, only then can you start to pay for things that you have just (supposedly) paid for. And so you will pay to educate your children in a manner that means they will be able to read and count; you will pay for your own private police force because ADT actually works; you will pay for your healthcare because you don't want to die of thirst in a state hospital in a puddle of urine *(see Qedani Mahlangu)*.

And only *then*, when you've paid for all that stuff twice, can you invest some money into the stock market. For most people, this is done on your behalf by a Jaguar-driving incompetent *(see The fund manager)* in Cape Town via your pension fund, which also comes with its own special tax. (They prefer the word "fees" but, as with taxes, it's not like you have a choice in the matter.) Here we come to the critical point.

What happens on the JSE is not only a rich person's worry. It's not even restricted to "middle-class problems" and above. This is the post-tax and post-second-tax, post-fund-manager-fees savings of pretty much anyone with a formal job, especially in the state sector where pension savings are, sadly, so often the only savings.

So we should always remember who got hurt most in 2017 after Deloitte refused to sign off Steinhoff's books, starting a cascade of revelations that boggled markets and minds alike and saw upwards of R100 billion evaporate.

Jooste's rise was impressive. He came from relatively little, had to go into significant debt to fund his chartered accounting degree, and quickly roared onto the business track, ambition flowing. In 1988 he helped put together the sale of a South African retail chain to Steinhoff's German owner, and by 2000 he was CEO of the company.

"Markus Jooste has transformed the South African manufacturer into 'Africa's Ikea' and the second-largest household goods retailer in Europe," gushed *Forbes* years later, before explaining that Steinhoff had purchased Pepkor Holdings for $5.7 billion in 2014.

But if Steinhoff's growth was stratospheric then its subsequent downfall was like a meteor crashing to earth. In December 2017 it shed 90% of its value in just a few days. The heavily invested former dollar billionaire Christo Wiese alone lost somewhere in the region of R50 billion. Steinhoff was found to have "released misleading information into the marketplace": it had overstated assets and profits to the tune of $12 billion. It was a staggeringly huge fraud, and the company was fined accordingly by the Financial Sector Conduct Authority (FSCA).

It would take nearly three years before Jooste faced any form of punishment in his personal capacity. In October 2020 the FSCA fined him at least R122 million for advising four Steinhoff shareholders to sell their stock before the shit officially hit the fan. But, as hefty a fine as that may be – the largest the FSCA has ever issued for insider trading – it is really a sideshow. The dodgy accounting itself has not been dealt with.

It will all come to court, one day, and much of the argument will be technical and indecipherable, as those in the world of finance like to keep it. We will follow it in the news, but our eyes will glaze over as the sterile details emerge, as will the eyes of the state workers, the teachers, the policemen, the nurses. (Christo Wiese may stay a little more attentive, but even he will acknowledge that these are the people most deeply affected.) The Government Employees Pension Fund (GEPF), South Africa's biggest pension fund, with R1.8 trillion belonging to 1.7 million current and retired state workers under management, is facing a R12 billion impairment, at least, from the disaster. This after lending an empowerment vehicle with links to Cosatu almost R10 billion to buy shares in Steinhoff. In those days, the share was trading at around R80 a share. Today it's a penny stock, with a "value", at the time of writing, of about 80 cents or so.

Deloitte, it is worth noting, had signed off at least two annual reports, in 2015 and 2016, that were, it appears, not representative of the truth, illustrating once more that it is not only the players who can be at fault, but the referees too.

Jooste quit the firm soon after the bombshell, and has lawyered up and hunkered down in his Stellenbosch laager, waiting for the weakened NPA to make its move. His Bentley Bentayga is sometimes seen cruising Hermanus, where his compound was the target of graffitied insults for a long while, so he's hardly under house arrest, but one would hope that his social circle has shrunk somewhat. He also faced "revelations" of marital infidelity in the aftermath: salacious tales of a much-younger kept woman who drove a matching Bentayga – some kind of polo-playing South Africanised wannabe Barbara Cartland-style cliché. For God's sake. Behind it all there's just a naked emperor riding a donkey.

"Steinhoff is going to struggle to process all the bad news in America for a long time, so there are better places to invest your money, immediately take the current price and delete this SMS and don't call anyone."

Text message from Markus Jooste to four Steinhoff shareholders the week before the irregular accounting scandal broke, as reported in the Financial Mail

Jooste exists in these pages for the scale of the Steinhoff hit on the savings and pensions of ordinary people, money intended to sustain the elderly in the evening of life, give their kids a fighting chance and allow them to spoil their grandchildren. Money for school fees and trips to the beach. To pay for uniforms and food and electricity bills.

He exists here, too, as the representative of corporate fraud: the stereotypical, philandering big-shot businessman who feels entitled to whatever he sets his eye on because who gives a toss for the little people (and Christo Wiese)? The exact person, along with the crooked politician, the world could do without.

And on that note, Jooste exists here also to make the point that listed businesses have public obligations, and that smart-looking businessmen in expensive suits are no more to be trusted than dressed-down politicians in ANC T-shirts.

The sorry story of Steinhoff's implosion on Jooste's watch reminds us of the importance of maintaining institutions and systems that police everyone who handles other people's wealth, be they the Gauteng Department of Health or a Steinhoff International. Now, as with the crooked politicians, we await Markus Jooste's day in court.

David Mabuza

b. 25 August 1960

*Deputy President of South Africa; Premier
of Mpumalanga (2009-2018); "Cyril's kingmaker";
Cyril's Mephistopheles; living insight into dysfunctional
ANC democracy*

DEMOCRACY IS, AS THEY SAY, THE LEAST-BAD FORM OF GOVERNMENT. Just take a look at "the greatest democracy in the world".

In the space of 16 years, two of three presidents of the United States were elected to office even though more Americans voted for the other candidate. This is because, technically, Americans don't actually vote for their president; they vote for state representatives and senators to choose him. And yes, historically, it's always a him, as Hillary Clinton discovered in 2016 when she won the popular vote but lost the Electoral College to Donald Trump. Al Gore did likewise to George W Bush in 2000.

That's democracy?

Apparently so.

During the 2016 presidential campaign, this perversity saw Trump and Clinton spending nearly three-quarters of their advertising budget and 57% of their appearances in only four swing states: Ohio, Pennsylvania, Florida and North Carolina. Between them, they are home to just 17% of the US population, and if you can name two cities in North Carolina, well done to you.

Push on down this road and you'll find that America is a democracy of gerrymandering and carpetbagging, and that the state of California has 40 million inhabitants and is represented by two senators, while the state of Wyoming has 600,000 inhabitants and is represented by... two senators.

But enough about the country that made modern democracy great and now seems to have totally buggered it up. What about South Africa, then?

Back here we have party-list proportional-representation elections every five years, which means you vote for the party with the presidential candidate you want, and if 50.01% of your fellow countrymen vote for him, he's in. Also, your vote is reflected in the party make-up of the South African National Assembly – assuming, that is, that enough people vote as you do. A party needs about 30,000 individual votes to get a seat, and if you gave your precious electoral cross to Agang or the Purple Cows in 2019, well, better luck next time.

It's a solid system, but this is South Africa; we have our own particular problems. There are two biggies.

First off, we're at best a "dominant-party state", which is the teeny-tiniest technical step away from being a de facto one-party state. And a one-party state in a country with free elections is a democracy in the same way that Hobson's choice is a choice. It's not, and it largely defeats the purpose.

To get the real benefits of democracy, there have to be at least two viable candidates when elections roll around, each serving as motivation for the other to perform their duties to a standard that earns the vote of the people. Intentional authoritarian one-party states in which opposition parties are outlawed used to be more of a thing when communism and fascism were the fashion, before we learnt that those forms of government inevitably result in the death and enslavement of millions of people.* So now de facto one-party states are *de rigueur*. Think of China calling itself a "socialist democracy", Russia holding elections for Vladimir Putin to win every four years, or the way politics rolls in Turkey, Equatorial Guinea and Zimbabwe. And South Africa.

We can thank our sordid history of colonial and apartheid subjugation for this fact of modern South African life, as we now find ourselves in a 26-year-old "democracy" in which the bulk of our voters were so brutalised by the past that they are unable to trust anyone but the party of liberation. Remember this the next time someone says you can't keep blaming apartheid for today's ills. Sadly, you really can.

The next problem of South African democracy is, of course, related to the first: the deep flaws at the heart of the ANC's internal electoral system. Just as the real democratic action in the United States tends to happen in Ohio, Pennsylvania, Florida and North Carolina, so ours happens every five years at the ANC's National Conference, where fewer than 5,000 party delegates hold the future of South Africa in the palms of their hands, effectively voting for the next president of the country.

The system is, as the likes of Gwede Mantashe, Thabo Mbeki and Kgalema Motlanthe have admitted over the years, affected to astonishing degrees by the manipulation and corruption of "careerist" cadres.

The key for those wanting to ascend to power is to find enough delegates to back them. Delegates are representatives of individual branches around the country, but there isn't, as you might imagine, a set number of branches proportionally representing the population by

---

* We learnt that lesson, right?

province. For an ANC branch to exist, you need 100 fee-paying members to join up, and you get an extra delegate for every 250 more members in the branch. Thus a motivated provincial leader can swell the number of his delegates by simply growing the number of members in the region. With annual fees at a mere R20 a pop, he or she could even rustle them up from scratch by starting branches for the low, low price of R2,000 each.

How do these delegates decide to vote? Supposedly as directed by their branch members on the back of robust policy debate that reflects an accurate representation of the people's opinion at grassroots level… But really according to what they're told by their provincial leaders, which might flatly contradict the members' popular vote.

Out of this reality emerges the importance of loyal and effective provincial premiers, our modern dukes of the realm. People who can do what it takes to ratchet up the membership numbers and ensure the designated voting slates are adhered to.

People like David Mabuza.

As premier of Mpumalanga from 2009 to 2018, Mabuza's profound skill was in boosting branch membership. At the ANC's National Conference at Polokwane in 2007, Mpumalanga had 325 delegates, sixth-most of all provinces and so mirroring its status as the sixth-most populous province in South Africa. By Nasrec in 2017, the province had 708 delegates, behind only KwaZulu-Natal. For comparison, Gauteng, with three times the population and almost five times the economy, had fewer than 500 delegates.

In what should have been, but isn't these days, a jaw-dropping piece of reporting, a 2018 *New York Times* profile of Mabuza outlined widespread allegations that he had lured new members with provincial contracts, cash payments from government funds and seemingly obligatory free meals. "He siphoned off money from schools and other public services," it explained, "to buy loyalty and amass enormous power, making him impossible to ignore on the national stage and putting him in position to shape South Africa for years to come."

Also in 2018, a disaffected ANC member in Mpumalanga, Ronnie Malomane, publicly slammed corruption in the province, in particular the existence of "ghost" branches and "cloned" members. "For every branch that is registered there is a cloned branch," he said. "People talk about state capture – here we have municipal capture." And that's not to overlook the persistent rumours that Mabuza had been linked to at least two political murders in his province.

The New York Times article went into great detail outlining allegations of Mabuza's trail of corruption. It claimed that "millions of dollars for education have disappeared into a vortex of suspicious spending, shoddy public construction and brazen corruption to fuel [Mabuza's] political ambitions".

For those interested in irony, Mabuza is a former maths teacher, chair of the South African Democratic Teachers Union (Sadtu) and MEC for Education. As the children of his province are still forced to make use of physically unsafe toilets, one wonders if he sleeps well at night, as the man behind the Bantu Education Act, HF Verwoerd, used to.

There is another, more satisfying irony, though. The story goes that Mabuza learnt his tricks from the master of provincial power plays himself, Jacob Zuma, and of course it was Mabuza's decisive tranche of Mpumalanga votes at Nasrec in December 2017 that cast Zuma into the political wilderness to suffer the indignities of being hauled into court and the general abandonment by those who once suckled at his ample teat. Readers who have seen the video of Zuma's mute yet horrified surprise when Cyril Ramaphosa was announced as the newly elected president of the ANC will appreciate the discretion with which negotiations must have been conducted. Had it been a scene from *Game of Thrones*, we might have seen the knife that had been slid into Zuma's back emerge through his chest right after his tight-lipped oral contortions had acknowledged the moment.

"If you want democracy, you have to join the ANC because the ANC never created democracy outside the party."

Siya Khumalo

The margin of victory was 179 votes.

There have been accusations, most notably from the pro-Zuma faction, that Ramaphosa had to have paid bribes to secure the win. Perhaps they're true, or perhaps the accusers are simply projecting from personal experience. What has been verified is that the #CR17 campaign spent hundreds of millions of rands to achieve victory, including R70 million just to ensure a backlog of branch membership fees were paid up, an apparently legitimate expense. As Marianne Thamm described it, this was "an indication of the deep corrosion... of the party's values and its internal democratic mechanisms", not to mention its capacity to organise.

At the end of it all, Cyril ascended to the throne and his quietly smiling Mephistopheles, David Mabuza, stood beside him as deputy.

For the record, Mabuza rejected the content of the now-infamous *New York Times* article as "baseless". In the same letter, however, he also declared that "the days of state capture are unilaterally over" which, in light of the Covid-19 PPE tender scandals, perhaps devalues his indignation somewhat.

And so we might thank Mabuza for saving us from a Nkosazana Dlamini-Zuma presidency – imagine for a moment that vision of political misery – but we should be wary of the debt to be paid for this Faustian pact. As a result of Nasrec 2017, David Mabuza, the thimblerigger of democracy, is first in line to the presidency of South Africa.

Ace Magashule

b. 3 November 1959

*Premier of the Free State (2009-2018);
Secretary-General of the ANC (2017-); "secretary-
gangster"; "Mr Ten Percent"; Zuma Mk II; the difference
between new dawn and interminable twilight*

*Dishonourable mentions: the Guptas, David Mabuza,
Supra Mahumapelo, Carl Niehaus, Jacob Zuma*

IT WASN'T LONG AGO THAT JACOB ZUMA was the most powerful person
in South Africa and thus, being the man he is, the most dangerous
person in South Africa. How, with a little help from David Mabuza, the
mighty have fallen.

Today Zuma has been reduced to Zooming with his son and Gupta employee Duduzane to try to work ersatz Bell Pottinger narrative diversions into the public discourse, and calling in sickies from Cuba to avoid his corruption trial and Zondo commission appearances. It's worth remembering what an untouchable and all-powerful king Zuma once was, not too many years distant, and comparing it to the pitiable figure he is today. Where he once instilled bogeyman fear in the hearts of South Africa's middle class, today it is contempt.

Now the most powerful person in South Africa is a far more contested position. Nominally it is the president, Cyril Ramaphosa, and we'd hope that really is the case, at least most of the time. But often it's hard to say. During much of the Covid-19 lockdown it was apparently Nkosazana Dlamini-Zuma, and often it seems to be the last person holding the microphone at the end of an ANC NEC meeting.

The most *dangerous* person in South Africa is rather easier to discern – a man with a load of power in his own right. That would be Elias Sekgobelo Magashule, otherwise known as Ace, a nickname from his soccer-playing younger days.

As we have seen in the previous entry, all indications are that the ANC National Conference at Nasrec in December 2017 was as rigged as a tall ship. Depending on which account you read, the voting for the ANC Top Six was either very corrupt or entirely corrupt, and the accusations that Mabuza was paid to support CR17 contrast well with the counting anomalies that saw Magashule pip Senzo Mchunu, from Ramaphosa's slate, to the position of party secretary-general. We've seen that Ramaphosa claimed his presidential victory over Dlamini-Zuma by a mere 179 votes, but Magashule squeaked in by just 24.

And here's the thing: when they added up the votes for Magashule and Mchunu, they found that 68 had mysteriously gone missing

Those in the Zuma faction agreed to a recount only if all the evening's voting was to be tallied again, but Ramaphosa hedged his bets, choosing to bank his position as ANC president rather than risking some more votes going missing next time around. The result is that the power dynamics of South African politics have been in a purgatorial state of paralysis ever since to the detriment of the entire country. Whereas Zuma used to have Gwede Mantashe as his wily SG enforcer, Ramaphosa has a similarly sharp operator working against him.

The reason for the antagonism is not hard to surmise. Magashule is a man swathed in allegations of corruption, fighting the same battle that Zuma has fought for the last 15 years, and using the same strategy to avoid going to prison: stay in power to retard the formal course of justice.

Unlike some of the players in this book – Zuma, for one – Ace Magashule's liberation credentials are not as glorious as they might appear on first blush. Whereas Zuma spent a decade on Robben Island with Mandela, and long years in exile and as an underground guerrilla, Magashule's past is less impressive than he would have you believe. This is the take of author Pieter-Louis Myburgh, whose book *Gangster State* did to Magashule in 2019 what Jacques Pauw's *The President's Keepers* did to Zuma two years earlier. Which is to say, it aired a lot of dirty laundry.

Magashule was brought up by his mother in the township of Tumahole in Parys in the Free State in the 1960s and '70s. He was a teenager when the Soweto uprising came to town, and when he went off to university he felt drawn to student activism – but he appears to have overstated his efforts somewhat, claiming to be co-founder of both the Congress of South African Students and of the United Democratic Front, and to have been charged with high treason when it seems he was arrested for accidentally being in the wrong place at the wrong time. In the mid- to late-'80s, he went into "internal exile" in Hillbrow where he developed a reputation as an effective fundraiser, but also as a possible requisitioner of those funds. This was a reputation that he has, it seems, never shaken. Magashule ascended steadily through the provincial ranks of the Free

"She only used to say, 'Do what will satisfy you; anything which will make you happy you must do.' That was the message always."

Ace Magashule, reminiscing about his mother

State, first as leader of the ANC and eventually as premier. By the time the era of Zuma came around he was, according to Myburgh, as keen as any of the pirates of Polokwane to have the Scorpions disbanded to avoid being prosecuted.

As one of the loyal dukes to Zuma's king, Magashule thrived in the Zuma Years, coming to dominate the Free State as Mabuza did Mpumalanga and the third of the Premier League, Supra Mahumapelo, would the North West. Magashule was said to have an interest in all activities in his province, earning the nickname "Mr Ten Percent" as he went about his business which, perhaps unsurprisingly, saw the Free State fall into general administrative decline. No surprises either that he struck up cordial relations with the Guptas at an early stage. His son Tshepiso was employed by them from 2010, and Magashule has been pinpointed as a key figure in the Vrede/Estina dairy farm and asbestos heist scandals, among others.

Today he is seen as the gangster heir of the Zuma mafia, a man who benefited from Zuma's patronage and protection and is willing to return the favour. In the three years since his acutely suspicious appointment as SG of the ANC, he has conspired with Zuma in public, defied Ramaphosa's explicit instructions not to use the ANC as a platform to defend himself (against allegations in *Gangster State*), and aligned himself with serial liar Carl Niehaus and the ragtag rabble of the Umkhonto we Sizwe Military Veterans Association. In August 2020, in a display of remarkably tone-deaf chutzpah, he put his name to an ANC press release headlined "We dip our heads in shame over Covid-19 corruption" shortly after his sons Tshepiso and Thato had been shown to have received nearly R3 million in Covid-19 tenders. Three days after the press release was circulated, Thato was reported to have bought a R2 million BMW X7.

"Limene mene makahambe." (He is a liar, he must leave.)
Free State ANC members singing about Ace Magashule outside Luthuli House,
October 2020

Many observers see Ace Magashule as a leader, if not *the* leader, of the Zuma faction, in diametric opposition to Cyril Ramaphosa. Analyst Ralph Mathekga prefers to see him as belonging to his own "interest group". Either way, the tiny gains we might have made as a country in the three years since Ramaphosa became ANC president and our supposed "new dawn" began pale into what might have been with a supportive, or simply not uncooperative, SG to rely on.

Today, we sit hobbled – Covid-19 notwithstanding – for the sake of an ace gangster and 24 miserable votes.

See The Guptas, John Hlophe, Cyril Ramaphosa, Edwin Sodi, Mosebenzi Zwane.

Supra Mahumapelo

b. 7 June 1968

Premier of North West (2014-2018); "Black Jesus";
"the essence of the absence of presence";
tyrant of the most forgotten; Premier League loser

DAVID MABUZA, ACE MAGASHULE... WHO'S MISSING?

He may have been consigned to political exile now, a fast-dating artefact on the *News24* search engine, but there was a time when Supra Mahumapelo was the inevitable third name on the list. Premier of Mpumalanga, premier of the Free State and premier of North West – they were the Premier League and, you might say, they were as thick as thieves.

There was something alphabetically determinative about Mabuza, Magashule and Mahumapelo.* These were the dukes of the lesser-known fiefdoms of South Africa, the types destined to insinuate their way into positions of power when a king such as Jacob Zuma reigns. As we've seen already, the price they paid for that luxury was absolute loyalty and ANC votes on tap. Mahumapelo's speciality was, it seems, simply dissolving branches that didn't follow orders and creating new ones that understood how the world worked. He was a self-styled nonsensical tyrant messiah, the "Black Jesus" who sought to "create the essence of the absence of presence" – whatever the hell that meant. If it meant not lifting a finger to serve his congregation, he nailed it.

Mahumapelo arrived on the scene a little later than the other two – pretty much at peak state capture – did what he'd come to do, and was the first to exit, literally hounded from office by North West residents he had abused with state looting and criminal negligence. The moment of judgment was an outburst of "chaotic protests" in April 2018 that he could have prevented had he been so inclined. Angry mobs burned buildings and buses and ransacked shops across the province, to such an extent that President Cyril Ramaphosa was forced to return home from a trip to the United Kingdom to quell the madness.

A government task team hurriedly despatched to investigate the state of North West found that it was truly rotten: wholesale institutional destruction from top to bottom. Twenty of 22 municipalities they visited had received qualified audits the previous financial year. Twelve were dysfunctional; things just didn't work. R15.3 billion had been lost to irregular expenditure, a figure on an upward trajectory. And the topper: these were all facts that had been established well before they arrived.

We have to be careful with statistics, though, as they have a tendency to reduce human tragedy to numbers on a page. (A point we'll return to.) What the task team found were tyrannised, neglected, unemployed people at their wits' end, so much so that they set their province aflame,

---

* Though we had to take a little bit of licence with the ordering of the book, as according to our logic Qedani Mahlangu should have been premier of Gauteng.

> "Common complaints… included insufficient governance, widespread corruption, poor service delivery, the appointment of incompetent officials, lack of consequence management in response to fraud investigations, dysfunctional councils, unemployment and a lack of support for youth initiatives."
>
> *Andisiwe Makinana, reporting on the findings of the inter-ministerial task team sent to investigate protests in North West*

from Mahikeng to Stella to Taung, just to gain the attention of those who might actually do something about it. Their violence barely made national headlines, but if you're ever wondering why enraged citizens out in the sticks take it upon themselves to burn down their local library and firebomb the buses that take them to work, it's because people in Pretoria (and Johannesburg and Cape Town) don't notice otherwise.

This time it worked. Despite the best efforts of his buddy Ace to stick up for him, Mahumapelo was soon sacked – the first of the Premier League to be relegated. He now sits in ANC purgatory while the party that became used to turning a blind eye as its cadres ran amok grapples with the PR problem of what to do about the endless list of delinquent officials it has spawned. Mabuza and Magashule will no doubt watch developments with interest.

North West is an unfashionable province known to the chattering classes for Sun City and not much else. But it is home to more than four million South Africans, almost entirely without meaningful influence in the corridors of power. When we think of Supra Mahumapelo, we should think of the desperate masses of the forgotten far from our major cities – out of sight and mind of those who can still make a difference in South Africa – and the service that Black Jesus has delivered unto them.

Qedani Mahlangu

b. 12 May 1968

*Gauteng MEC for Health (2014-2017); reaper of the
Life Esidimeni tragedy; MEC of torture by cold,
starvation and thirst; humanity at its worst*

FORMER DEPUTY CHIEF JUSTICE DIKGANG MOSENEKE manages to
exude such extraordinary humanity in dealing with the worst of society
that at times you just want to reach out and hug him. An anti-apartheid
activist in his younger days and then a judge in South Africa – to say the
least, he's seen the worst of humanity.

You can imagine, then, that it would be worth steeling one's soul to
hear him answer the question: "What was the worst moment in your
career?" The answer is what we came to know as the Life Esidimeni
tragedy, the commission of enquiry into which he chaired.

"Just the sheer human pain, the lack of care, the disregard," he told *Daily Maverick*.

Life Esidimeni is our destination writ large. It is where this road goes. If you hollow out the state, impose incompetent and corrupt people to administer to the basic rights of poor and vulnerable people, Life Esidimeni is what happens.

It is shocking, it is inevitable, and it will happen again.

It seems unlikely that former MEC for Health and Social Development in Gauteng Qedani Mahlangu ever set out to be an especially evil person. As philosopher Hannah Arendt captured so tellingly in the phrase "the banality of evil", ordinary people who do monstrous things seldom do. Arendt coined the expression while watching the trial of Holocaust architect Adolf Eichmann.

In the months up to June 2016, Mahlangu presided over the removal of 1,700 mentally ill and disabled patients from privately run facilities that cared for state patients. This was done to save the department some cash. And it was done despite repeated warnings and court action from the South African Society of Psychiatrists, the SA Federation for Mental Health and families of many of the patients.

The cluster of facilities from which these state patients were moved were known as Life Esidimeni, and the "care homes" to which they were taken were in many cases suburban residences that had been hurriedly repurposed by operators who knew nothing about how to care for people with special needs. They were not licensed, they did not have the infrastructure to care for the patients, and in some instances it appears they cared absolutely nought for the dignity of human existence.

These vulnerable people – these sons and daughters and sisters and brothers – were packed off to their fate without IDs, without medical records or medicines or files. Families were not told where or when they were moving. In some cases, they had their hands tied and were carted off in the back of bakkies.

The result was that 144 people died from causes that included starvation, dehydration and hypothermia. Years later, dozens of people were still missing. At one monstrously named facility, Precious Angels,

> "It was a bundle of bones. You could count the bones. I stood there and cried… It looked like they never gave her food."
>
> *Daphne Dubree, describing her granddaughter, Mehmona,*
> *who died at the Takalani facility in Soweto*

23 of the 57 people transferred there were dead within a year. At another, Mosego Home for the Elderly in Krugersdorp, the health ombud would find that patients were fed "rotten bread, meals of cabbage and porridge, and only one meal a day", despite the institution having received R13 million from the provincial budget.

The health department had made commitments not to move any patients to substandard facilities, and yet there is no evidence they bothered to run the most basic checks. They may even have actively suppressed inconvenient information. "We knew full well that Life Esidimeni patients would never cope," said veteran mental health worker Joyce Orritt, speaking to *The Guardian*. "They were there under the Mental Health Care Act. They were committed. They couldn't care for themselves. They couldn't be 'deinstitutionalised'." Orritt raised red flags about the conditions of the facilities the patients were earmarked to go to, but she was conveniently suspended shortly before transfers began.

Families spent months trying to find their loved ones, and in many cases they were dead when they did. Some were refused post-mortems, despite clear signs of neglect, starvation and abuse. One man found that his sister had died and simply been buried in the garden of the "care home". A woman had to identify her brother among a pile of decomposing corpses in a disused butcher's shop in Atteridgeville.

Those who managed to find their loved ones alive recount horrific tales. Forty people crammed into a garage with no food or water. People sitting in filthy, urine-soaked clothes. According to *The Guardian*, one man, Lucas Mogwerane, found his brother in appalling conditions and offered him a banana to eat. Soon he was surrounded by starving patients who ate their bananas whole. They were too hungry to peel them.

> "[A]n insider from within the Gauteng health department told that the actions of Qedani Mahlangu were not an aberration, but merely a continuation of standard practice... The only unusual thing about Life Esidimeni was that she got caught."
>
> *Mark Heywood*

People were tied to beds. They were beaten, starved and denied water. How might we explain this extended horror story?

Here's one way: the 1,700 Life Esidimeni patients were booted out of specialist facilities in order that the department could save more money to spend on "irregular expenditure" and "consultants". Those making the decisions couldn't have given less of a damn about what happened to those 1,700 people, but what happened was that 144 of them were, in effect, tortured to death.

Mahlangu had been insisting for some time that the process was necessary due to the savings to be made by cancelling the decades-old contract with Life Healthcare. Budgets were tight, she insisted, and the auditor-general was increasingly concerned about the ongoing contract.

Except that this was nonsense, as Moseneke's investigations would reveal. Gauteng Finance MEC Barbara Creecy rubbished these claims – there had been no such concerns shown by the auditor-general on that front, though "irregular expenditure" was proving to be a problem.

In the 2015-2016 financial year, the Gauteng Health department managed to lose R483 million to irregular expenditure, and it spent R90 million on "consultants". According to the Bhekisisa Centre for Health Journalism, "The body paid R30 million to a consulting firm for 12 weeks of work at Chris Hani Baragwanath Hospital. And the controversial global consultancy group, McKinsey & Company, was paid R485,000 for a two-day workshop." Almost R60 million was paid to two firms of attorneys for ten months of work – equating to R300,000 a day. Remember, this is a *provincial* department. The use of "consultants" didn't stop either – but the care of the weakest people in our society did.

And so to brass tacks. Why on earth did Mahlangu do this? Why didn't she care? Why did the people working under her not intervene? Moseneke tried and tried to find out. He wept, and kept on asking questions. Why did nobody stand up to Mahlangu? Why was everybody more interested in appeasing the minister's inhuman demands than applying the Constitution? Why did civil society and doctors need to scream to be heard? Why did she ignore the pleas and the threats and the warnings and even the court actions?

When confronted, Mahlangu simply denied everything, blamed her subordinates, and arrogantly and dismissively explained that her lack of interest as the crisis unfolded was because she was "busy with political work", as if this somehow justified things. She showed the same disregard for the victims' families as she had shown for the victims themselves.

Moseneke reminds us that "the premise of democracy is insecurity of tenure, the pain and risk of people changing their minds about whether or not you should be in office". Let us never forget that it is actually possible to get rid of people like Mahlangu who, like Eichmann before her, took to claiming she was just a cog in the machine.

Eichmann, at least, faced justice and was hanged in Israel. To its shame, the NPA declined to prosecute Mahlangu. In fact, nobody has suffered any consequences of any significance for the death of 144 people and the traumatisation of hundreds more.

"There is a need to draw a line between the leaders responsible and the people like me forced to serve as mere instruments in the hands of the leaders."

Adolf Eichmann, 1961

"I cannot carry personal blame because I wasn't working for myself. I was an elected official."

Qedani Mahlangu, 2018

Mahlangu was moved on from being Health MEC, but then, true to form, the Gauteng ANC saw fit to re-elect the person who had presided over the worst human-rights disaster in modern South African history to its Provincial Executive Committee in July 2018. It was a move almost as astonishing as the Life Esidimeni story was horrific.

Four months passed before the ANC's National Working Committee eventually overruled the decision and she was fired for good. The consultants and irregular spenders no doubt expressed the gravest sorrow at her departure.

Julius Malema

b. 3 March 1981

Leader of the EFF; fascist; businessman; clickbait

Julius Malema is one of two inhabitants of these pages whose stamina for stuffing up has endured the decade since *50 People Who Stuffed Up South Africa* was published. (No surprises for guessing who's Number One.) This can be attributed to his evolution from "fat little man", as we had it in 2010, to a slimmer, strategically effective fascist today.

We noted back then that for Malema "obesity, in the absence of an enlightened mind, is said to speak of significance". Well, blow us down with a feather if the kid didn't have a shot at banting, that favourite pastime of the radical revolutionary.

Malema and the EFF – for they are the same phenomenon – haven't moved their core offering since inception. An extension of the ANC's

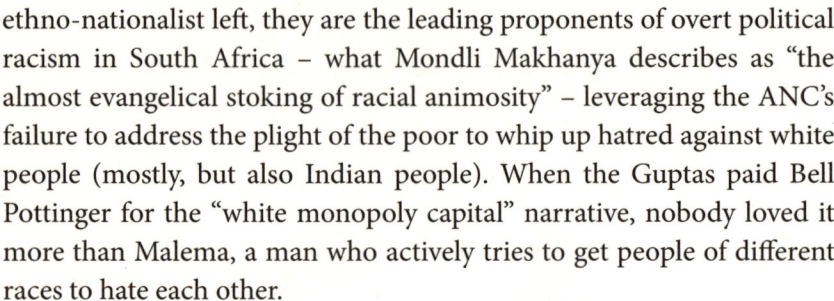

> "It is not a secret that I wear Louis Vuitton and Gucci."
>
> *Julius Malema*

ethno-nationalist left, they are the leading proponents of overt political racism in South Africa – what Mondli Makhanya describes as "the almost evangelical stoking of racial animosity" – leveraging the ANC's failure to address the plight of the poor to whip up hatred against white people (mostly, but also Indian people). When the Guptas paid Bell Pottinger for the "white monopoly capital" narrative, nobody loved it more than Malema, a man who actively tries to get people of different races to hate each other.

Malema remains a selective moralist, jumping on whatever cause suits his agenda. What *has* changed is that he has learnt to wait, like the ethical vulture that he is, for crises to appropriate for his unconvincing performative rage – just ask the folks at H&M, Vodacom and Clicks.

In representative terms, the EFF is small (10.79% in the 2019 election), and yet Malema and the Swarovski *Sturmabteilung* make a Very Big Splash in our media. This is because Malema represents the darkest fears of an editor's white readers, and generates a lot of Twitter noise on the feed of the junior "content producers" populating our big news websites. Seeing Twitter as a wire service, not a curated ideological bubble, they set the Google Ads cycle churning.

In October 2020, a simple Google News search for "Julius Malema" yielded 53,700 results. At the same time, a search for "John Steenhuisen", the leader of the opposition, yielded 35,300 results. Now, news is not a democratic process, but the fact that the leader of a 10% party gets 50% more coverage than the leader of the 20% party reveals much about our society, and the media that serves it.

We leave it at that. Malema's ongoing contribution can be summarised in under 500 words. A bumbling fascist in 2010, a slicker fascist in 2020. The stench of his keto-breath politics may be with us a while longer.

Mugwena Maluleke

*Secretary-General of Sadtu (2009-); principal figurehead
of the dismal failure of South African education;
representative of the economic and societal handbrake
that our unions have become*

MUGWENA MALULEKE IS PROBABLY THE MOST INFLUENTIAL PERSON in South African education today. He is also, it would appear, proficient at his job, having retained the same position for 11 years and consistently delivered what has been asked of him. How can it be that he is performing so well when our education is suffering the greatest crisis in its history?

The answer is simple and sad: because the crisis is all about schoolchildren who are unable to read or write, whereas Maluleke represents the teachers, and by comparison they're doing just fine.

Maluleke is Secretary-General of the South African Democratic Teachers Union (Sadtu), the largest public-sector trade union in the country; and in the world of unions, the SG is essentially the CEO. The buck stops with him, though any free-market metaphors may not be welcomed. Maluleke's interests and influence were well illustrated during one of the most preposterous government pronouncements, of many, to have emerged during the ruinous Covid-19 pandemic. In July 2020 the news came that permissible minibus tax occupancy would be raised to 100% while government schools would be closed for four weeks for fear of teachers becoming sick, despite other civil servants going back to work.

Infection disease expert and government adviser Professor Shabir Madhi explained what was happening: "It seems government is more keen to listen to taxi owners and trade union leaders than to the scientists, because the scientists have come out uniformly to say that you shouldn't have 100% occupancy of taxis, you shouldn't shut the schools… They're going against scientific advice that has been provided to them; they're doing exactly the opposite."

"Teacher unions are undermining our pandemic response," summarised Nic Spaull, a long-time observer of our educational woes. But that's just in 2020. Since the 1990s, they have been undermining the very fabric of our society by perpetuating an educational system that takes malleable young minds and produces young adults who are largely unemployable in the knowledge economy.

The sorry fact of the matter is that science and educational outcomes play second fiddle to politics in South Africa. In particular, we have been outmanoeuvred by unions that have become adept at holding our government to ransom because of their ability to mobilise by the hundreds of thousands and to withhold votes where needs be. (Look out, 2021 municipal elections.) Often, union members sit in the ministries that do the negotiating. The argument for the protection of workers' rights is undeniable, but you don't have to be Maggie Thatcher to see the damage we're suffering at the hands of our unions, especially in education.

South African education is consistently ranked as bad or exceptionally bad in international comparisons, whether it's the Southern and Eastern Africa Consortium for Monitoring Educational Quality or the World Economic Forum doing the measuring. According to a 2017 headline in *The Economist*, "South Africa has one of the world's worst education systems." Some of the stats are unforgivable; for instance, more than a quarter of pupils cannot read after six years of schooling, compared to rates

"With more than 260,000 members, Sadtu is labour federation Cosatu's largest and most influential union. It has been a grooming ground for ANC leaders who have gone on to become ministers, MECs and senior government officials. Many of its members are active ANC branch leaders, and the union provides foot soldiers in election campaigns."

Sipho Masondo, 2016

of 4% in Tanzania and 19% in Zimbabwe. The number of matriculants who achieve university exemption rattles along at less than 30%.

One of the worst crimes of the apartheid era was Hendrik Verwoerd's declared intention to keep the black population poorly educated, as "hewers of wood and drawers of water", for whom the teaching of mathematics was "quite absurd". The apartheid government thus offered the poorest levels of education to those it sought to isolate. The Bantu Education Act was written by Verwoerd himself and passed in 1953 to this end. By the 1970s, black schools received anywhere from one-fifth to one-fifteenth of the funding of white schools.

How, then, is it even possible that our state education has become worse than it was then?

Bantu education was vile, but it seems undeniable now that today's is, practically speaking, worse. In 2016, Statistician-General Pali Lehohla noted that black South Africans between the ages of 25 and 34 were less skilled than their parents. Our long-suffering minister of Basic Education, Angie Motshekga, observed at the time that "educational attainment in South Africa's poorest schools is falling".

Lack of spending isn't the problem. Throughout the 2010s, South Africa budgeted from 5.7% to 6.5% of GDP on education versus a European Union average of under 5%.

No. It really is the teachers who, while feeling entitled to consistent above-inflation salary increases, are abysmal and often abusive. All too many teachers in schools across the country buy positions with cash, sex and favours; physically and sexually abuse pupils; collude to leak matric

"[T]eacher unions at present carry the burden of supporting political movements, of holding the education system together at some provincial and local levels, and functioning in support and defence of their members. They are rendered almost incapable of thinking and acting educationally as a result."
Volmink Report, commissioned for the Department of Basic Education, May 2016

exam papers; refuse to teach extramural activities; and deliberately strike during exam season for best effect. Most damagingly, they are themselves poorly taught, and the hours they teach on average have been whittled down by teacher absenteeism to the point of criminal negligence. A 2012 study of teachers in North West revealed that they taught just 40% of their scheduled lessons. In 2016, Motshekga revealed that teachers at former African schools teach for 3.5 hours a day, compared to those at former Model-C schools who teach for 6.5 hours a day. In 2017, it was reported that 10% of all teachers didn't arrive for work on any given day.

In any other world, there would have been a revolution from above and below to hold our teachers accountable. But Motshekga and her department have, for so long, had nothing on the power of the unions. In South Africa, a third of our budget goes on civil service wages – around R630 billion in the 2020 financial year. The deal, then, is reciprocation come elections, and sharp realpolitik operators such as Maluleke use this leverage as the most ruthless of CEOs might.

It's perhaps revealing that unions have something ironically in common with the corporations that the cadres who run unions so despise (in this case rightly so). They are both entirely beholden to their shareholders; everything else, including the welfare of the greater community, is secondary – merely an afterthought.

So when you read that "Sadtu has a duty to children and their future", as it declares without shame in Maluleke's official biography, this is akin to the marketing gumpf from a Steinhoff-like corporate outlining its commitment to civil servants whose pensions are invested in the PIC. In other words, lip service. Coincidentally, Maluleke is a board member of the PIC. One wonders who taught whom the lesson.

Maluleke believes that the challenges facing South African education are "systemic". No doubt he is correct, but we can be equally sure that he doesn't see the problem when he's looking at himself in the mirror in the morning. May the time soon come that someone with real power – and here we're looking at our ex-trade unionist president – takes seriously the welfare of our future generations, and sets him and his shareholders straight.

Nosiviwe Mapisa-Nqakula

b. 13 November 1956

*Minister of Defence and Military Veterans; member of
the presidential establishment; CIC of an ever-declining
national embarrassment; proof of the lie of the Arms Deal*

Dishonourable mention: Kebby Maphatsoe

IF YOU'RE NOT ENTIRELY AU FAIT with your contemporary South African politics – if at some point in the last decade you had to, for the sake of your sanity, take a step back from the relentless media reportage of ongoing governmental calamity and capture – then you might struggle to place Nosiviwe Mapisa-Nqakula. Which one is she again?

You'll know she's a cadre, of course. Cabinet-level to make these pages, presumably, so something of a heavyweight. Leading a department swathed in allegations of incompetence and corruption, most likely.

But that doesn't really narrow it down, does it?

If you apply your mind a little, you might link the Nqakula in her surname to her husband, Charles, who was famous, while minister for Safety and Security back in the day, for saying that people who complained about the crime rate in South Africa should stop whining and just emigrate already.

Now we're getting somewhere.

Nosiviwe Mapisa-Nqakula has, in fact, been in Cabinet for 16 years, as minister of Home Affairs, Correctional Services and, since 2012, Defence. In deference to the last role, perhaps, she has managed to camouflage her Cabinet career by distinguishing herself positively in precisely no way. Perhaps the only incident she is remembered for is the bizarre claim, wrapped in much juicy speculation, that she smuggled a young Burundian woman into South Africa in an air force jet in 2014. Nevertheless, she provides a thread that connects the reigns of Mbeki, Zuma and Ramaphosa. Together she and Charles, also a previous minister of Defence, are literally a power couple in South Africa, effectively ruling aristocracy – which makes her dismal legacy that much sadder. Here we are focusing on her leadership of our military during the last/lost decade – and what a shambles it's been.

If the Arms Deal was the story of the ANC's original sin of corruption, then the record of the South African National Defence Force since then reveals just how unabashed this rooting of the government till was intended to be. Even for a virgin effort, there were no qualms offered or intended, and the proof is in the dilapidated state of our army today. Had those in government chosen *not* to endow our military with billions of rands worth of unnecessary equipment as a means to funnel the spillover into their pockets, then its subsequent decay might not be as galling. Instead, there's gall just about everywhere, as our military proffers up embarrassment after embarrassment while the once-shiny fighter jets don't fly and the frigates rust gently at anchor.

As we outlined in the entry on Joe Modise in the original *50 People*, the Arms Deal had us purchasing equipment the country neither needed nor could afford to run. Nothing has changed on that front. For instance, in June 2016 Mapisa-Nqakula explained in Parliament that just half of the air force's 26 Gripen fighter jets were on active service while the other half were on "rotational preventative maintenance", a technical way of saying "not exactly gathering dust because they're cleaned on a regular basis". And in September 2019, our most senior sailor, Vice Admiral Mosiwa Hlongwane, reported that the navy was receiving approximately a quarter of the annual funding needed to maintain its vessels. Of three frigates and two submarines in urgent need of refitting, they had 70% of the R400 million required for a single submarine. They needed another R400 million for the other submarine, R700 million each for the frigates, and who knows how much for the rest of the navy.

That's the high-tech stuff. But it turns out we couldn't afford, or didn't know how, to run even the bare basics of a military force. So while the Gripens sit meekly in their hangars and the frigates are tethered in Simonstown, Mapisa-Nqakula struggles to find the available cash just to pay her soldiers' wages. And when those soldiers go out and about and try to do actual army stuff, the result is comical farce bookended by the deepest human tragedy.

Sexual exploitation and abuse within the military has become so "rampant", Mapisa-Nqakula's own term, that she admits to dreading its abbreviation – SEA – because she deals with it so regularly. Our reputation as peacekeepers in central Africa is such that the United Nations now regards the SANDF as one of the worst sex-offending armies on global duty, and Parliament was compelled to form a dedicated task force in 2019 to investigate allegations going back years. At this point, it's worth recalling that Mapisa-Nqakula was president of the ANC Women's League in the mid-2000s, when it gave its vociferous support to one Jacob Zuma, a man who faced a high-profile rape trial and has been argued by many to be a sexual exploiter of women.

Meanwhile, only around a third of our 35 Oryx helicopters, the workhorses of the army, are operational at any one time. As a result, our ability to respond to humanitarian crises such as Cyclone Idai, which struck Mozambique in March 2019, is a fraction of what it was in the past.

In May 2019, an SANDF parachutist crash-landed into a pole at Cyril

Ramaphosa's presidential inauguration. He appeared not to be too badly injured, but the metaphor about competence and capability was hard to ignore. (It also proved to be a portent of things to come for the president.)

Another crash landing followed in January 2020, this time for the air force's only serviceable Lockheed C-130 Hercules, at Goma airport in the Democratic Republic of the Congo. Built in 1963, the transport plane is unlikely ever to fly again, though the SAAF will be hoping to get a couple of its remaining seven Hercules airworthy at some point. Without them they have effectively no logistics capabilities, and have to hire Russian Antonovs to do the job.

The following month, a video did the social media rounds, showing a battalion of soldiers unable to respond to the order to march while preparing for Armed Forces Day in Cape Town. Onlookers could be heard laughing as the battalion commander, to use a well-known military phrase, lost his shit. A separate clip that same month showed an SANDF Rooikat armoured vehicle careening out of control and scattering shrieking soldiers before ploughing into a barricade at the Roodewal bombing range in Limpopo. Both are scenes straight out of *Sgt Bilko*, and they're hardly the only ones in circulation. The army's response is to bemoan the intentions of those "casting doubts about its personnel and equipment to the unsuspecting public".

But, dear army, the public is no longer unsuspecting. The doubts are well and truly suspected. Confirmed, even. Many times over.

In April, Professor Lindy Heinecken, author of *South Africa's Post-Apartheid Military*, outlined the difficulties facing the SANDF following the deployment of troops to help maintain lockdown regulations during the Covid-19 crisis. "For the past 25 years," she wrote, "there has been little to no organisational transformation to reconfigure the force structure and design to meet current realities." As it stands, in short, there is no battle plan and it's being terribly executed.

Heinecken went on to express concern that our soldiers were not adequately trained for community policing, and that "excessive force against civilians" may be used. And, lo, it came to pass that her worst fears were realised. A week later Collins Khosa was dead due to blunt force trauma to the head following an encounter with SANDF members in his own home, in which numerous witnesses claim he was doused with beer, choked and beaten with a rifle. Khosa's wretched and unnecessary death, along with the peremptory SANDF response to it, was just one of many similar distressing incidents – incidents that Heinecken had suggested were almost inevitable, given that the SANDF is not fit for the purpose of policing our cities.

Sadly, the SANDF is not fit for the purpose of much these days. Most of its equipment is obsolete or defunct, while the new stuff is, as we've seen, too expensive to run. The average age of its personnel is estimated at a ludicrous 43 years old, and the bulk of them are considered by knowledgeable observers to be unfit and unhealthy. Political analyst Greg Mills, for instance, reckons that only 10% of our 76,000 soldiers, sailors and airmen are fit for military deployment.

The situation has become so dire that there are those who believe the army should simply be abolished in its entirety. This is not necessarily a philosophical question about the role of the state and the moral implications of spending money on arms versus social good; rather, it is a practical and desperate observation. As it stands, our defence budget sucks upwards of R52 billion a year, and yet all indications are that this is insufficient for it to successfully deal with potential external threats or humanitarian missions; in other words, its reasons for existence. On the contrary, it is evidently becoming an internal threat to the citizens it is mandated to protect. So why not just get rid of it?

This is a flawed argument, to be certain. Armies *are* important for successful modern states – look up successful modern states; they all have working armies – and whatever the budget limitations, there is always a way ours could be reconfigured as an efficient and honourable organisation. For this, however, it would need a bold strategic overhaul with long-term horizons and decisive leadership at the top. Without either, Mapisa-Nqakula finds herself promoted into the pages of this book alongside her fellows in arms who have wrought destruction on the country over the last decade.

Before we move on, however, a mention in dispatches must go to her former 2IC, Kebby Maphatsoe, if only because *his* tale is a perfectly apt little microcosm of the ANC factionalism and absurdity that has allowed our military to become what it has become. For six years, until 2019, Maphatsoe was both deputy minister of Defence and Military Veterans and the veteran chairperson of the Umkhonto we Sizwe Military Veterans Association, a position he still occupies, which receives public attention only, it seems, when he is accused of being a fraud, a crackpot or someone's useful idiot.

Despite being the face and fist of Umkhonto we Sizwe today, he hasn't been able to shake long-running allegations that, far from being a veteran of gallant service in the name of the struggle in Angola, he is in fact a veteran of little more than being a camp cook, twiddling his thumb and even deserting under dubious circumstances. A fraudulent image, many would conclude, backed up by accusations of actual fraud (for example, "using state money to fund an elective conference"). He is also on record as saying – crackpot claxon! – that he thinks Thuli Madonsela was a CIA agent.

And that someone to which his idiocy has proved useful over the years is, of course, the one and only Jacob Zuma. Maphatsoe has long been seen singing for his supper outside various courthouses then occupied by his hero, and whenever the message that "we will fight back with anything at our disposal" needs to be conveyed with blunt urgency.

But Kebby the cowboy doesn't quite make the military grade here, because for the acme of ANC absurdity you can turn to Carl Niehaus in a few pages' time, and because those in ultimate charge must take ultimate responsibility (Cyril Ramaphosa, take note). And so the gong goes to Mapisa-Nqakula, who has been commander-in-chief for eight long years. As her fellow ministers in arms have been decimated around her on a regular basis, the victims of presidential whims, state capture convenience or their own incompetence, she has dug in and fought an enduring stand. For that, she deserves a medal. But she is a veteran of undistinguished service who has overseen the steady decline of our armed services to its current state of embarrassment, and although the Arms Deal was before her time, she has come to personify the shameless intention on which it was born.

Andy Marinos

b. 13 November 1972

*CEO of SANZAAR; figurehead of professional
rugby gone wrong; goose killer*

IF WE'RE GOING TO TALK SOUTH AFRICAN RUGBY in the 2010s – and we are – then we absolutely have to start and finish with the 2019 Rugby World Cup. A team of no-hopers that loses the respect of the sporting world and then somehow emerges from the abyss of despair to stand in triumph. A kid from a township called Zwide outside Port Elizabeth, who loses his mother and grandmother as a teenager and can't afford shorts for his first rugby trial, then becomes the first black captain of the Springboks *and* leads them to triumph. A canny, unknowable coach, so different from the predictable meatheads we're famous for, who talks openly about transformation and has actual playing strategies to implement and can manage players *and* has that all-important magic dust in his pockets.

If there have been countless downward trajectories in the 2010s, of which the Springboks were certainly one for seven or eight years, their redemption in Japan in November 2019 must be the sports story of the decade. With the greatest respect to the teams of 1995 and 2007, we had never needed a win more, and we did it with a squad that actually represented, and was supported by, most of South Africa. That was the potential future of our country right there.

What a tale of decline and redemption.

But this is a book about colossal stuffer-uppers, and that's enough with the uplifting reverie.

We *could* discuss the Springboks losing to Japan in Brighton, in September 2015, the greatest rugby upset of all time. Or our first-time losses to Argentina (Durban, 2015) and Italy (Florence, 2016), or losing four times in a row to Wales, or humiliating record losses to New Zealand (0-57 in Albany, 2017) and Ireland (3-38 in Dublin, 2017). But you know what, let's cut Heyneke Meyer and Allister Coetzee a philosophical break. Without the journey they took us on, redemption in Japan would not have been as sweet.

So we'll drop the national game altogether and take a look at where rugby has gone to die. That would be on the playing fields of Super Rugby, once an events calendar around which fans used to plan their late-summer weekends, today a wasteland of forgotten glory.

For South Africans, Super 10 rugby was our post-pariah, pre-democracy, still-amateur admittance to international provincial rugby in 1993. It had Transvaal, Northern Transvaal and Natal up against seven teams from New Zealand, Australia and even Western Samoa, and what a novelty it was. Transvaal, led by a certain Francois Pienaar, won the inaugural final at Ellis Park.

Two years later, at the same venue, Pienaar would lead South Africa to World Cup triumph, and then, cunning operator that he was, into a new age for rugby. By 1996, the professional era had dawned, and with it Super 12 rugby, a competition so undeniably exhilarating that South Africans would get up at – or, if they were students, stay up until – 4am to watch the Auckland Blues play the Wellington Hurricanes on a Saturday morning. Then they'd settle in for five more games to come, even if they would seldom remember the last two, involving nominative animals, colours and meteorological phenomena.

By this stage the rugby boards of South Africa, New Zealand and Australia had formed the SANZAR consortium to administer the game professionally across the three southern hemisphere powerhouses. The CEOs of the Aussie unions led the way, while Rian Oberholzer ensured South Africa got a reasonable deal, no doubt under the leery eye of his father-in-law, Louis Luyt.

The potential, the rugby bosses in their ill-fitting suits soon found, was astonishing. Super Rugby, along with the new six-match Tri Nations Test competition, attracted a $550 million broadcast deal from Rupert Murdoch's News Corp for TV rights for the first ten years. Ooh, a golden goose, you can imagine them thinking, as Carlos Spencer and Christian Cullen lit up screens across the globe on a weekly basis, and the cash rolled in.

At first, the goose was well tended. Hesitant observers worried that the Tri Nations would kill extended international tours, with dirt-tracker midweek games and series honours on the line – which it did, and that's a profound loss to this day. Strike one. But Super Rugby was magic. For a decade South Africans loved it, even though a local team couldn't win the thing.

Then, when the original News Corp deal came to an end, SANZAR figured the goose could work a little harder. From 2006, the Tri Nations would include nine Tests, and Super 14 would be the order of the day. It was the basic dumbo capitalism of more must equal better coming into effect. No-one gave the new teams – the Free State Cheetahs and the Perth-based Western Force – much of a chance, and now there were a couple of games a weekend that weren't worth the bother. But still, no dramas, as the Aussies might have figured. And with the Bulls finally winning the tournament three out of four years from 2007 to 2010, South Africans didn't complain.

Then came Super 15, in 2011, with five teams from each country, and the hare-brained thinking of committee compromises was suddenly that much more apparent. There would now be three "conferences", one for each country, and within each conference teams would play each other twice, while *between* conferences they would play each other once – except that they wouldn't play one randomly selected team from each of the other conferences because, of course, they didn't want too many games. Oh, and there would be a three-week break at some point so they could get in some Test matches against northern-hemisphere opponents.

Huh?

This bizarrely nonsensical model was originally unveiled in 2009, the year after Andy Marinos had taken over as CEO of SANZAR. Now

Marinos is by all accounts a decent chap with a solid history of playing and administrating the game, and there's no way the extended dog-show that Super Rugby would become can be pinned entirely on one guy. You can imagine the hard-nosed Aussie and the patronising Kiwi and the entitled Saffer union bosses all jostling to have their say, convinced their particular non-negotiable additions to proceedings would help produce a glorious new sporting creation rather than the rugby equivalent of Frankenstein's platypus flapping its way through a half-year ultra-marathon. But Marinos really should have known better than putting his name on the masthead of this abomination.

Having played for the Western Stormers in the late '90s, he had experienced the competition at its peak, when it really had something to offer. Genuine excitement. Wall-to-wall quality. Depth. Common sense.

Instead, he found himself overseeing a diluted system that would flog home-derby matches to death – with the likes of the Stormers/Western Province playing the Bulls/Northern Transvaal effectively four or five times a year across Super Rugby and Currie Cup competitions – while eliminating a couple of international contests, in which case a team might miss playing two of the most powerful sides in the tournament because *sommer so*. Imagine an English Premier League season where one team avoids playing Manchester United and Liverpool based on the luck of the draw.

The goose had gone mental.

Marinos moved on from the job in 2010, but then returned as CEO in 2016 just as the competition switched to Super 18. It may as well have been Super A Million. Or basketball. Now there were extra franchises from Japan and Argentina involved – pretty much their national sides – and the conferences didn't even have the same number of teams. A competition that was 12 weeks long when it began in 1996 now ran from February to August. Amazingly, there were calls within SANZAAR (the extra A was for Argentina) to make the competition even bigger, to crack the American market with all its American dollars.

At what point, one wonders, did Marinos and the boys in the administrators' boxes realise they had taken a wrong turn? Were they aware that the parables we learn at a young age about golden geese and whatnot actually apply in real life? That the rapidly declining gate takings and TV viewership were a reflection of the "product" on offer?

The Stormers, for instance, held the record for having the highest regular match attendance of any non-Test rugby team in the world as recently as 2018. Yet average crowds have dropped from 43,000 a game in 2010 to 32,000 in 2015 and 15,300 in 2019. TV viewership for their games has dropped from 600,000 in 2015 to 200,000 in 2019. It's a familiar story elsewhere. If it weren't for Fantasy Rugby, SuperBru and sports betting, the numbers would be a fraction still.

Come on, Andy, there really were clues. A playing season that lasted longer than actual seasons. The absurdity of "taking a break" to play Test matches, the real crucible of rugby. Teams seldom fielding their full-strength sides; playing some opponents three times in a season while others not at all; coming in the bottom half of the log (eighth in Super 15) yet still making the playoffs. Ultimately, the absolutely obvious fact that the rugby on display was, in the main, being dialled in by uninspired, exhausted teams – that it had become stupefyingly boring.

The ultimate verdict for Super Rugby: not so super.

The Covid-19 pandemic has basically deep-sixed the entire world, but of the rare positives to pluck with tweezers from the devastation, the death knell to Super Rugby is most welcome. Ten years ago this might have been considered a tragedy. Today's it's a blessed mercy, like putting down your beloved old bulldog who's taken to barking at the walls and weeing in your slippers at night. It was well past time, and now the major South African franchises will venture to play in northern climes. Let's hope lessons have been learnt, specifically – as New Zealand's superb makeshift Super Rugby Aotearoa tournament showed – that the soul of any sport is well nurtured by fewer, better matches.

And if you think franchise rugby is beyond the pale and irredeemable, no matter what, just cast your mind back to the Springboks and the 2019 Rugby World Cup.

Glorious.

Fikile Mbalula

b. 8 April 1971

Minister of Sport and Recreation (2010-2017);
heavy lightweight fixer; ball dropper; one explanation
for the demise of South African sport

IN OUR PREPOSTEROUSLY BLOATED CABINET, of which a good chunk of the ministries are literally designed as tax-sucking patronage outlets, the department of Sport and Recreation is a bullshit hangover from apartheid days when politics and sport went hand in glove. Most countries don't have one. Why bother?

One reason, to play devil's advocate, is to harness the unifying power of sport. It has wonderful potential to inspire and uplift the poor. At grassroots, it could be about getting kids off the street and strengthening communities. More visibly, at representative level, it could be about reinforcing culture, nation building and, dare we think it, racial reconciliation. A number of prominent countries that do have sports ministries include them under a broader title incorporating youth or culture – so yes, there's something there, perhaps.

If we take the optimistic view, then when might be the best time for this lightweight portfolio to land in a politician's lap? How about he takes over mere months after his country has successfully hosted the Soccer World Cup – all the goodwill, all the generosity of spirit and open chequebooks available to him, all those collective feelings of patriotism and togetherness. You might say the opportunity was teed up perfectly, just waiting to be driven gently down the fairway – then along comes Fikile Mbalula in his blindingly loud golf pants that look like they were regurgitated by the 1980s.

Fikile Mbalula was appointed as minister of Sport and Recreation in November 2010, four months after the World Cup was concluded at Soccer City, the end of a wonderful tournament that defied the naysayers and turned out to be a remarkably successful advertisement for South Africa. It started with Siphiwe Tshabalala firing in *that* goal against Mexico, and it ended with joy and hope in our hearts, the country's eyes lifted to the sporting horizons. What a decade this might be!

Mbalula was the face of sport in South Africa for six-and-a-half years, and by the end of his tenure he could point to no meaningful legacy for the country. Bafana Bafana, who many believed had a bright future after the World Cup, dropped 30 positions in the global rankings in that time. The Springboks were at their lowest-ever ranking when he left. The Proteas were heading in that direction too. We had secured no major sporting events despite the success and leftover infrastructure of 2010. In fact, Mbalula suspended our rugby, cricket and athletic codes from even bidding for events due to a lack of racial transformation. But then there were no meaningful governmental youth programmes he could identify that might have encouraged such transformation from the ground up.

Instead, we just got Fikile tweeting a lot, and making inane, semi-decipherable comments whenever he could pretend to be a celebrity in front of a camera. He called Bafana Bafana "a bunch of losers" and made a spectacle of flying to Las Vegas to watch Floyd Mayweather in the most expensive fight of all time (despite boxers in South Africa not being paid their purses). Seemingly inevitably, he made headlines when he felt obliged to explain that a picture of a penis that had gone viral on Twitter was, in fact, not his penis. Because, given his idiot antics, it may well have been.

Mbalula has, somehow, been moved on to two serious ministries in recent years, Police and then Transport, but in the process he has only managed to transfer his very *un*serious me-me-me antics to the way they are run. At Police, he styled himself as "Mr Fearfokkol", as a child might, and now at Transport he is "Mr Fix", apparently unaware that this makes him sound like the local drug peddler. It was also grimly ironic when we witnessed the country's railway stations being stripped to nothing and endless cables thieved – literally the system being unfixed – during the Covid-19 lockdown because of security personnel shortages.

A confirmed political palooka since the Youth League days of drinking Johnny Blue with Brett Kebble, it is astonishing that a guy of Mbalula's calibre can have held positions in national Cabinet for the entire decade covered in this book. And yet here he is, still, doing his thing, mouthing off whenever the mood takes him, not afraid to pick hypocritical fights with others in power, a source of mild entertainment and a principle-free political bellwether for his ANC colleagues.

As we saw in the previous entry, South African sport can be turned around in short order with the right people in charge, leading to tremendous success and real-world positive outcomes. So too, we must remember, can the country itself. But not with the likes of Fikile Mbalula in charge, it can't.

Baleka Mbete

b. 24 September 1949

Speaker of the National Assembly (2004-2008; 2014-2019); National Chairperson of the ANC (2007-2017); Nkandla defender; mixer of church and state; living embodiment of partiality

Dishonourable mentions: Nkosinathi Nhleko, Thulas Nxesi, Jacob Zuma

NO ROUGH-AND-TUMBLE JOURNEY through the last decade of South African politics would be complete without a trip to that most remarkable of country homesteads, Nkandla. A place where a swimming pool miracles itself into a fire pool; where the security wall is, on closer inspection, a chicken run; where the soundtrack on permanent loop is *'O Sole Mio*.

At first glance, the obvious personification of this particular scandal is the owner himself, the man with his name on the title deed (maybe!), Jacob Zuma. But Jacob Zuma is the personification, and indeed the cause, of so much that has gone wrong in our country that devoting his entry to some overpriced home remodelling would underplay his hand somewhat. Like convicting Hannibal Lecter for identity fraud.

Rather, we're filing it under Baleka Mbete.

Nkandla really was, in many ways, small fry. The extent of the misappropriation of public funds spent on upgrades to Zuma's private homestead was eventually calculated to be a trifling R7.8 million. Whether or not you buy that maths, even the actual spend of R246 million, the figure that stuck so firmly in the public craw, pales next to the real damage of state capture that would emerge in time. Compare it to the half a trillion rand that evaporated from our economy in the days after Nhlanhla Nene was fired as finance minister or the countless billions looted from SOEs – it's chicken feed for the chicken run.

Nkandla's importance was its absolutely unavoidable symbolism – initially of Zuma's abuse of power and ultimately his fall from power. Most devastatingly for South Africa, though, it came to symbolise just how far those in the upper echelons of the ANC were prepared to go to prioritise their party before their country. None more so than Baleka Mbete.

If the ANC sees itself as a broad church *(see Jessie Duarte & Gwede Mantashe)*, then Baleka Mbete is the embodiment of the manner in which it has chosen to defy the separation of church and state. Mbete will go down in our history as having served as both speaker of Parliament and national chairperson of the ANC, for ten years each. These are two mutually incompatible roles, and yet from 2014 to 2017 she juggled them at the same time like Molotov cocktails, and so she will also go down in our history for a third role: pre-eminent defender of Castle Nkandla.

Before Mbete would be called on to secure the ramparts, however, there was an army of other defenders before her. We must, therefore, lay out the basics of the battle that played out over seven years, from

2009 when "security upgrades" for the newly elected president of South Africa's residence were initiated, to 2016 when the second-term Zuma (and Mbete et al) faced humiliation before the Constitutional Court.

It was in 2012 that minor skirmishes around the burgeoning costs of "Zumaville" erupted into open warfare on the back of persistent reporting by the *Mail & Guardian*. An early figure of about R20 million for the expansion of the compound was now being dwarfed by revised estimates of around a quarter of a billion rand. Not only was this a multiple of the amounts spent on previous presidents' residences, but the vulgarity of it was made that much starker by the living standards of Zuma's neighbours. In 2011 in the Nkandla Local Municipality only one in three homes was considered a "formal" dwelling, one in six was serviced with piped water and one in 12 had flush toilets.

Opposition parties sensed a scandal and the Public Protector, Thuli Madonsela, was asked to initiate an investigation, one that would keep it in the public eye for a further four years, attracting ever more condemnation. Countless Zuma allies were called on to run interference during this time, and the two reputations initially most damaged in the process were those of Minister of Public Works Thulas Nxesi and, most laughably, Minister of Police Nathi Nhleko. In late 2013, Nxesi put his name to an inter-ministerial report that may as well have been titled "Nothing to see here", and introduced South Africans to the curious new concept of a "fire pool".

The actually believable assessment of the situation was released by Madonsela in 2014. The Nkandla report, as it came to be known, found that unlawful upgrades that had nothing to do with the president's security had indeed been made, that he had "unduly benefited", and that he should be compelled to pay back an appropriate sum of money to

"For the opposition, Nkandla is the gift that keeps on giving. For the ANC, Nkandla has turned foot-shooting into an art form."

Ranjeni Munusamy, 2016

cover those costs. To mix our military metaphors just a tad, this was the torpedo that would eventually sink the entire Zuma presidency, though there were nearly four years still to run before that moment of realisation occurred at the ANC National Conference at Nasrec in 2017.

Zuma's response, as delivered by his minions, was to deny that the Nkandla report was legally binding, and to drag things out as per standard Stalingrad defence operating procedure. In short, he didn't like Madonsela's report and thought one of his mates could do a better job. Nhleko obliged, releasing his take on proceedings in 2015; this was the one that came with a video demonstration of the fire pool in action set to the evocative tones of 'O Sole Mio. It went on to explain that the chicken coop was necessary because it prevented the chickens from running around and setting off the alarms, and that the cattle kraal, visitors' centre and amphitheatre were also security features. Other stitched-up reviews followed.

Despite these efforts, Nkandla hung around in the press like the smell of cow pats – or bullshit, if you prefer. The media kept digging, and it was used with sensational effect in the National Assembly by EFF MPs chanting "Pay back the money!" During Zuma's 2015 State of the Nation Address, Parliament was overcome with chaos, and by this point it had

"The truth is that the ANC has forgotten its intellectual roots. Since 2007 it has become an organisation dedicated to protecting its leader, Zuma, at the expense of providing leadership on burning societal issues. Consider, for instance, the party's zeal in dealing with the Nkandla issue. Virtually every brain in the party has been engaged with spinning the looting of R246 million of taxpayer funds to build Zuma's house. Yet the party postponed its crucial national general council – scheduled for June 2015 but pushed out to October – because no-one could be bothered to write up policy papers. That's the ANC under Zuma: morally bankrupt, ethically compromised and intellectually lazy."

Justice Malala, We Have Now Begun Our Descent

become clear that Mbete was his pivotal defender. In that instance, she had the EFF ejected by heavies not afraid to use their fists, and the rest of the time she consistently ruled against opposition parties on the matter. Perhaps most damningly, she oversaw the passing of a parliamentary resolution that effectively nullified Madonsela's report in favour of Nhleko's amateur opera clip.

In March 2016, the Constitutional Court delivered a decisive blow, declaring that the Public Protector's findings were binding under South African law and that, in ignoring them, Zuma had "failed to uphold, defend and respect the Constitution". All MPs swear an oath to uphold the Constitution, which meant that Parliament, under Mbete's guiding hand, was absolutely culpable in the process: "There was everything wrong with the National Assembly stepping into the shoes of the Public Protector," ruled Chief Justice Mogoeng Mogoeng.

The next day – April Fool's Day – Zuma was forced to make a squirming apology to the nation, in which he ducked and dived and generously interpreted the Concourt ruling in his favour, but conceded that he would indeed have to pay back *some* of the money. A resignation announcement it was not, but it marked the end of his once-untouchable hold on power and the shamelessness that went with it. Most tellingly, the Guptas left South Africa for Dubai the following week.

Zuma went on to pay back R7.8 million to the state, which he raised with a loan from an obscure bank based in the former Bantustan of Venda, one VBS Mutual Bank. To very few observers' surprise, VBS was later found to be an institution riddled with corruption *(see Floyd Shivambu)*. Thus, for now, Zuma is technically living in his house legally, as it were, though when he walks the grounds these days and takes it all

"The problem today is that the Speaker has simply allowed the president to go scot-free without accounting for what is clearly in everybody's version a prima facie impeachable offence."

Advocate Tembeka Ngcukaitobi, Constitutional Court, September 2017

in one imagines there may be a few vexations playing on his mind. That the place is seemingly falling into disrepair, the legacy of a government build, no doubt. That the homestead he pulled so many favours to save ultimately led to, and now symbolises, his fall from grace. And that, when he looks out beyond his taxpayer-funded boundary fences, he sees locals in the distance who refused to support the party that backed him, the ANC, and rather voted in the IFP to govern the Nkandla Local Municipality in 2016.

Baleka Mbete, meanwhile, has followed a similar trajectory. As speaker of the house she had been, after Zuma, the second-best-remunerated politician in the country, with a salary of R2,716,798 in 2017. She had, for a time, been a likely candidate to succeed him even – imagine, for a moment, that horrific vision – and had run for ANC presidency that same year. By then, however, Zuma had annointed his ex-wife over his loyal speaker and party chair, and so she didn't make much of a showing. Today, she pops up in an embarrassing interview on Al Jazeera here (2019) and as a special envoy to Zimbabwe there (2020).

Mbete's hostile and defensive demeanour came to be reflected in much of her most prominent political work, and in the end it seemed to exude that sad inverted priority of the modern politician: self-party-country. Which may as well be on the welcome mat at Nkandla.

Nomvula Mokonyane

b. 28 June 1963

*Minister of Water and Sanitation (2014-2018); presider
over corruption on an infrastructural scale; polluter of our
waterways; personification of government's failure
to provide the basic human right to water*

Dishonourable mention: Jacob Zuma

THE SOUTH AFRICAN CONSTITUTION IS A DOCUMENT of which its citizens have been famously and rightly proud since it was signed into law in 1996. It is perhaps most famous for, and we are perhaps most proud of, the Bill of Rights, which makes up its second chapter. "This Bill of Rights is a cornerstone of democracy in South Africa," the Constitution explains. "It enshrines the rights of all people in our country and affirms the democratic values of human dignity, equality and freedom." Powerful stuff.

Here follows, then, a story that illustrates how, a couple of decades down the line, the South African government demonstrates less care for its citizens' rights than it once did. It is a deeply uncomfortable story that sees the violation of a child's right to water, dignity and ultimately life – the unforgivable price to be paid for human greed dressed up in politics. We tell it in inverse acknowledgement of the Stalinist rationale that one death is a tragedy, but a million deaths are a statistic. In South Africa we can be grimly thankful that we don't face the million-plus death tolls of the Soviet era, but certainly millions are affected by the immoral behaviour of our supposed leaders. The death of six-year-old Nsuku Mhlongo bears the worst witness to this.

* * * *

They say that death by drowning is a nice way to go but, so far as we can tell, "they" have seldom tried it out themselves.

The mechanism of death by drowning is a terrifying confluence of conscious reaction to your submersion in water and your body's involuntary responses. When Nsuku Mhlongo fell into an uncovered, water-filled trench in Giyani, Limpopo in January 2019, his first reaction would have been terror and panic. Unable to swim, he would have held his breath and thrashed about for something to hold on to. He may have tried to scream for help. Tiring fast, and still frenzied with terror, his blood carbon-dioxide levels would have risen quickly, driven upwards by his anaerobic flailing attempts to survive.

Eventually, a harrowing minute or so of panic later, his blood CO_2 levels would have reached a threshold called the "breath-hold breakpoint"– when you simply cannot hold your breath any longer. Involuntarily, Nsuku would have taken a desperate deep breath, filthy water flooding into his trachea.

Exactly how Nsuku died we will not know. He may have been "lucky", as much as one can consider this a way to describe losing consciousness as a result of gasping asphyxia, his paroxysms dissipating weakly in the brown filth of a roadside ditch – after which his vocal cords, constricted by involuntary laryngospasm, will have relaxed, water will have flooded his lungs and, within six minutes or so, brain death would have occurred. Or, perhaps, he would have suffered cardiac arrest while still conscious, still writhing, still desperately trying to live.

Either way, the media reported that a boy had drowned in a trench. That's journalism for you – the cold business of cutting a long story short.

History does not record whether Nomvula Mokonyane knows the name Nsuku Mhlongo, but given the rather conspicuous fact that the provision of potable, safe water is critical to life and dignity, and indeed is a right all South Africans are supposed to enjoy, perhaps expecting the former minister of Water Affairs and Sanitation to remember the names of all those who have died as a result of the pillaging of her department's coffers is a bit much to ask. It is important to be fair in these things.

The trench in which Nsuku Mhlongo died was dug by Khato Civils, a contractor working on the Giyani Emergency Project, which was ostensibly designed to bring safe drinking water to impoverished communities in Limpopo as a matter of urgency. We say "ostensibly" because that's not what the Giyani Emergency Project was actually designed to do. The clue is in the fact that "emergency" expenditure circumvents standard procurement regulations.

The playbook goes like this: declare it a humanitarian emergency, talk in sombre tones about dignity and the ravages of apartheid, avoid the procurement regulations, get your buddies a few billion and Bathabile's your uncle! It's such an easy win!

Let's allow then-CEO of Lepelle Northern Water (LNW), Phineas Legodi, to get the patriotic juices flowing: "The project received the blessings of President Zuma, Premier Stan Mathabatha and the Minister of Water and Sanitation Nomvula Mokonyane. During his State of the Nation Address, President Zuma applauded the winning team of LNW for their efforts of ensuring that the people of Limpopo are emancipated from water and sanitation challenges that have been troubling them for years. Ours is to ensure that the dignity of the community is restored!"

Heavens! *Emancipated* no less! Dust-in-the-eyes stuff, isn't it?

Yet the trench in which Nsuku Mhlongo died had stood open for two years – that's how much of an emergency the job was. It had stood open for two years because Khato Civils hadn't been paid. And they hadn't been paid because the national department was bankrupt. The money was gone, as nonexistent as Nsuku Mhlongo's Grade 1 report.

The Giyani Water Project provides a helpful example of what happened to corruption under Zuma and his goons. What was once relatively small-scale jobbery exploded into massive fraud and theft that ran into the billions. What had existed before suddenly existed on a scale so large that it bankrupted a ministerial department. This could only be achieved with the right person running that department.

Like so many of the current ANC bigwigs, Mokonyane has been around a long time. Her lifelong activism, from her church group in the West Rand through to her activities for the SACP and the ANC, and the undeniably good work she did during the '90s in various MEC roles in Gauteng, are almost enough to blunt a chap's pen. She was banged up for her activism in a mid-'80s apartheid jail when she gave birth to her first child, for crying out loud – what lessons in the importance of dignity might that have endowed? She had been a member of the NEC since 1994. And, unlike a few of the younger guns in Cabinet, she was no moron either, having completed courses at Penn and Harvard, as well as in Sweden.

In so many ways, the Nomvula Mokonyane one encounters on paper before the Zuma Years appears to be precisely the kind of person you want as a minister: experienced, smart, committed, grounded. By 2014, however, her form was dipping. What's more, we had a different kind of presidency, for whom government existed for a different purpose.

Having performed poorly as premier of Gauteng, helping to push the ANC to its weakest position in the province in its history, Mokonyane lost her position to David Makhura. And it is here that we see come into play the instinctive political talent of the spymaster at the heart of so much damage in this book, Jacob Zuma. Rather than letting her drift, in her moment of vulnerability, into the political wilderness, President Zuma sensed an opportunity. So he didn't just promote her to

Cabinet; he made up a brand-new ministry specially for her to run, the Department of Water and Sanitation. We will never know if there was an overt understanding of what her role was really to be but, as they say, let's judge Mokonyane by her actions, not her words. For she didn't just run the department; she ran it into the ground.

In this case, the plan to connect the Giyani waterworks to the Nandoni Dam 45 kilometres away had been initiated in 2010. There was an initial false start. A company was awarded the tender for the project, but in a feat of tenderpreneurial brass neck to doff your cap at, the company managed to achieve the conspicuous feat of being founded after the contract was awarded. The courts got involved, and enough time passed for Mokonyane to arrive on the scene. She would show more than brass neck in the coming years.

As outlined in the extraordinary Corruption Watch report, "Money Down the Drain", one of Mokonyane's first big decisions was to ignore the Supreme Court's order to issue a tender for the completion of the Giyani project while lying to Parliament that she was complying with the order. Her ethical constitution thus laid out for all to see, Mokonyane intervened in the project and had LTE, a consulting firm, appointed to complete the work. LTE's boss Thulani Majola, in a freak incidence of uncanny happenstance, was a buddy of Mokonyane's.

To sweeten the Giyani deal, it seems that Majola sent LNW chairman Kennedy Tshivhase a token thank-you note comprised of a Mercedes-AMG G63 (retail price without options as of 2020: R3.1 million), with R1.4 million for sundries stuffed into its capacious boot. This was the allegation for which Tshivhase was suspended in 2019. Either way, LTE was appointed; whether it knew anything about water reticulation was besides the point. It in turn appointed sub-contractors to do the work, one of which was Khato Civils.

With the right people in the right kind of car, contracts for the project exploded from the original R250 million to almost R3 billion. Work was done by Khato but LNW didn't pay, so Khato ordered its staff home. As of mid-2020, the pipeline did not exist, and the people of Giyani were without a reliable water supply.

> "Corruption and mismanagement in the South African water sector cannot be attributed to just one powerful person, although Nomvula Mokonyane certainly showed that one determined individual can have a devastating impact."
>
> *"Money Down the Drain", Corruption Watch report*

This all raises the question, who killed Nsuku Mhlongo? In law it was a tragic accident. But we all know that the existence of the trench in which he drowned was no accident all.

In the Giyani project, Mokonyane had created the enabling environment required for massive graft to thrive. As so succinctly noted in "Money Down the Drain", construction projects are "the traditional magnet for corruption because they involve large amounts of money, are complex and difficult to monitor, and because, since each one is different, they are difficult to benchmark against each other in relation to cost". Quite so, and one key lesson we've learnt is that if the solution to a problem proposed by the government is ever a massively expensive project, chances are it's all just a vehicle for theft.

This all brings us neatly to Phase 2 of the Lesotho Highlands Water Project, the much-needed plan to increase the quantity of water provided to Gauteng. In 2016, with the playbook now well established, LTE started throwing its weight – that is, Mokonyane's name – around at the Water department and in Lesotho, demanding contracts.

In the end, Mokonyane delayed the project, overtly declaring that she didn't want "the usual companies" to be involved. The procurement lead in her ministry was fired, then reinstated by the Public Protector (for indeed there was such a person in those days), and then promptly resigned after being paid out for her full contract. Her Basotho counterpart suffered a similar fate, and was fired for "insubordination", among other things.

While it is not yet clear who has been awarded what contracts, we do know from news reports that LTE received contracts worth R5 billion between 2014 and 2016. We also know that the company donated R3.5 million to the ANC in June and July 2016, that the overall budget for the project had ballooned to R26 billion, and that, as *City Press* wrote, "the standard fee for consultation is 10% of the total cost, meaning a spot on the water project could net the company as much as R2.6 billion".

To borrow from disgraced children's entertainer Rolf Harris, can you see what it is yet?

* * * *

The relationship between Mokonyane and Zuma was one of such trust that, in 2017, she was made head of elections at the ANC's National Conference at Nasrec – a little insurance policy that, as it happens, didn't pay out in the end. Not surprisingly, given that she had very publicly backed Zuma's candidate, Nkosazana Dlamini-Zuma, for the top job, she didn't last under Cyril Ramaphosa. Having laid waste to her brand-new Water ministry, she spent time at the Communications and Environmental Affairs ministries – happily not long enough to bankrupt them – before being "deployed to the party's Eastern Cape provincial leadership structure", which sounds rather like cadre-speak for fuck off. She interrupts her work there from time to time to give testimony at the Zondo commission about her relationship with the generous management of Bosasa, which we will return to later in the book. *(See Gavin Watson.)*

Meanwhile, the department of Water and Sanitation no longer exists as a ministry, and Phase 2 of the Lesotho Highlands Water Project is said to be back on track, with completion expected in 2026. This delay means new property developments in Gauteng have been held back – and, to be absolutely clear, the province's water supplies, the national economy, and all those millions of livelihoods that it sustains, will not endure a serious upcountry drought.

And so, like Nsuku Mhlongo's parents, we are left looking to the heavens. Pray it rains, because Nom-Nom-Nomvula's people needed to eat.

Brian Molefe

b. 1966

CEO of Eskom (2015-2016); weeping face of the corruption and catastrophic failure of South Africa's power generation, and its economy along with it; shebeen-goer

Dishonourable mentions: Lynne Brown, Salim Essa, Malusi Gigaba, the Guptas, Matshela Koko, Abram Masango, Collin Matjila, Anoj Singh, Eric Wood, Jacob Zuma, Mosebenzi Zwane

AT TIMES IN THIS BOOK we've suggested that a particular example of thievery or departmental despoliation is relatively minor league compared to the worst manifestations of state capture and institutional buggery that is to be encountered elsewhere. Well, welcome to elsewhere.

This is Eskom, the vast entangled quagmire where the Zupta mafia has gone to town and the South African economy has gone to die.

This is the power utility that might have been the beating heart of modern South Africa, efficiently run and future-focused, but is rather a sickly arrhythmic pacemaker, half a trillion rand in debt, that falls to pieces whenever you're on deadline, and must be stuck together with masking tape and fervent prayers before it's coaxed back to life.

This is a grotty shebeen filled with any number of thieving rats, though the bawling face in the shop window belongs to Brian Molefe.

In years to come, the historians will write – on their solar-powered laptops, most probably – the story of Eskom, and they will fill reams while doing so. It will be a drawn-out tale of personality clashes, epic mismanagement, calculated plunder and opportunistic grabbery, including the obligatory not giving of any damns by the clashers, mismanagers, plunderers and grabbers. At this relatively early stage in proceedings, we'll do well just to cover the basics.

To 2008, then, when the first rolling blackouts began and we came to be introduced to the curiously regressive idea of load shedding. Where once we had electricity whenever we wanted it, now we didn't. This was the result of our government's excellent efforts to encourage growth in our economy while, moronically, doing nothing about increasing the power capacity needed to sustain this growth. One day someone flicked a switch, and there it was – we were in a new era of intermittent darkness. For more on how we got to that particular point, see the entry on Alec Erwin in *50 People Who Stuffed Up South Africa*.

Once the problem was diagnosed – a shortage of power generation – the plans could be made. We would need to build new power stations, manage the grid properly and in around nine years, according to the experts, we would be back on track. My god, we all thought then – we'd have to wait till 2017! If only.

Because just a year later we entered the age of Zuma, and just as no plan survives contact with the enemy in war time, so great sectors of South Africa, and Eskom in particular, quickly came under attack, and our plans for recovery evaporated.

Eskom was prime looting territory: an absolutely massive operation with enormous annual budgets, two colossal capital projects to get started in the Medupi and Kusile power plants, all manner of tenders and contracts, and general decaying of management and oversight.

The looting began in earnest with Zuma's appointment of Malusi Gigaba as Minister of Public Enterprises in 2010, a position that allows a wayward minister to become an architect of corruption and mismanagement at any number of state-owned utilities, should the mood take him or he be instructed so. Gigaba began by reconstituting Eskom's board and executive, driving out trustworthy and capable employees and replacing them with amenable individuals who would award contracts, take bribes and craft dodgy deals to order.

His interference in Eskom's board and executive led to the resignations of CFO Paul O'Flaherty in 2012 and CEO Brian Dames in 2013. Both played key roles in steering the utility's build programme, most importantly Medupi and Kusile, two of the largest coal-fired plants in the world. Originally scheduled for full commercial service by 2013 and 2014 respectively, neither plant is fully operational as of writing, and there is industry talk that the builds have been so defective that they may never run at planned capacity. Completion of the former is now due in 2021 and the latter in 2024, with both now estimated to come in at more than three times their initial costings, perhaps R460 billion – nearly as much as Eskom's outstanding debt in 2020.

Dames was replaced by acting CEO Collin Matjila, who brokered procurement deals in favour of businesses owned by the Gupta brothers. Among other things, he facilitated a R43 million Eskom sponsorship for their propagandist rag, *The New Age* – a figure to remember next time you're topping up your electricity meter.

Zuma then stepped in to move Gigaba along to Home Affairs in May 2014 (due, it seems, to his inability to take orders from Dudu Myeni at SAA). In his place was new Minister of Public Enterprises Lynne Brown, but normal service was not interrupted for long. She continued with the process of questionable board appointments at the utility as its finances deteriorated. In April 2015 she brought in Brian Molefe as Eskom's new CEO, with Anoj Singh as his CFO, and the two then presided over what is now seen as the height of Eskom capture and thus the height of state capture.

During their tenure, Eskom paid fees of R1.6 billion to consulting multinational McKinsey and Trillian Capital Partners – the local advisory firm controlled by Gupta business associates Salim Essa and Eric Wood – for a turnaround strategy for Eskom. Leaked documents and emails revealed plans to extract a total of R9.4 billion in fees from the utility, including for consultation on the trillion-rand Russian-sourced nuclear programme which would have bankrupted the country. How's that for a business model? Break something, then offer to fix it at insanely overinflated prices while actually breaking it a whole lot more in the process.

Singh allegedly facilitated the illegal diversion of R3.8 billion from Eskom to support the purchase of Glencore's Optimum coal mine from the Gupta-linked Tegeta in 2016, a deal which got the green light from Mineral Resources Minister Mosebenzi Zwane.

Molefe's role in all this came to a very public head in late 2016 after the release of the Public Protector's report on state capture. It revealed, on the basis of cellphone records, that the Eskom CEO had paid regular visits to the Gupta residence in Saxonwold, though Molefe denied the claim through public displays of *snot en trane*. He was merely visiting his regular shebeen, he explained, hidden away among the mansions of one of the wealthiest suburbs in the country. No-one was buying it, and he was forced to resign.

It was a profound fall from grace for a man who had seemed to have a golden future ahead of him in the 2000s, and who had seemingly done good work as CEO of Transnet. But allegations of improprieties would in time emerge from his tenure there, and he would later be ordered by a court to pay back the R10 million he had received from an illegal R30 million Eskom pension payout after a mere 18 months at the utility. Today, the blubbing Molefe remains a running political joke.

Meanwhile, acting CEO Matshela Koko, who replaced Molefe, was also implicated in the Optimum deal, and his stepdaughter won contracts with Eskom worth R1 billion. So, a different guy in charge but pretty much the same guy.

Another prominent player in Eskom's corruption saga was Abram Masango, who headed its capital projects, including Medupi and Kusile. He is now facing corruption charges for receiving kickbacks for ensuring that Tubular Construction Projects won a R745 million contract at Kusile power station in 2016, which then ballooned to R1.2 billion.

When Cyril Ramaphosa was elected president in February 2018, the laborious process of unravelling the web of capture spun under his predecessor began. Jabu Mabuza, appointed as acting CEO, described the extent of recycled tenders with inflated prices as unbelievable.

Today South Africa's Special Investigating Unit has referred more than 5,000 Eskom employees – more than a tenth of its workforce – for disciplinary action for offences ranging from the failure to declare their interests to doing business with Eskom and leading suspicious lifestyles. It is investigating build contractors, diesel suppliers, coal supply and

transport contracts, and contracts for cloud computing. Along the way it has identified 135 employees who did business deals with Eskom worth more than R6 billion.

The clean-up continues under new CEO André de Ruyter, who is driving a maintenance programme for neglected infrastructure, addressing the debt burden and design faults at Medupi and Kusile, and backing policies to create new generation capacity with the help of the private sector. De Ruyter faces an epic challenge. The business of refloating a sinking behemoth such as Eskom is, by necessity, a ruthless one if it's to have any hope of success. Defaulting municipalities that owe the utility billions are now being temporarily cut off to encourage payment. Who suffers? As usual, the poorest of the poor.

And how's it all going?

Load shedding in 2020 is already the worst on record, and by 2030 South Africa needed to generate a further 27,000 megawatts of new power – nearly equivalent to the utility's reliable supply at present.

No more Brian Molefes and Matshela Kokos in charge, then...

See Malusi Gigaba, The Guptas, Jacob Zuma, Mosebenzi Zwane.

Lucky Montana

*Former CEO of Prasa; face of the farce of parastatal
governance and of the country's infrastructural failure*

Dishonourable mention: "Dr" Daniel Mtimkulu

YOU MAY HAVE NOTICED, BY NOW, A RECURRING THEME emerging in our little journey through our lost decade. Corruption. Like the *Macarena* in late 1996, it's everywhere. Just a little bit of it is technically evil, but a lot of it, especially if you're not actually doing it yourself, makes you want to strangle people. Soon you just can't get it out of your head. Seeing as we're now well into the heart of the malodorous maladministrative Ms, we need to be careful not to overdose. So let's chug through Lucky Montana's story at a bit of a clip, shall we?

In fact, just one vignette will suffice to convey what he was all about and what he epitomises in our ten-year retrospective of corruption upon chicanery upon jiggery-pokery.

In November 2014, the Passenger Rail Agency of South Africa (Prasa) took delivery of its first Afro 4000 diesel and hybrid locomotive from the Spanish manufacturer Vossloh España. Resplendent in sky-blue livery, it was to be the pride of our railways, one of 70 such locomotives purchased for all of R3.5 billion. There was, however, a problem.

On closer inspection, the locomotive was found to be nearly a foot too high for our railway system. And that was just the first layer of the problem. The second was that senior management had – quite predictably, because there are still some competent people left at our SOEs – identified the problem in advance. Yet the powers that be had rammed through the order anyway. The third problem, then, was that the powers that be were out-and-out fraudsters.

Being the resourceful Saffers that they are, the engineers at Prasa did what they could to make the locomotive work. You can imagine them up on the roof, walking around with a tape measure and a monkey wrench, banging here, tapping there, scratching their heads, wondering about the maximum approach speed at Driehoek Bridge. But in the end they were trying to jimmy a size-12 foot into a size-8 shoe, and inevitably there was a nasty derailment – a locomotive pulling 11 carriages ran off the tracks in August 2015. And just when you thought the farce was complete, it turned out the engineers couldn't assess what had happened because the data logger was in Spanish.

The Afro 4000 Prasa purchase is as mad as it sounds – a deal that Milo Minderbinder couldn't have put together. No, it took Prasa CEO Lucky Montana and his chief engineer "Dr" Daniel Mtimkulu to come up with it. You will not be shocked to learn that "Dr" Daniel was a doctor of nothing other than his curriculum vitae.

To no-one's surprise after that debacle, Montana appears to have been up to his eyeballs in graft as he ran Prasa into the ground. A year after he was fired, it emerged that the SOE had nearly R14 billion of irregular expenditure on its books, and he has subsequently joined the chorus line at the Zondo commission, which has found out that, among other things, his skill for acquiring inexplicably expensive Johannesburg properties outshines his ability to put a train on a track.

Meanwhile, the BEE front company that helped set up the purchase in the first place, one Swifambo Rail Leasing, has been ordered by the courts to pay back R2.6 billion to Prasa – but there's another problem. Swifambo has been liquidated, as you'd expect, and Prasa, in a new decade and under new leadership, has worked out that the most effective way to recoup costs is… to try get most of the trains back on our tracks and only run them on compatible sections of the network. The only practical alternative is to sell them for a song on auction. What a hand they've been dealt by those who came before them.

Corruption in South African politics is so endemic, so built-in, so *draining* that narrowing down the people in this book was, in the main, a process of mass exclusion, not inclusion. Bog-standard corruption in the tens, or even hundreds of millions, just isn't good enough. But Lucky Montana cracks the nod for two reasons. First, the wholesale degradation of our railway system, as occurred under his watch, is the destruction of the basic infrastructure of our country – literally, the system we need to function.

And second – that story. Honestly. That's what it came down to when the scoundrels like Lucky had free reign.

Lucky he's not in jail.

Thabang Moroe

*Cricket South Africa CEO (2017-2020); disgraced
frontman of our national cricket administration; the type
of guy who sends our best players running for the hills;
scapegoat for all the others still at the trough*

*Dishonourable mentions: Haroon Lorgat, Gerald Majola,
Chris Nenzani, Beresford Williams*

LET'S BE HONEST, IT'S NOT LIKE TOO MUCH OF SOUTH AFRICA was best in show in 2010. Our politics, economics and corruption was pretty dire back then and, somehow, we've just plumbed deeper, darker, more disastrous depths in the intervening decade to get to where we are today – which is, by our estimates, somewhere near the bottom of Mponeng gold mine in Carletonville, Gauteng. Meanwhile, the bits that *were* really good actually still are: the Joburg buzz, the Cape restaurants, the Saffer can-do attitude, Table Mountain. So where, then, have we fallen from truly lofty heights?

Ah, cricket.

You can so easily forget, looking at the great big steamy rhinoceros midden that is Cricket South Africa (CSA) today, just how consistently superb and uplifting our national team was in the not-too-distant past. In 2008, we beat England in England in a Test series for the first time since readmission, then we travelled to Australia to endeavour to do likewise to the Aussies. We chased down the second-highest target in Test cricket to win the first match in Perth against Australia, and came back from the dead, courtesy of JP Duminy and Dale Steyn, at the greatest cricket cauldron of them all, the MCG, to win the second Test against Australia. With it, we had claimed the series, the Australians' first loss at home since 1993, and as a result the number-one ranking. Did we mention this was against Australia?

Superb stuff, and perhaps our finest single moment in cricket. Ever. In the years to follow, we battled it out with the Aussies, the Poms and the Indians for top spot, before returning to England and Australia in 2012 to repeat the feats of 2008. After that, finally, we could spend three fine years at the top of the rankings.

We had battled an itinerary that did us no favours, we had won away from home with remarkable consistency and, surprisingly to many neutral observers, we had done it in a fashion that was often glorious to behold. We were led by a hard-nosed captain in Graeme Smith, who could take a beating and score a fourth-innings hundred in a series-deciding chase; we were blessed with one of the greatest all-rounders in history, Jacques Kallis, anchoring the team; we had magicians in the middle order in Hashim Amla and AB de Villiers, who vied with each other from match to match as the most entertaining batsmen in the world; and we had a fast-bowling attack of such fear and beauty, led by the greatest bowler of his era, Dale Steyn, along with Vernon Philander and Morné Morkel, that it was only fair to compare it to the West Indian attacks of the 1980s. What memories.

We dedicate much of this entry to those glorious times because when it comes to sport in South Africa it's just that much better for your health and wellbeing to avoid the inevitable incompetence, corruption and politics that underscore the rest of it. We've got enough of that everywhere else, so wouldn't it be nice if we could keep it from the spectacle that is cricket? (And soccer and rugby and the Olympics and tiddly winks.) But, to our profound diminishment, we can't.

So, to the latter half of the decade – the fall. Where once we stood proud at the top of the game, today we have a national cricket team that scraps it out with the likes of Bangladesh and Pakistan for fifth spot on the Test, ODI and T20 logs. We languish here despite the fact that we still have the fast bowlers, now led by another great-in-the-making,

Kagiso Rabada; and we have the world's pre-eminent wicketkeeper all-rounder in Quinton de Kock; and we *could* have one of the world's greatest batsmen, AB de Villiers, who is still seeing the ball as big as a watermelon and is still fit and healthy enough to walk into any team anywhere. Including the Proteas. And yet, for some reason, he doesn't.

AB de Villiers has scored 22 Test centuries (only one of them in a losing match), and it's a crime against cricket that he won't end his career with 30 or more.* One reason is that the modern game and its players have sold their souls to the insatiable god-kings of jewel pots and shiny trinkets, as epitomised in a competition that can see 60 matches played in seven weeks after which not a single one registers a lasting memory. But the IPL is an entry for another book. No, the real reason we've watched, with tragic hearts, our national team play so much cricket since 2016 without its best batsman is because of men like Thabang Moroe.

Moroe was the CEO of CSA from 2017 to 2020, initially acting then official then suspended then fired. A rite of passage for the professional gravy-trainer, you might say. The details of why he was sacked are not important here – HR shenanigans, abusing the company credit card, wasteful expenditure in an organisation haemorrhaging cash. Whatever. Moroe may well face criminal charges at some point, which is why he's our headline act here, but if he does it will likely be a diversion encouraged by those equally complicit in the ruination of South African cricket in recent times. The likes of former CSA CEOs Gerald Majola and Haroon Lorgat, former president Chris Nenzani, and Beresford Williams, who became acting president despite being implicated in the very same report that saw Moroe fired. Between them, and so many on the CSA board, they are a toxic mix of possibly psychopathic, certainly self-serving and ultimately inept and unpatriotic functionaries who seem to actively reject the essence of the roles they are there to fulfil – that is, to be guardians of the game for those who love it.

---

* Ian Bell has scored 22 Test centuries, for God's sake!

> "CSA is riddled with self-serving bureaucrats whose main agenda is jostling for space at the rapidly emptying feeding trough that holds CSA's dwindling riches. Money, reputation, stakeholder confidence and players' support, which were abundant at one stage, have all but gone. The trough is nearly bare, and a multitude of looming crises are unresolved."
>
> *Craig Ray, 2020*

Their and the board's behaviour makes a lot more sense when you read that directors are paid R350,000 a year plus perks these days to attend quarterly meetings. As veteran cricket commentator Neil Manthorp puts it, "It has taken the 'honour' out of honorary and made the majority of the current incumbents believe that the game belongs to them rather than to the players and fans. Instead of serving the game, the game is serving them. And rather nicely."

In October 2020, the entire board of CSA finally took the hint after a year of administrative chaos, and stepped down. It has been an age coming. With traitors like these in charge, our best talent has fled to the IPL and county cricket, the sponsors have likewise jumped ship, and New Zealand and Sri Lanka have fancied their chances.

And yet, the real heroes – Faf, QDK, KG and mates – remain to battle against the cronies, the odds and sometimes even professional opposition. In their honour, here are a couple of departing stats to lighten the heart, which exist despite the best efforts of our useless administrators. As of 29 February 2020, South Africa is the only team in the world to have a positive win ratio in One Day Internationals against all opposition. We achieved this by beating the Aussies – that is, in case you missed it, the national team of Australia – by 74 runs at Boland Park in Paarl. It was our ninth win against them in ten matches, at which point we had 49 victories to their 48.

There is glory yet.

Hlaudi Motsoeneng

b. 1968

De facto head of the SABC (2011-2017); third-person-referring media lunatic; hugely influential propagandist to tens of millions of South Africans

"IN MY VIEW HLAUDI MOTSOENENG IS HLAUDI MOTSOENENG, and there is one Hlaudi Motsoeneng in South Africa, is this one called Hlaudi Motsoeneng."

So, that's clear then. Classic Hlaudi Motsoeneng, who ran the SABC almost into the ground.

There's a temptation – given the utter idiocy with which he, a supposed media man, presented himself to the media – to do a meta-hatchet job on Motsoeneng with an example of the most egregious scourge of modern "journalism", the listicle. Headline: Hlaudi With A Chance of Say Whaaaaaaaat!? Click click, tjing tjing, thank you very much.

But, sorry, the SABC matters too much. It matters because for the vast majority of South Africans the SABC is the only source of news that's not Facebook and, as we know, Facebook is a magic mirror that tells you how lovely you look, not an actual news service.

Consider this. *Business Day,* still the country's foremost serious print newspaper, has a circulation of 20,000. Widen the search parameter to the *TimesLive* website, the online home of *Business Day, Sunday Times, Sowetan, Financial Mail* and others, and this was getting around 5.8 million unique monthly browsers in 2019. Okay, so there's some proper influence there.

Now consider South Africa's most popular radio stations. Ukhozi FM has more than 7.5 million *weekly* listeners, Umhlobo Wenene more than 5.8 million. If you prefer your radio in English, then Metro FM has 4.3 million listeners.

In fact, SABC radio is a news and commentary lifeline for tens of millions of South Africans. According to the Broadcast Research Council of South Africa, 13 radio stations had more than a million listeners per week in the year to March 2020. Here's the list by radio station, listenership, predominant broadcast language and owner. Note the last column in particular.

Ukhozi FM	7,607,000	Zulu	SABC
Umhlobo Wenene FM	5,850,000	Xhosa	SABC
Metro FM	4,331,000	English	SABC
Lesedi FM	3,346,000	Sesotho	SABC
Thobela FM	2,925,000	Sepedi	SABC
Motsweding FM	2,755,000	Tswana	SABC
RSG	1,329,000	Afrikaans	SABC
Munghana Lonene FM	1,208,000	Tsonga	SABC
Gagasi FM	1,191,000	Zulu/English	MRC Media
Jacaranda FM	1,120,000	English	Kagiso Media
Ikwekwezi FM	1,090,000	Ndebele	SABC

| Ligwalagwala FM | 1,090,000 | Swati | SABC |
| East Coast Radio | 1,022,000 | English | Kagiso Media |

How is it, then, that so many of the wealthy among us can with one hand dismiss the SABC as irrelevant propagandist bilge, and with the other complain about a perceived lack of education among our fellow voters? Really, those of us fortunate enough to not have to rely on the SABC for our view of the world ought to be a great deal angrier about its parlous state, because it is, comfortably, the most important media organisation in the country.

Which brings us to Hlaudi, whose rise to power in the Free State SABC newsroom was accompanied by his status as an embedded hack for the ANC powers in that province, not least a certain Ace Magashule.

The moment Thabo Mbeki was out, Hlaudi was in as head of "special projects" which, fortunately for the Zuma camp, included elections and the State of the Nation Address. Mbeki's embedded head of news (and a star of *50 People Who Stuffed Up South Africa* in 2010), Snuki Zikalala, lasted less than a month under the new regime.

The fact that Motsoeneng is, by his own utterances, a strange man, was neither here nor there. Zuma's gangsters dispensed with the facade of governance early on in proceedings, so Motsoeneng would do just fine.

Motsoeneng's years as the head of the SABC were easily mocked and caricatured, but they were far more disgraceful than amusing. He battered an already politicised newsroom. In 2016, eight brave journalists stood up to his interventions and suffered the consequences. In a typical abuse of power, Motsoeneng had banned the airing of protest footage. His reason – "If you always put crime on media, you report about crime… actually what you are doing, you are encouraging young people to commit crime" – was of course imbecilic, but contrary to the clickbait listicles, there was nothing funny about this. It was policy designed to support the ruling faction of the ruling party.

The SABC8 were fired for airing these concerns, but when a court overturned this decision, they came under the most appalling attack. In 2017 one of them, Suna Venter, died of stress cardiomyopathy, usually caused by prolonged and serious stress. *TimesLive* outlined the attacks on her as follows: "She received threatening SMSes. Her flat was reportedly broken into on numerous occasions, the brake cables of her car were said to have been cut and her tyres were slashed. Her family said she was abducted and tied to a tree on the Melville Koppies while the grass around her was set alight. Earlier [in 2017], she was shot in the face with an unknown weapon and had surgery to remove the metal pellets. During the past year, she was assaulted on three occasions."

Venter was 32 when she died.

So, no LOLs or listicles here. Motsoeneng was a vital cog in the state capture coup d'état, the man tasked with overrunning the national broadcaster, which happened to include dozens of stations for tens of millions of citizens. In the process he didn't just ramble like a madman; he destroyed lives. The fact that he had a mildly amusing side-gig as a halfwit is only the distraction it was meant to be.

Motsoeneng's performative state censorship was predictably unsustainable, though it took several years for common sense to prevail. He was booted for good in 2017 for, among other things, lying about his qualifications. He didn't have a matric.

Unusually for a South African institution, the SABC has, since the departure of its boss from hell, along with the worst of the state capturers, recovered to some extent as a journalistic entity. SAFM is increasingly the talk radio station of choice. Great hires such as Phemelo Motene and Stephen Grootes are winning over listeners in crucial slots from a struggling Talk Radio 702. Its newsroom is in better shape, if not exactly thriving. If it can sort out its finances, there is hope, at least, for the SABC.

Given that so many millions of South Africans rely on it for news and entertainment, it's critical we get this right, and that the likes of Hlaudi Motsoeneng (and Snuki Zikalala) are in no way involved.

Tom Moyane

b. 31 January 1953

Officially disgraced former Commissioner of SARS; "rogue unit" fabulist; destroyer of South Africa's once high-functioning government; one of the president's keepers

Dishonourable mentions: the Guptas, KPMG, Jacob Zuma

SOME PAGES BACK, UNDER THE ENTRY FOR JOHN HLOPHE, we discussed the idea that justice delayed is justice denied, and how our politicians have perfected the art of high-profile foot dragging when facing legal censure – the upshot being that the long-suffering South African public is denied justice year after year. One approach that seems to take this notion to heart, with the same ultimate effect, is our recent presidents' obsession with Commissions of Inquiry*.

---

* Always Officially Capitalised because that shows how Important they are, and that they're absolutely Not a Distraction from real Justice being served.

The website for the Department of Justice and Constitutional Development outlines no fewer than nine commissions that have been completed or instigated in the past decade. They generally take years to run their course, cost millions, if not hundreds of millions, and come to be known by the name of the judge chairing them. So we've had, in chronological order: the Donen commission into the UN's Iraq oil-for-food programme (2006-2011), the Seriti commission into the Arms Deal (2011-2016), the Farlam commission into the Marikana massacre (2012-2015), the Cassim commission into Mxolisi Nxasana's fitness to hold office as National Director of Public Prosecutions (2015, *see Shaun Abrahams*), the Heher commission into higher education (2016-2017), the Zondo commission into state capture (established 2018, ongoing), the Nugent commission into the state of the South African Revenue Service (2018), the Mokgoro commission into advocates Nomgcobo Jiba and Lawrence Mrwebi's fitness to hold office at the National Prosecuting Authority (2018-2019), and the Mpati commission into the state of the Public Investment Corporation (2018-2020).

If you thought it took a long time to read that sentence, try following a commission – you could have watched two Rugby World Cups in the time it took Judge Seriti to interview a few people and scribble together his report on the Arms Deal. And, of course, he didn't even interview the right people: the findings of his commission were set aside by the North Gauteng High Court because it was essentially a whitewash. That was in 2019 – a couple of months later, and you could have caught a third World Cup. Did we mention that the whole thing cost R137 million?

The real elephant in the room of inquiries is Judge Zondo's drawn-out theatre-piece analysis of state capture, begun in 2018. Officially known as The Judicial Commission of Inquiry into Allegations of State Capture, it is a process that to the casual observer appears to have produced several smoking guns that have required impressive measures of self-restraint for the Hawks not to respond to. In some instances, the guns have been produced by the perpetrators themselves, as when they casually announce that they were party to bribes because that's the way things rolled at the time and it would have been unbecoming not to join in. Perhaps more astoundingly, it was revealed in July 2020 that the commission had cost R700 million to date and a further R130 million had been allocated to get the production to the finish line in 2021. That's closing in on a billion rand for an official version of the Gupta Leaks – which anyone can read online.

Sometimes, however, after all the paint drying and teeth pulling and leading of horses to water, there is an actual result that tilts the balance of justice back towards the light. Case in point: the Nugent commission into the shenanigans at SARS, which cost a mere R8.8 million and found that the boss of our revenue services was, indeed, the force of darkness that we all thought him to be.

That boss was SARS Commissioner Tom Moyane and he was, in the title of Jacques Pauw's decade-defining book, one of the president's keepers.

SARS as it was before Moyane took office is the vital starting point in understanding the damage that he has done to South Africa as a whole. Before Moyane, SARS was broadly taken to be the most impressive state institution in the country. It was "a post-apartheid success story… the jewel in the civil service crown", in Pauw's words. "Once the inefficient and clumsy Inland Revenue Service and a separate Customs and Excise department, it was remodelled into a mean tax-collecting and customs machine to serve as the engine driving South Africa's social democracy, including the funding of over 17 million grants to more than 10 million people very month. Its transformation has been chronicled in at least two international business school journals."

SARS, itself a success story, was the beating heart of one of our country's greatest post-democratic achievements: the upliftment of the poorest of our poor.

Much of the credit for its performance goes to its commissioner for ten years, Pravin Gordhan. Under his guidance, it started to attract the brightest and best in tax, accounting, law and forensics. Morale was high. Employees spoke of "the higher purpose". When Gordhan moved to the Finance ministry, Oupa Magashula took over without a perceptible knock in performance – but he was then forced to resign in 2013 for the now quaint offence, in light of all that was to come, of offering a job to a pal.

Enter Tom Moyane.

With the commissioner's position vacant for more than a year, President Zuma chose to ignore 104 legitimate candidates for the job, avoid the usual practice of endorsing the finance minister's preferred choice, and fill the role with a handpicked, wholly unsuitable man. Was Moyane, who had been forced out of his position as correctional services commissioner and would later be implicated in tender scandals in the department, fit for the job as head of SARS? Quite apparently not. Did he use to babysit Jacob Zuma's children while in exile in Mozambique? Quite apparently so.

In the politics of the Zuma Years, there was no greater attribute than loyalty to the king.

"As soon as Moyane arrived, all hell broke loose," writes Pauw in *The President's Keepers*. He goes on to paint a picture of subterfuge, scandal and shame in the ensuing years at SARS, as the new commissioner took a sledgehammer to the place, targeting specific agents who, it turned out, had opened the wrong cases against the wrong people, and shaking the very foundations of the institution in the process. The book offers a seemingly endless supply of backstabbing cigarette smugglers who were apparently either financing people in high places or ratting on them for protection. The Guptas, Edward Zuma, Mark Lifman, Roy Moodley, Robert Huang – these names all litter the pages. But ultimately it came down to the usual suspect: Jacob Zuma.

The nub of the problem, it seems, was that Zuma's dog-show of a tax situation was a real threat to his presidency at the time, more so than the distractions of Nkandla or any other scandal that magnetised itself towards him. An investigation taken to its full completion would have proved highly problematic.

Hence the brutal decision to tear apart SARS. The decisive game plan rested on what was a propaganda ploy with some real depth – what the Nugent report would describe as "a premeditated offensive against SARS, strategised by the local office of Bain & Company... for Mr Moyane to seize SARS". A story was fabricated of a "rogue unit" that had been running amok at the revenue collector and required censure; it was endorsed by a world-renowned auditing company, and it was leaked to eager journalists at one of the country's most influential weekly newspapers.

The supposed rogue unit included acting deputy commissioner Ivan Pillay, group executive Johan van Loggerenberg, group executive for strategic planning Pete Richer and head of enforcement Gene Ravele. What did they have in common? They were competent officials who had been targeting politically connected tax delinquents. Eventually, Pravin Gordhan was dragged into the muck.

Allegations were made against the unit – from spying on Zuma to running a brothel – investigations triggered and ultimately a report signed off by none other than KPMG, previously one of the world's most trusted auditing firms. No longer now, though, after it came to light that Moyane's lawyers had drafted instructions to KPMG, dictating findings and recommendations that appeared almost verbatim in the report.

In October 2014, the month after Moyane was appointed as commissioner of SARS, the *Sunday Times* started reporting on the imaginary rogue unit. It would, to its great shame, go on to publish another 30 articles and reports on the matter over the next two years before finally cottoning on to the fact that it had been played for a useful fool in 2016. The Press Ombudsman ordered it to retract all stories about the unit. After an internal investigation the following year, KPMG retracted the findings of its report and repaid the R23 million it had charged SARS for effectively ensuring its demolition.

By then the damage had been done.

As analyst Khaya Sithole later wrote, "In lending legitimacy to the hoax, KPMG and the *Sunday Times* enabled the proliferation of dubious actions that decimated the nucleus of a well-functioning state agency – in a country where state agencies are defined by dysfunctionality."

The cases against Zuma and his cronies that might have been had simply disappeared, and while Moyane remained in office things fell apart around him. He installed CCTV cameras to spy on staff, he fast-tracked VAT repayments for the Guptas and he even had a SARS official "kidnapped" in his own office. Moyane was, in fact, so delinquent, so obviously in thrall of an agenda entirely at odds with the public good, that the famously circumspect Cyril Ramaphosa suspended him in March 2018 shortly after he assumed the presidency and months before the Nugent inquiry was due for completion. He then fired him, on the good judge's recommendation, before the final report was even submitted. In that report, Nugent notes that the staff at SARS had been cowed into such a sense of fear and paranoia under Moyane's reign that there was "a palpable shift" in willingness to contribute to the commission once he had been fired, such that that last month of the commission was "as demanding as all the time that had preceded it, which was a manifestation of the fear and anxiety that existed when the inquiry commenced".

SARS had fallen into a downward spiral of decay by then with predictable results: the talented people who had done so much to build it into the efficient tax revenue collection service that it was had started to leave. Around the country, accountants were finding that their company VAT refunds weren't being processed on time and that SARS officials weren't responding as efficiently to queries as they once did. Over the course of six years SARS had increasingly fallen short of tax collection targets, with post-Covid estimates of around R300 billion in accumulated shortfall by March 2021.

The knock-on effects of Moyane's reign of institutional annihilation will, tragically, be felt for years. In the time it takes for us to get our tax returns assessed, in the higher taxes we will have to pay to try to make up the growing shortfall, in the worsening economic conditions that will follow. Ultimately, the poorest of the poor will once again bear the brunt.

The Nugent commission did well not to beat around the bush. It described the situation at SARS as "a massive failure of governance". It got Moyane fired. It recommended prosecutions. But the commissions of which our presidents are so fond have, after all the time they consume, no power to actually punish people. How Tom Moyane is not on trial for treason is the most astounding thing here.

Dudu Myeni

b. 29 October 1963

Chairwoman of SAA (2012-2017);
delinquent director; JZ's good friend with a nice handbag;
pilot at the wheel as SAA went down in flames

Dishonourable mention: Jacob Zuma

SINCE 1994, THE SOUTH AFRICAN GOVERNMENT has given South African Airways almost R70 billion. This is Zuma territory, so we'll spell it out: that's seventy thousand million rand.

Over the same period, the South African government has given Comair, the operators of the British Airways franchise in Southern Africa, as well as low-cost local shuttle service kulula.com, exactly zero rands and zero cents.

South African Airways has not posted a profit since 2011. Comair has, at the time of writing, never failed to report a profit. To avoid such an indignity, it voluntarily went into business rescue due to the Covid-19 aviation crisis. Meanwhile, SAA had to be dragged kicking and screaming into the process, along with its new imbongi-in-chief, Pravin Gordhan.

SAA can be absolutely swell. The pilots are world-class and the cabin staff are often tremendous. Once, returning from an unforgettable trip to Mexico, your correspondent was exhausted to the point of tears when trudging up the air bridge to catch the last leg home from Buenos Aires to Johannesburg. The greeting upon arriving at the aircraft – "Howzit!" – was wonderful. It was like being home already.

But, now, isn't this precisely the point? Isn't it just preposterous that R70 billion has been poured into a money hole so that an already reasonably well-off person may enjoy a South African welcome in Buenos Aires? Isn't it very, very clear that this should not be a priority?

In any case, SAA was just another truck of taxpayers' cash to be scrapped over by the Zuma gangsters, and a means to ensure there were business class flights to George and East London for politicians who needed them. Zuma needed a friendly figure to run the thing, so he chose his "intimate friend" Duduzile Myeni.

Now, that's some gall. Many side-chicks are lucky to get taxi fare home in the morning; Myeni got a whole damn airline.

What kind of person is Myeni? Turns out the absolute worst.

Myeni acquired non-executive director status at SAA in 2009, the year Zuma became president – another less-than-remarkable coincidence in these pages, and never mind that she lied on her CV about having a degree. She quickly set about shimmying her way up aviation's greasy pole, and after a mass board exodus in 2012 she became acting chair and then official chair until 2017. In those years, according to Tim Cohen, the airline haemorrhaged R250 million a month – more than R18 billion in total.

Midway through the bloodbath, Myeni was intent on inserting a shady third party into the leasing of five Airbus A330s, an obvious attempt at graft, though in her words "to promote South African business opportunities". Our finance minister, Nhlanhla Nene, saw it for what it was and said no. Zuma sacked him nine days later, and the result was Nenegate and all that came with it. *(See Des van Rooyen.)*

Myeni also scuppered, on her bae's orders, a code-share deal with Emirates worth $100 million a year on the morning it was due to be signed. It was horrifically embarrassing, a humiliating moment for South Africa and its businesses. We don't know why Zuma – in contravention of all the fiduciary and board processes – ordered Myeni to can the deal, but we can make some educated guesses.

After all, this is the Myeni who ordered that state housing money, channelled through her son's company, be funnelled into the Jacob Zuma Foundation, of which she is chair.

This is the Myeni who looted to the point of near-destruction the Mhlathuze Water Board, of which she was chair.

This is the Myeni who, according to Angelo Agrizzi, received R300,000 a month from Bosasa stuffed into Louis Vuitton handbags, of which she was apparently rather fond.

It appears, in retrospect, that she was an effective plant, doing whatever it is she was expected to do, no matter the shame, no matter the evident damage to the airline she chaired or the country it represented. Now formally a delinquent director, there is at least a little taste of justice. Judge Ronel Tolmay summed it up nicely in her judgment in May 2020:

> "She was a director gone rogue, she did not have the slightest consideration for her fiduciary duty to SAA. She was not a credible witness. As already stated, she changed her versions, contradicted herself, blamed others and played the victim."

Despite the delusions of those who would have prevented it, SAA eventually did go into business rescue during the Covid-19 crisis. Then, in October 2020, Finance Minister Tito Mboweni announced yet another R10 billion bailout for the airline, having previously explained what a stupid idea that would be.

Pravin Gordhan, who fought such a noble battle against state capture when Zuma ruled with his iron and wandering hand, seems to have chosen the national carrier as the hill on which to have his political reputation shot to pieces. But his argument – that a national carrier will help attract private investors to South Africa – has prevailed for now. Money earmarked for higher education, among other things, must be diverted to make it happen, which just illustrates how a little bit of graft and BEE fronting and overstaffing here translates into the likelihood of more Fees Must Fall protests over there. Blade Nzimande must have had cold-sweat flashbacks to burning campuses when he got the news. *(See Blade Nzimande.)*

Can SAA be saved? Once upon a time, perhaps. But after a decade of losses and morale implosions with Dudu Myeni at the controls, we think they're smoking their socks.

Either way, Captain Myeni can go jump in a lake.

Carl Niehaus

b. 25 December 1959 (maybe)

*Former spokesman of Nelson Mandela; unofficial
spokesman of Nkosazana Dlamini-Zuma and Ace
Magashule; almost Spokesman in the Presidency;
walking, breathing embodiment of the ANC's journey
from high morality to absurdist farce*

To many, Carl Niehaus is a running political joke, a man with the credibility of Richard Nixon circa 1974. Yet in some ways he is one of the more tragic of our 50 f***er-uppers, someone who sacrificed much for the moral high ground in his younger days, and who then sacrificed his reputation entirely with his subsequent behaviour. In so doing, he represents the greater reputational downfall of many in his party.

In 1980, Carl Niehaus was booted out of Rand Afrikaans University, weeks before his final exams, for distributing posters supporting the release of Nelson Mandela. He joined the ANC and transferred to Wits, where he excelled and graduated with a BA *Summa cum Laude* in 1983. That same year he was arrested with his fiancée Jansie Lourens. Aged 23, he was sentenced to jail for 15 years for high treason for, among other things, reconnoitring the Johannesburg municipal gasworks as a possible target for attack.

Reporting in *The Washington Post* at the time, Allister Sparks described him leaving the court: "As he left, Niehaus turned towards the public gallery where his parents, supporters of the segregationist government, sat among black Africans. Niehaus raised his fist and called out the congress slogan of 'amandla', which means 'power'. As he did so his parents fell into each other's arms and wept."

He had joined the ANC underground and been rejected by his friends and family, because he was a principled young man who felt that apartheid was abhorrent. About this Carl Niehaus was irrefutably right, and brave to boot. Whatever may have followed – and good grief, a lot did follow – there was a time when he appeared to have more principle in his pinkie than a good many of his white compatriots. For betraying "the Afrikaners", he suffered the horrors of being gang-raped by more than 20 men the night before he was sentenced.

The story of Niehaus's younger years makes what followed so much more outlandish, because the Carl Niehaus we know today – the Zuma-loving, Magashule-supporting, faux-combat-fatigue-wearing, gibberish-spouting, money-grubbing court jester – has gone further off the rails than Prasa under Lucky Montana *(see Lucky Montana)*.

Niehaus married Lourens in jail and earned a degree in theology through Unisa while incarcerated. Lourens served her full four-year sentence, while Niehaus served nearly eight years along with other ANC political prisoners. He was released in 1991. Like the ANC, Niehaus might have had a gilded future ahead of him, but from this point his fortunes track, with remarkable overlap, the fall of the ANC from iconic inspiration to insipid embarrassment.

On his release he became the media liaison for the ANC and even one of Mandela's spokesmen. After the 1994 elections, he was elected to the ANC's National Executive Committee and made an MP. By 1996 he was chairing parliamentary committees. He was a genuinely senior guy. That same year he was sent to the Netherlands as South Africa's ambassador, where he gained a doctorate from Utrecht University.

It was after his return from the Netherlands that the wheels came off. It's not clear exactly why this happened, but he ran into huge financial problems, defaulting on loans and mortgages, both formal and personal. Having allegedly used his relationship with Nelson Mandela to secure a job at Deloitte, he left in 2003 under a cloud of embarrassment due to his financial affairs. Later, he admitted to forging signatures of senior Gauteng officials to secure loans while CEO of the Gauteng Economic Development Agency. He was evidently not terribly good at being corrupt, which in the context of this book is a strangely endearing trait.

That was 2009, the year Zuma came to power. With doubts about Niehaus's past pouring forth, things came to a head in a *Mail & Guardian* interview that blew the lid on the shambles of his life filled with tall tales, broken promises and bad debt. It was clear he had been living far beyond his means, and he tearfully admitted to not having done a lot of what he said he'd done. Much of his CV, it turns out, was a complete invention.

He did not, in fact, graduate from Wits, let alone *cum laude*. He does not have a doctorate from Utrecht. He was not on the boards of the *Maatschappij der Nederlandse Letterkunde* or the South African Netherlands Chamber of Commerce or the *Afrikaanse Skrywersvereniging* or Civirello (Pty) Ltd or the African advisory council of Heineken or the President's Awards for Young Achievers. He was not the chair of the finance committee of the South African Council of Churches. And while he *was* head of South Africa's delegation to the Organisation for the Prohibition of Chemical Weapons (OPCW), he was not South Africa's Permanent Representative on the OPCW Executive Council.

Perhaps most disturbingly, the story of his gang-rape in prison appears to have been a piece of fiction, "revealed" in an open letter to his 11-year-old daughter. The pathology behind that particular story must be quite something to unravel.

By this stage he had managed to run up debts that make the eyes water. R700,000 from Rhema church. R300,000 rent owed on a vast property in Midrand. R2 million on a mortgage for a home in Morningside. He was sued by Magula Makaana, a businessman, for failing to repay a loan of R350,000. He was sued by the advertising agency Mortimer Harvey for R900,000 for work done for the Children United Foundation of South Africa, plus a R600,000 personal loan to boot. Legacy All Suites Management, which manages the luxury apartments at the Michelangelo Towers, wanted R230,000 for unpaid rent. And there was the unfortunate travel agent called Cheryl Clur, who told *The Star* that Niehaus "stiffed" her of R90,000 for a Mauritius holiday. He and his family had been in desperate need for the holiday, you see, on account of the "leukaemia treatment" he was undergoing, and so she'd been persuaded to advance him the payment…

In all, Niehaus's debts appeared to be to the value of more than R4.5 million. This all starts to look less and less like incompetence and more and more like brazen, abusive entitlement. Sound familiar?

Niehaus was forced to leave the ANC. He dropped out of the headlines for eight years, only to reappear in 2017 as a rabid pro-Zuma man, suddenly now with a background in the MK. It was the same year he fictitiously killed off his 88-year-old mother – having done the same to his father five years before – to avoid legal action over the R4.3 million he owed for rental of two luxury apartments in Sandton "as well as damage to expensive furnishings and artwork, unpaid concierge charges and interest", according to Toby Shapshak writing in *Sunday Times*. Nevertheless, he felt he had something to offer to the Nkosazana Dlamini-Zuma campaign for presidency of the ANC and, most astoundingly, her campaign managers felt justified in welcoming him on board.

> "What we know is that he is a pathological liar. He needs help. He was never in MK and he knows it. He should just ask for forgiveness for his lies and deceit."
>
> *Tweet by Derek Hanekom, December 2017*

Stephen Grootes asked and answered the obvious question: "Why would someone employ a known liar and cheat? It can only be because they need that person to lie and cheat for them."

For Niehaus, a victory for NDZ might have signified a chance at redemption and a second time in the sun. Instead, a landlady at the luxury Zimbali resort in KwaZulu-Natal told the *Sunday Times* of how he had promised her government jobs in lieu of rent once Dlamini-Zuma was running South Africa, and that once she had lost at Nasrec, he "ran away in the middle of the night". Of course he had.

Thus aligned with what we may describe as the "more bad" ANC faction, Niehaus has fared poorly in the Ramaphosa era, descending to the level of a clown in the court of Zuma and Magashule, dancing for his dinner alongside fellow clowns Kebby and Des, running Twitter battles against the weathervane clown in the opposite court, Fikile Mbalula, appearing as trial support for the relevant accused cadre as needed, and – again, really quite astoundingly – apparently writing Magashule's press releases.

Niehaus's perpetual defence, mentioned practically every time he appears in front of a camera, is that he spent eight years in jail. It seems hard to refute this particular fact, but literally everything else he has done is now up for question.

The scary thing is that Niehaus, like NDZ herself, so nearly made it. This career liar was a few votes away from being the spokesman in the presidency. Perhaps the tale of Niehaus's spectacular fall from moral authority and personal sacrifice to self-deluded hollow vessel parallelled that faction of the ANC's own trajectory so closely that they couldn't resist him. He just fits in so well.

Blade Nzimande

b. 14 April 1958

*Secretary-General of the SACP (1998-); Minister of Higher
Education and Training (2009-2017); BMW driver;
symbol of leftist contortionist thinking; fiddler
as our universities burned; fallist fall guy*

THE HARD RIGHT HAS BARELY CHANGED in living memory. Intolerant,
closed-minded, racist, ethno-supremacist authoritarians.

The hard left, however, has. It's become an absolutely contradictory
mess within a mess, such a cesspit of opportunists, imposters and infant
thinkers that they can't even agree on what they are. But intolerant, closed-
minded, racist, ethno-supremacist authoritarians isn't far off the mark.

One reason why the hard-left has reinvented itself in this batty
fashion is because it's had to. It hasn't won a serious political contest in

decades. In the UK, for example, various attempts at hard-left politics have floundered upon the rocks of common sense. Labour's recent return to the extremities of leftist thinking under Jeremy Corbyn was accompanied by its chronic predilection for anti-Semitism, and rather mirrored Oswald Mosley's personal political journey in the 1930s from old-school Labour worker-focused politics, through anti-Semitic identitarian fascism to political irrelevance. This was so distasteful to the British electorate that they gave a man no less absurd than Boris Johnson a prodigious 80-seat majority in the House of Commons in 2019 – something not seen since the last time the electorate was faced with a kleptocratic left-wing rabble and therefore duly elected Margaret Thatcher.

In the United States, the gently centre-left Barack Obama managed, to some extent, to cut through that country's political tribalism with his authenticity and substantial charm. But in 2016 the electorate was faced with a Democratic candidate, Hillary Clinton, who had embraced urban identity politics and toxic new-progressivism in the mistaken notion that America and *The New York Times* were in the same place politically, denouncing everybody between New York and Los Angeles as "deplorables". The Republican candidate was a bright-orange property-development scion, reality TV star and tax-dodging incoherent lunatic.

Clinton is so transcendentally unlikeable, and the Democrats so blind to the concerns of working Americans, that they voted for the latter. Extraordinary, really.

Bernie Sanders supporters might scoff at the idea of Hillary Clinton being described as a leftist – she's a faux-lefty, if anything, the opportunist imposter telling the infant thinkers whatever they want to hear, never mind the compounding contradictions from audience to audience. But if leftist thinking once meant making incremental strides towards social equality then "faux-lefty" is almost a redundancy for the Democrats in this ideologically polluted modern era.

For the 2020 elections, the party responded to their appalling 2016 strategy by choosing for president an evidently good guy in Joe Biden. Back in the day his speeches against apartheid were stirring stuff, but today he's a million years old, he appears to forget where he is while making speeches, and he clearly has no answers to those who loot in the name of Black Lives Matter, whose votes he needed, and whose intolerance and violence kept the deranged naartjie in the race.

Just as right-wing ethno-supremacy has been for so long, so the new Western "progressive" political left has become a real cancer on the modern world. It is made up in the main of middle-class, downwardly mobile and highly indebted graduates of an elite urban university system, the degradation of which they have participated in. They have gone to university to be protected from arguments and ideas they might not like or might find hard to hear, and they are now out in the world. They are not so much educated as they are re-educated, and they have the degrees to show for it.

They behave with all the entitlement you'd expect from a powerful, indoctrinated, angry and technologically savvy elite. With its cultural diktats and insistence that people must constantly seek to attain some kind of elusive ideological purity in spite of the various original sins of their birth, this is not a body of people who helps to win an election. It doesn't take much quiet reflection to realise that a heady mix of communism, racial segregation and intersectional prescriptivism, as touted by this new progressive hardline, doesn't have much broad appeal or staying power to it. That's why the left has to appropriate other people's fights, without their permission, and usually buggers them up.

For example, consider the problem of climate change. It's not difficult to accept that the climate is changing and that this is not necessarily a good thing. Serious people spend a great deal of their lives trying to come up with solutions that reduce carbon emissions and pollution while protecting our collective prosperity. But then here comes the hard left with their PhDs in Media Studies – in the form of Extinction Rebellion – demanding full socialism as (fancy that!) the only solution to environmental degradation. The rest of us yawn and switch to Netflix, and in the process ignore the great work of serious climatologists, policy experts and economists who are looking for functional solutions.

This infantile essentialism, always political, destroys progress.

A version of this phenomenon happened in South Africa in the mid-2010s, in the form of the Fees Must Fall movement that overwhelmed our universities and wrought inestimable long-term damage to our tertiary-education system. Being South Africa, however, it had its own singular features.

In March 2015, UCT student Chumani Maxwele ignited the Rhodes Must Fall movement when he poured human crap over a prominently positioned statue of Cecil John Rhodes. The excrement was from one of the notorious plastic boxes used by residents of Khayelitsha that are placed for weekly roadside collection, and it formed the basis of a political performance to protest against the indignities and oppression suffered by black South Africans, along with the university's slow pace of transformation. The merits of throwing around human poo notwithstanding, Maxwele was making a really pertinent point. What *was* the arch-imperialist Rhodes still doing presiding over the university rugby fields, in a spot that saw hundreds of students pass by every day? It sparked a debate – #RhodesMustFall – that flashed around South African campuses and made it all the way to Oxford in the UK, and it ultimately led to the removal of the statue in question.

The point, if not the process, seemed justified, but the political theatre proved an ominous precedent. Here was a societal fight for dignity being appropriated by an individual with his own agenda, whether he was conscious of it or not at the time. As genuine as his anger and motives appeared to be, it's worth noting that in 2020 he would be appointed to a Department of Water and Sanitation task team under Lindiwe Sisulu – so he would do alright out of the whole thing.

But back to October of 2015, and Rhodes Must Fall evolved into Fees Must Fall. This spark was ignited at Wits, following a 10% hike in fees, but again the movement resonated across the land, from the universities of Johannesburg, North West and KwaZulu-Natal to Fort Hare, Rhodes and NMU, and of course to UCT. This time, things got very messy very quickly. Within days riot police were involved and arrests were made. Classes were disrupted and cancelled, exams postponed.

The fee hike was the *casus belli*, but at its heart this was once again a protest fuelled by an overwhelming sense of inequality, injustice and exclusion felt by black students, and a distinct cross-generational disagreement with how best to approach the problem. Many of those involved were poor, and genuinely struggling to pay their fees and find accommodation. How hard must it be to battle through university when you don't know where you're sleeping at night or how you're going to pay the bills? Being unable to afford it is a deeply unjust reason to fail at university. But once again the protests attracted bad actors, criminals and politicised operators looking to profit from the chaos. Predictably, the EFF got involved.

The rhetoric was all over the place: fees had to be eliminated, university workers "insourced", the syllabus "decolonised", Western paradigms such as hierarchical meetings and gravity done away with. The violence was ongoing and extraordinary. Cars were set alight, buildings vandalised, petrol bombs thrown, teaching staff assaulted and intimidated. In February 2016, students at UCT took to burning piles of historical "coloniser" art torn down from the walls of nearby residences, though it was discovered that a couple of the cremated paintings were, in fact, by black activist artist Keresemose Richard Baholo. They may as well have thrown the university's reputation into the flames.

Around the country the vice-chancellors and administrators appeared to have no answer, or simply lacked the political backbone, to respond to the destruction and racial invective that accompanied every new incident. At a time when they desperately needed an adult in the room to calm the waters and provide a rational way forward, they succumbed to the intersectional mental gymnastics that allows petrol bombers to be released on warning and Archbishop Njongonkulu Ndungane, UCT's head of council, to be verbally abused by screaming students.

"This is my inherent contradiction in life. I enjoy mocking Rhodes and yet he pays my university fees."

Kgotsi Chikane, son of Frank Chikane, fallist, 2015

The most tragic consequence of this mayhem was the suicide, in 2018, of acclaimed cardiologist Professor Bongani Mayosi, then dean of the Faculty of Health Sciences at UCT. According to his sister, Mayosi's soul had been "vandalised" by the ongoing vitriolic attacks he had faced from Fees Must Fall activists.

There was certainly cause for the anger and indignity. As we saw with protests in the North West *(see Supra Mahumapelo)*, there is some meaning to be had for a struggling person simply to be seen and acknowledged, even if they have to throw poo to achieve it. But the objective assessment – for such things exist in the real world, no matter your opinion on critical theory and post-modern politics – is one of an enormous net negative for the country. When protesting students close down a campus and stop their fellow students from writing exams and gaining their degrees, this causes real-world consequences. International students literally just picked up and left, taking their funds, goodwill and potential future investment elsewhere. Top professors followed suit. There was grave reputational damage – not to mention the physical stuff. It was later revealed that damages to South African campuses in the years 2015-2017 amounted to about R800 million, enough to put thousands of students through university. The University of the North West's Mahikeng campus alone cost nearly R200 million to repair after buildings were set alight (no coincidence that it was Mahumapelo's neck of the woods). This was actual criminal activity made possible by the criminal negligence of those nominally in charge.

UCT was ranked 124th on the World University Ranking in 2015, the year that the "fallist" movements began. It was at 171 by 2018, with worryingly low scores for the critical metrics of Teaching and Research – scores that will only be improved by attracting, rather than frightening away, top talent.

Racialised inequality and the alienation of black students at South African universities, very obviously, is a massive problem that needs solving. Maintaining a viable, high-quality tertiary-education system is vital for the ongoing success of the country. Both statements are true, *and they are true at the same time*. This is not hard to see for those who will attempt to hold two vaguely complex thoughts in their head simultaneously. What is hard is solving them both at the same time. So we're not here to say there was an easy fix to the problems that underscored the Fees Must Fall movement. But we *are* here to say that the supposed fix – or, rather, the complete inability to implement a fix – was utterly appalling for all concerned, to the point of national negligence.

The problem with being in a position of authority when you've wandered down the cultural Marxist pathway of grievance fetishism is that, when things come to a head, the far-left extremists will eat you for breakfast. By the time you have to make meaningful, critical decisions in front of an angry crowd, your thinking has become so contortionist and concessionary because the mad logic involved means you cannot win no matter what you do. This is the moment the moderate traditional left discovers that the extreme new left really isn't its ally.

Thus South Africa's university administrators and vice-chancellors – the Max Prices and Adam Habibs, who found themselves between the rock of the horrified observers and the hard-left of the insatiable activists – were in a Kafka trap. Whatever action they took proved how wrong they were. So there could be no meaningful action, and the system paralysis filtered upwards through all the layers of administration and oversight to the ultimate buck-stopper in this instance, South Africa's highest-profile lefty (in name, at least), Blade Nzimande.

Have the perils of ideological thinking manifested themselves in South Africa any more obviously than in the actions of the supposed communist Blade Nzimande? A man so dedicated to his vision of bringing prosperity and justice to the poor and downtrodden masses of the country that he sacrificed all inklings of moral authority by helping to manoeuvre Jacob Zuma into the presidency – the means to the end, he presumably argued – and in so doing set back the cause of prosperity and justice for the poor and downtrodden masses in the country by a decade, at least, and possibly indefinitely? A man whose furrowed facial expressions alone convey the furious righteousness with which he seeks action against capitalist oppression, and with which he denounces those who query the ethics of a figurehead of communism approving multimillion-rand government limousines for his use during his time in Cabinet? (Originally a BMW 7-series, later an Audi Q7.) Which is to say, in South Africa, the Communist Party is a wholly-owned vassal of the ANC, with a controlling share bought from Blade Nzimande with a ministerial car and a cushy job doing nothing about higher education. Bish bosh.

There's not much more to it than that. Nzimande's personal history was steeped in academia and social justice – his sociology PhD from the University of Natal was on "corporate guerrillas" – and yet he looked on with what appeared to be very little regard for the damage being done as the vice-chancellors flailed about and the campuses burned. He had the opportunity to channel the fallists' righteous fury into something constructive and yet nothing he did was hailed in any way by the various parties involved, and there was no resolution on the matter by the time he moved on from the ministry of Higher Education in October 2017. The result was that, just two months later, Jacob Zuma could announce, as a parting middle-finger to all in the dying weeks of his reign of destruction, "Free university for all!" – a populist promise so cynical that even his own pocket finance minister, Malusi Gigaba, advised against it. The cost to make it happen, estimated at anywhere between R15 billion and R50 billion a year, is another magic-money pipe dream that will sink South Africa deeper into debt, and there are already early indications that Basic Education, specifically school infrastructures, will suffer due to the diversion of funds.

The real harvest of Fees Must Fall and Nzimande's dereliction of duty will be reaped in years to come as the quality of engineers, mathematicians and doctors expected to build and tend to our country and its people declines. Because yes, despite some of the fallists' fantastical ideas, gravity must be taken into account – for instance, when constructing a bridge or a building or a future university campus.

Ebrahim Patel

b. 1 January 1962

Minister of Trade, Industry and Competition (2019-);
Minister of Economic Development (2009-2019); communist;
trade unionist; wrong guy in the wrong job at the wrong time

Dishonourable mention: Rob Davies

BEFORE WE GET TOO CARRIED AWAY WITH SELF-FLAGELLATION over
our Covid-panic mismanagement, it's good to remember that, on this at
least, we have not been alone. South African exceptionalism in its many
flavours is an important force behind our entitlement pandemic. It can
lead us to believe that this country has a special ability to make the worst
of a situation. Often this is true.

In the vaguest terms, imagine having a small but rapidly growing
economy in the mid-2000s that was starting to absorb the unemployed
into its embrace, all the while dispensing hope and dignity to people
who had known no such thing for 350 years or so. Imagine that, and
then imagine stealing R1.5 trillion and spending it on Mercedes-Benzes
and the New-Money-No-Clue uniform of Louis Vuitton-emblazoned
handbags and Gucci sunglasses.

As South Africans that's the level, right? That's the kind of abuse we've
been taking. So when Covid-19 hit these shores in force in March 2020,
it was probably reasonable to expect that we would concoct a uniquely
South African way to compound a deadly pandemic and turn it into an
epic disaster. We did, for sure, but there is some succour to be had in
knowing that most of the rest of the world, from Italy and the UK to the

US and Brazil, set itself on fire too. Even the Aussies were appalled by their government's showing, and that's saying something. Covid-19 has caused mayhem all over, but mayhem is contextual, and our context is the missing R1.5 trillion and the Cartier comrades.

But heavens above, did we make a special hash of the pandemic. The numbers are horrendous – less the immediate life-stopping horrors than the longer-term lives-affecting damage that has followed. In four months of hard lockdown, the country lost more than a decade of employment growth, shedding something like 2.8 million jobs, where the nation's workers, bankers and businesspeople had, in spite of all the obstacles put in their way, added 2.2 million jobs between 2009 and 2019.

We did this because we thought it was the best thing to do. Rich countries had done it, and there was genuine alarm that this particular virus would sweep through vulnerable poor communities with high incidences of diabetes, TB and HIV, with the potential to kill tens of thousands of people.

Hindsight is 20:20, and it never cannot pass. We didn't die in the numbers we feared in March 2020, and that was in all likelihood because Covid-19 kills the elderly while South Africans don't get old. They usually die young because living here while poor is a death sentence, Covid or no Covid.

Thing is, we knew that last bit back then. Below a certain income, wealth correlates directly with health and life expectancy. This isn't even basic economics. It's the common sense possessed by those who have the means and inclination to put their heads out the window and look at the world. It's a cause-and-effect chain that a child can understand.

Ebrahim Patel is no child. He is a communist and radical unionist who has found himself as minister of Labour, exactly where he would want to be. No, wait, sorry, that was a typo. Patel actually ended up as minister of Trade and Industry. This after a long stint as minister of Economic Development, which is basically the same difference. Funny, no? How a guy with no formal economics training ended up in the very engines of the economy he despises?

If ever a fox has been put in charge of a henhouse… Except that there is something cunning and streetwise about a fox. Patel is more like a plague of locusts in charge of a field of wheat. Maybe not so funny, come to think of it.

So, when the Covid excrement hit the windmill, our minister in charge of making commercial policy decided to make things worse than they could have been by implementing the dumbest regulations imaginable. He stood by while Nkosazana Dlamini-Zuma banned the sale of alcohol and cigarettes, instantly transferring billions in potential tax revenue to bootleggers and smugglers. He made a buffoon of himself defining "essential" clothing with the command-economy enthusiasm of a Warsaw Pact left-shoe factory in swathes of sub-sectioned 3.9.11-style regulations that served to convey little more than a sense of impending doom. Worst of all, he banned "unfettered e-commerce".

Think about that for a moment. He banned the one way that promoted economic activity while encouraging people to stay at home – rather the holy grail, you'd think, for literally the minister of Trade and Industry. But no, this was – in classic Soviet kneejerk dumbthinkery – "unfair" on the physical retailers, apparently.

As heavyweight investor Michael Jordaan commented, "Not allowing e-commerce because it's unfair to physical retailers is the same as not allowing mobile phones because that's unfair to landlines."

Problem is, Comrade Patel would have taken the implicit advice on offer there exactly backwards.

Was this profound failure malice or ignorance? Who knows. Only those entirely au fait with magical Stalinist thinking, where everyone being equally dead is the pinnacle of egalitarianism utopia, will be able to offer some kind of explanation for this madness.

One outcome, though, is that it clearly illustrates where the minister stands on technological progress in the economy. The man from District Six who spent his formative youth in the now-dead textile industry in Woodstock, Cape Town, does not seem to want to move with the times.

Patel found a breeze in his sails from an unexpected source: the comfortable middle class. How cringingly embarrassing it was to watch

> "[A]t the moment, the government is behaving like the well-meaning relative who comes to visit you in the intensive-care unit. They dutifully sanitise their hands at the door and bring you flowers, and while they lean in to gently touch your shoulder to reassure you they are there for you, they stand on your oxygen pipe. As you flail for breath, they physically restrain you to make sure you don't do yourself any harm. Finally, as you stop resisting, the last thing you see is a look of relief on their faces because they believe you've finally seen sense, as the heart monitor flatlines."
>
> *Bruce Whitfield, May 2020*

the revelation of the bubbles in which people live. For some of us, the lockdown was more nuisance than anything – even a bit of a lark. We were downcast by our cancelled holidays in Provence and Tuscany, but we shared memes and witty enjoinders on social media. We downloaded Zoom. We clicked on dumb "Mzansi reacts" stories on *TimesLive* and *News24*. We baked endless rubbish sourdough and put it on Instagram. We wrote Facebook posts about taking stock, about remembering what matters in life, about making the best of this crazy time and really connecting with our kids.

South Africa really is Benjamin Disraeli's "Two Nations". Because so few of us ever visit that other place, and because we are so inured to its relentless suffering, we didn't even look over the fence to notice that in the other South Africa, 2.8 million people were losing their jobs and battling to feed their kids. That's because carpenters and plumbers and labourers and shop assistants and cleaners and cooks and builders and gardeners and nannies and hairdressers and cabinet makers and bartenders and drivers and desk clerks and parking guards and waiters and petrol-pump attendants and mechanics and manicurists don't work from home. While we vexed about our dwindling alcohol supplies and called our local bootleggers in desperation, the farm labourers and glass-makers that the industry should have been employing went hungry.

At Groot Constantia they even decided to virtue signal their support of the government's ban on alcohol sales, despite the catastrophe it was wreaking in the winelands and the alcohol industry at large. "Patience," the vineyard tweeted. "Much as we love sharing our wines and estate with you, we believe in teamwork, and right now Team South Africa is focused on saving lives. At Groot Constantia we are South Africans first, proud winemakers second. #FeelGrootConstantia"

This at a stage, at the height of a wet Cape winter, when the industry had lost a reported 117,000 jobs. If you take nothing else from this book, please remember to never drink Groot Constantia ever again.

Patel's active moves against e-commerce and his distrust of technological change illustrate the type of thinking that has been applied to our economic policy during the lost decade. They are likely to be rooted in his fears that they have the potential to threaten people's jobs. This would not be a new observation. We all know that the advent of the driverless car will herald the end of the Uber driver. Electric cars charged at home will herald the end of the petrol-pump attendant. Online grocery deliveries will spare Checkers shoppers the dubious charms of the check-out staff – and so on. But Patel's head-in-the-sand approach to what the government keeps calling the Fourth Industrial Revolution is harmful at best. Change is inevitable, and history teaches us that progress improves people's lives and generally creates jobs elsewhere. The Luddites railed against steam power, but steam power made the world better in the end by providing mobility, supply chains at scale and, eventually, electricity. Our government should be hard at work trying to facilitate what they call in the energy space a "just transition" from one power source (burning the Gupta brothers' coal) to another (solar, wind, gas, hydroelectric) in a way that doesn't leave the whole of Mpumalanga unemployed. At the very least, our government should be getting out of the way, cutting out reams of diktats and allowing private business to do this.

Any casual observer of the economy will have seen that business owners have either had to shutter their businesses and let their staff go, or reimagine their businesses from the bottom up. They have, as economist

Nic Spaull observed in the *Financial Mail*, the means to "pivot away from labour" to a new reality:

> "Businesses are choosing not to rehire those they retrenched, reflecting their pessimism about SA's future as well as their unwillingness (or inability) to absorb the costs of re-employing staff. On a cynical view, businesses may be using the crisis to pivot away from labour they see as costly, risky and possibly unnecessary.
>
> "If that is the case, then Covid-19 and the lockdown will not only have revealed our inequalities like never before, but actually made them far worse, accelerating a disjuncture that has been long in the making."

It will also expose the minister of Trade and Industry. At a time when our economy is desperate for vision, efficiency and leadership, we have a guy running the show who appears to exist in a 1950s ideological dichotomy that no longer reflects any kind of reality, and lacks any meaningful ideas as to how to salvage anything from this catastrophe.

As Spaull says, the Covid crisis may have forced the country into a new and necessary paradigm in terms of grants. The Covid-19 Social Relief of Distress Grant may already be a de facto Basic Income Grant, which is a Very Good Thing if we accept the reality that "full employment" is a pipe dream in our country.

Now, to fund the thing we need a working economy, which means Patel needs to start thinking about and acting on the move to tech-driven efficiencies, not avoiding it – a point the Covid crisis hasn't just made loud and clear, but also accelerated rapidly.

Patel gets it hard from us because of his prominence during the lockdown debacle. His timing is unfortunate. If there'd been no global pandemic, Rob Davies, minister of Trade and Industry for ten years before him, would probably have his spot here for overseeing a steady decline in annual economic growth from around 3% to next to nothing even before Covid hit. Then again, they're effectively the same guy, representing the same disastrous government approach. Both cut from the same red cloth

(Davies's is cut particularly badly); both acolytes of a communist party that still calls its leadership body the Politburo (really); both exemplars of magical economic thinking who have no real ideas for growth, who cannot comprehend the workings of the modern business world, let alone debt and its future implication, and who would rather look for inspiration to the failed economies of decades past.

From what we can see, Patel and Davies are not corrupt in the Zuma-as-state-capturer sense of the term. They are not incompetent in the Zuma-counting-big-numbers sense of the term. They are not disloyal to their fellow countrymen in the Zuma-as-president sense of the term. But what a slave to backward ideology they are.

However you see the world, South Africans deserve better than this.

Riah Phiyega

b. 29 May 1958

*National Police Commissioner (2012-2015); poisoned
chalice inheritor; one example of our dysfunctional
police force; Marikana scapegoat*

*Dishonourable mentions: Bheki Cele, Jackie Selebi,
everyone involved in the Marikana massacre*

ON 16 AUGUST 2012, SOUTH AFRICA EXPERIENCED a profound and utterly tragic moment of time travel, transported back to the early afternoon of 21 March 1960. Back then, in the previously anonymous township of Sharpeville, between the industrial towns of Vereeniging and Vanderbijlpark, policemen in the employ of the apartheid government of South Africa opened fire on a crowd of black protesters. When the gunfire stopped, 69 people were dead, many of them shot in

the back as they fled. The Sharpeville massacre attracted international condemnation, from the United Nations among others, and marked a turning point in the increasing isolation of the apartheid state.

More than half a century later, in the platinum mining town of Marikana, about two hours' drive north of Sharpeville, a similar scene played out. Policemen in the employ of the democratic government of South Africa opened fire on a crowd of black protesters. When the gunfire stopped, 34 people were dead, many of them shot in the back as they fled. The Marikana massacre attracted much local condemnation and remains a festering scab on the fragile landscape of the "new" South Africa, the moment when our post-democratic police force reverted to apartheid-era stereotype.

There were some differences between the cases. The policeman at Sharpeville were white, at Marikana mostly black. The protesters at Sharpeville, objecting to the much-hated passbooks or *dompasses*, were mostly unarmed. The protestors at Marikana, striking miners from the Lonmin platinum mine, were armed and had demonstrated extreme violence in the preceding days, in which ten people had died, including miners, policemen and security guards.

And yet the effect was the same: horrific widespread loss of faith in the South African police; deep shock and sorrow that the state could turn on its own people and shoot them down in cold blood; whatever pretence of collective innocence that may have existed beforehand irrevocably shattered; in the aftermath a heartless response from government, doubling down on the crimes of its police force.

Riah Phiyega had been National Police Commissioner for all of two months before the massacre. Coming from a corporate background, she had no experience in policing, and she inherited the mantle of a position that had been steeped in ineptness and embarrassment for at least a dozen years. She had taken over from Bheki Cele, who had been found unfit for office and fired on the back of a leasing scandal, and he'd taken over from Jackie Selebi, who was jailed for corruption. Both were hopeless, Selebi essentially denying that crime was a problem in South Africa while being a criminal himself, and Cele strutting about in his jaunty hat, actively encouraging his employees to shoot to kill (though he contested the actual wording).

Combine that with the harsh winter reality of a violent highveld wildcat strike, and Phiyega was on a hiding to nothing. She would go on to blame the events on a "catastrophic system failure", which would appear to be a fair assessment, given the state of the South African Police Service, though nothing she or anyone else would say could penetrate the mist of fear and loathing that possessed those cops who had hunted down fleeing miners far from the cameras.

Many of those who were there and who investigated the massacre in detail, such as the photojournalist Greg Marinovich, are convinced it was premeditated, and orchestrated in "collaboration" with the police, the state and those with vested interests. But out of the 600-page

"Even a chicken protects all of its eggs... We put our cross next to Zuma's face, and then he sends his police to kill us."

Lonmin miner, August 2012

"It is becoming clear to this reporter that heavily armed police hunted down and killed the miners in cold blood."

Greg Marinovich, August 2012

"If our recommendations were implemented, I have no doubt that there would have been prosecutions."

Judge Ian Farlam, August 2019

"If we allow police and our elected politicians and our officials to do this, it's a precedent, it means it will just keep on going. If we offend them with our actions, if we want people to be accountable, if we want capitalism to be just, as it isn't at the moment, it means our people are gonna get mowed down again for being disobedient."

Greg Marinovich, author of Murder At Small Koppie, August 2020

R153 million Farlam commission that investigated the scandal, not one prosecution has emerged. It did, however, find that Phiyega had misled the commission, and it recommended that her fitness for office should be investigated. Having been suspended, she was moved on in 2015, a quiet scapegoat, found to be absolutely out of her depth.

Her successor as police commissioner, in an acting capacity, was Khomotso Phahlane. He lasted nearly two years before he ended up in court on corruption charges in 2018. That same year, the chalice was passed back to none other than the guy previously found unfit for the job, Mr Shoot-to-kill himself, Bheki Cele. This is the state of our policing in the 2010s – an ongoing crisis, forever tainted by the most infamous single incident in post-democratic South Africa, while the tragic mini-Marikanas resurface all too frequently with names like Andries Tatane and Nathaniel Julius.

Oscar Pistorius

b. 22 November 1986

*Paralympian wunderkind; embodiment of all that can
be great about South African sport; killer; self-pitying
contemporary Icarus; embodiment of South Africa's
particularly violent version of broken masculinity*

IN SOUTH AFRICA WE ARE IN THE MIDST of an ongoing war between men and women. Of the various atrocious social phenomena that trouble our nation's soul – widespread poverty, government corruption, debilitating unemployment – few, if any, deliver as much shame and ignominy as the manner and frequency with which our men murder and rape our women. We might say that the murder and rape of women by men in South Africa is like braais and Nando's – one of those rare pastimes that crosses all of our country's barriers of race, wealth and cultures.

All reasonable people know that there is a severe and fundamental crisis of masculinity in South Africa. That way too many of our men take out their pathologies, insecurities and self-loathing on women. That way too many of them are bad bastards. But the statistics are contested and perhaps even unknowable, so a lot of the discussion is based on educated guesswork. It seems, as reported in an earlier entry, that there really were 450,000 rape reports in the decade to September 2019, and yet we know that rape is grossly underreported. Some say that as few as one in 25 is reported; multiplying those numbers produces a frankly terrifying statistic.

Here are some additional ones.

More than 2,700 South African women and 1,000 children were killed in 2019, most at the hands of people they knew. Some estimates have it that more than half of our women have experienced violence at the hands of their partners.

The Medical Research Council reports that "a dedicated GBV [gender-based violence] population-based study on women in Gauteng (2011) has shown that more than 1 in 3 women (37.7%) have experienced physical and/or sexual intimate partner violence (IPV), 18.8% reported sexual IPV, and 46.2% reported economic or emotional abuse".

According to a Wits-Sonke Gender Justice report, a 2016 study of 2,600 men in Diepsloot, north of Johannesburg, revealed that 56% of them "reported that they have either raped or beaten a woman in the last 12 months. Of those men using recent violence, 60% committed multiple acts of violence against women during that period."

But to kill off one particular canard, this pandemic of ours is not limited to impoverished townships. To illustrate its cross-cultural, class-pervading, non-racial nature, South Africa's most globally famous purveyor of misogynistic violence and rage is Oscar Pistorius. He did not live off "an average monthly income of R1,500", as per the men interviewed in Diepsloot, he didn't live in a shack or single room, and he had finished high school. In the three months before he did what he did, he had experienced neither food insecurity nor unemployment.

The spectacular fall from grace of this once-revered Paralympian athlete can be neatly illustrated by the sheer scale of the embarrassment felt by the authors of *50 Flippen Brilliant South Africans*, who included Pistorius in their 2012 book. We didn't just include him; in the first edition of that book we described him as an "incredibly nice guy". That certainly didn't age well. Our conclusion, however, was not quite as dramatically wrong. "[I]t seems likely that gold medals and sprinting will not be the beginning and end of the Oscar Pistorius story," we wrote. "What will Oscar do next? It's unlikely to be accountancy."

Indeed, it wasn't. Within four months of publication, in February 2013, Oscar Pistorius had murdered his girlfriend. We don't know exactly what happened in that startlingly tasteless house on his Pretoria security estate, but Pistorius was (eventually) convicted for shooting to death his girlfriend who had been so frightened that she had already locked herself in a lavatory before the shots were fired. Pistorius was so angry he shot her through the door. He pulled the trigger four times.

By all accounts Reeva Steenkamp was a lovely young woman. It was her youthful misfortune to be drawn into the circle of Oscar Pistorius which, as it turned out, contained a hyper-macho lifestyle of speedboats, supercars, guns and rage – all the standard accoutrements of South African male success and bravado.

We need to be careful here. There are those who will tell you that "all men are trash". This is essentialist, divisive and untrue. It is even true that gender-based violence doesn't always flow in one direction. However, among the boys, we know that many of our male acquaintances are incapable of having meaningful relationships with other men – relationships that are not based around bawdry misogynistic jokes and talking down their wives and girlfriends on the guys' WhatsApp group (a group that is otherwise limited to discussing sport, politics and hot chicks). And the extension of this lack of meaningful relationships with other men is that their relationships with their wives or girlfriends are something we'd rather not explore in too much depth. Something to keep behind closed doors, as it were. These men are the fathers that raise their sons to be "tough" and aggressive, sons who see their fathers treat their mothers poorly.

South Africa's crisis of masculinity is an intergenerational toxic miasma, passed from father to son and nurtured by an education system that adopts the morality and measures of success of Victorian English schools, which the actual English schools abandoned in the 1970s. And ultimately it feeds off violence, and in particular the powerless righteous default of "I'm angry, you suffer".

There is much to despise about Oscar Pistorius and his trial. The shattered dreams. The shame we were forced to endure as the international press descended on the Pretoria High Court and relayed our femicide rates to the world. The doltishly inept and criminal police who stole watches and despoiled the crime scene. The true believers, the Oscar cultists who – like the Hansie cultists a decade before – refused to countenance their idol's awful crime.

Oscar the double-amputee celebrity Olympian was few people's prediction for poster child of domestic abuse, and yet the lesson is more blistering for it. Male-on-female violence is endemic in South Africa. It's in the townships and townhouses, hostels and the house next door.

Some say Oscar was insane when he did it – temporarily, in the heat of the moment or perhaps maddened over time, incrementally isolated from reality in his bubble of ego, celebrity entitlement and high-octane manly pursuits. Whatever the case may be, there is an undeniable collective madness that is echoed day in and day out across our land in countless cases that are never even reported, let alone brought to trial, let alone validated with a conviction.

Of the many things Oscar became when he murdered his girlfriend, a symbol of one of the plagues of our time was not an obvious one, but it is the most enduring.

Pistorius will be eligible for parole in 2023. "Lock up your daughters," the boytjies on WhatsApp will laugh. How deeply unfunny it all is.

Cyril Ramaphosa

b. 17 November 1952

*President of South Africa (2018-); Deputy President
of South Africa (2014-2018); star of 50 Flippen
Brilliant South Africans; slow mover;
grand dreamer or grand fantasist?*

OH, CYRIL.

We hoped, we really did, that we wouldn't have to include our current president here… And yet, just as he appeared in *50 Flippen Brilliant South Africans*, so he is here.

How can he not be?

There are those who have argued for years now that as deputy president of the country and, more importantly, of the ANC under Zuma, Cyril Ramaphosa should bear his share of shame and responsibility for the fetid swathe of corruption that enveloped our land in the Zuma Years.

He was there, in influence, at peak capture. Plus he was even given direct charge of turning around Eskom, SAA and the Post Office in 2014. Firefighter-in-chief, they called him. (How JZ must have heh-heh'd when he handed him that turd sandwich of a job.)

But it wasn't just his failure to bring about meaningful fixes in the Zuma presidency that was the problem. The greater criticism was that he was lending it the legitimacy of his presence – a respectable businessman, a trustworthy figurehead, a great South African even. Might the fall of Zuma have come sooner if Ramaphosa had taken a bold stand in defiance?

It was a long and dangerous game that Ramaphosa played – a game that risked him being cast into the political wilderness once again, as had happened when Mbeki outmanoeuvred him in the 1990s, and yet one that he eventually won, by the narrowest of margins, at Nasrec in December 2017. And so the naysayers had to concede that the plan had worked. He'd made it. Zuma was forced to resign in February 2018 and Ramaphosa was our leader. He had bided his time, did what he had to do to finally take power – and now he could… do what exactly?

Ramaphosa's rise to the presidency of South Africa was an impressive feat in itself, a truly Machiavellian tale. But once victory had been declared he, like George W Bush after the invasion of Iraq in 2003, seems to have had no plan for the real challenge that followed. How would he manage the toxic factionalism within the ANC, the pervasive corruption across all levels of government, the utterly enormous economic challenges facing the country?

In some circles it appears that the anger the majority of South Africans once directed with such vehemence at Zuma and the Guptas has been transferred to Ramaphosa. Of course, it's unfair. Zuma and the Guptas and all who ran with them are the scum of the earth. Ramaphosa is a decent guy. And yet people are tired of waiting. Because as much as Ramaphosa can count with apparent ease and isn't fathering children with his friends' daughters and doesn't look to be selling the country to foreigners, the president's softly-softly slowly-slowly approach is reminiscent of quiet diplomacy in Zimbabwe at the turn of the century, or Captain Smith having tea with John Astor as the *Titanic* bears down on the iceberg.

Things have happened, yes, but at what glacial pace, when time is of the essence. Zuma is gone (2018). Zwane (2018), Dlamini (2019) and Gigaba (2019) are gone, along with some of the other most implicated Cabinet ministers – yet others remain, three years later. Shaun the Sheep at the NPA has been replaced with someone who appears to be competent (2019). Ditto Tom Moyane at SARS (2019). There have been a handful of low-level arrests (2020), with some chatter of higher-level arrests to come.

The number of obviously despicable people in positions of power is shrinking ever so painfully slowly, the political interpretation of *Waiting For Godot*. And yet they are still everywhere.

"South Africa will soon be corruption-free," Ramaphosa declared with such optimism in November 2018. What a tragically delusional line that turned out to be, as though our state wasn't still largely captured by municipal patronage and localised corruption. Fast-forward to the worst humanitarian and economic challenge of our time, the Covid-19 crisis, and the scale of procurement corruption that emerged from it is unfathomable, and perhaps as immoral as anything that took place under the Zuma presidency. One estimate had it that, as of October 2020, two-thirds of the R15.6 billion spent to date had been stolen.

Ramaphosa, we must conclude, is either far less powerful than we might have hoped or he is living in a realm of semi-fantasy, perhaps brought on by too many years in the rarefied world of BEE billionaire-dom. The way Nkosazana Dlamini-Zuma and others muscled into proceedings with such authoritarian gusto during the ruinous lockdown would point to the former. The talk of smart cities and bullet trains and multiple state-operated mega-projects in a time when more than half our tax revenue goes to civil service salaries and another 20% to paying off our debt would point to the latter.

So a combination of the two, then.

Either way, we must wonder why Ramaphosa worked for so many long years, why he spent all that time and energy and moral capital,

"South Africa's greatest adversary remains itself. The government's failure to assess the failure of its policies and admit error, and thus to view the current situation as a problem only and not a crisis, has brought us to this point... This is compounded by a pathological unwillingness to make tough choices, and insufficient ability to manage complexity."

Greg Mills and Ray Hartley, July 2020

putting his reputation and ethical heartland on the line, to finally get to the top and twiddle his thumbs. If you're going to make that deal with the devil, we would suggest you make it count.

Is there some kind of philosophical point of no return that a man crosses when surrounded by vagabonds and thieves for too long; when the salvation he thought he could render no longer equates with the reality and morality of real-world existence?

We place Cyril Ramaphosa here oh-so-gently because he is more fragile than can be imagined, and president of a fragile country teetering on the edge. Covid-19 was a sledgehammer blow after a decade of continuous hammering. It might have been an opportunity of sorts. Perhaps it still is. But only if a powerful, decisive, clear-thinking, practical leader is there to take it.

This is the first year of the 2020s. Might we hope that such a person exists to make the next ten years somewhat more fruitful than the last?

Mamphela Ramphele

b. 28 December 1947

Black Consciousness co-founder; struggle activist banished to Tzaneen; mother of Steve Biko's children; former Vice-Chancellor of UCT; former MD of the World Bank; former trustee of the Nelson Mandela Foundation; founder of Agang South Africa; former DA presidential candidate; formerly the politician most uniquely and favourably positioned to bring about real and positive change in South Africa

OKAY, YOU CAN'T EXACTLY BLAME HER for stuffing up the country in the last ten years, but she must be the worst person at politics in the world.

"I offered her the world, she wanted the galaxy, and she ended up with a shack in Pofadder."

Helen Zille, April 2015

Floyd Shivambu

b. 1 January 1983

*Deputy President of the EFF; Malema's Number 2;
beneficiary and embarrassingly public face
of the VBS bank looters*

In 2018, Floyd Shivambu was arrested for speeding in the Free State after doing more than 180km/h in his Range Rover Sport. Not much to note there other than the fact that 180km/h is pretty brave on the N1 unless you feel, for some reason, you're immune to prosecution and the laws of physics.

At the time, a Range Rover Sport went for about R1.1 million, a touch less than the annual salary of an ordinary MP. These poverty rations might explain why the white Range Rover Sport regrettably had to be bought with money stolen from VBS Mutual Bank. A big important chap like Shivambu can't not have a Range Rover, you see.

We are, in a jurisprudential sense, fairly fresh on our journey that will, in a just world, see Shivambu, Julius Malema and their friends shifting their sartorial focus from red to orange. At the time of writing, one VBS official had pleaded guilty and been sentenced to seven years in jail, another eight had been arrested, and the Zondo commission had recently expressed its desire to have a chat with Floyd and Julius about the R16 million-plus that ended up in a slush fund paying for the holidays, the birthday parties, the inevitable Gucci habits and, of course, the Range Rover. This follows some cracking reporting on the looting of VBS Mutual Bank by Pauli van Wyk of Scorpio, the investigative unit for *Daily Maverick*.

The truth is the ultimate protection in matters of libel, and the plain speak of Van Wyk's award-winning journalism is almost as illuminating as the detail itself. "Money robbed from VBS Mutual Bank" funded EFF activities, she writes. And: "In a scheme designed to mask the origin and ultimate beneficiaries of the funds, VBS money flowed through companies over which Julius Malema and Floyd Shivambu have ultimate control."

Boil it down and we find that Shivambu, the jackboot on the foot of our country's fascist political party, stole the meagre savings of elderly and poor people in Limpopo, and spent it on a fast car (and some other stuff).

The EFF's racism is common cause. For instance, the party's insistence on calling Pravin Gordhan by his middle name, Jamnadas, is a dog

"Floyd Shivambu's Limpopo wedding to Siphesihle Pezi, his Range Rover, some of his property rental leasing contracts and his lifestyle have been funded by VBS loot and private businesspeople wishing to do business with the state. This is detailed in reams of bank statements, WhatsApp discussions, documents and Scorpio's conversations with his benefactors. In return, Shivambu uses his political power to assist his benefactors, the evidence suggests."

Pauli van Wyk, Daily Maverick, October 2020

> "We are going to state here, categorically clear, without any fear of contradiction, that the EFF and ourselves as MPs never benefited anything from the VBS Mutual Bank looting and the so-called heist that happened there."
>
> *Floyd Shivambu, speaking in Parliament, October 2018*

whistle to its mob of nationalist troglodytes. But when the anti-Indian racism angle became a thing, it seemed so weird and unnecessary (in the weird and unnecessary world of EFF logic, that is). Shivambu, in a parliamentary committee meeting, suggested that a treasury official's presence in the meeting "undermined African leadership" because the man was of Indian ancestry. There followed unmistakeably racist and seemingly unhinged attacks on the official in question, Ismail Momoniat.

Once the story was blown open, and it was clear that Momoniat was directly involved in trying to sort out the VBS debacle, it all started to make sense. As the National Treasury and SARB closed in on the VBS heist, so Shivambu's rhetoric escalated. Support came from EFF spokesman Mbuyiseni "Che" Ndlozi (the best-looking fascist of them all) with a classic party line: "It was very odd that the Reserve Bank does not want to save a black bank. Many other banks have been saved, and so it is wrong to not save VBS."

In other words: bail it out and stop asking difficult questions.

The VBS scandal was, in fact, a fairly common or garden-variety ANC looting mission. An early indication that there were politically amenable figures making important calls at the bank came when it was revealed that VBS had lent Jacob Zuma more than R7.8 million to pay back the money he was found to owe for upgrades to Nkandla. This despite him not qualifying for a bond of that amount. *(See Baleka Mbete.)*

One of the challenges for the VBS robbers was finding enough money to steal from a bank that catered to the low-income residents of Limpopo and focused on stokvels and burial societies. The trick was for ANC deployees in about 15 local municipalities to deposit municipal funds into the bank – suddenly, there's a lot more loot. But in terms of the Municipal Finance Management Act, which Momoniat had helped write, municipalities may not bank with mutual banks, so when National Treasury got wind of this, Momoniat instructed the municipalities to withdraw their funds. This forced a liquidity crisis and an investigation ordered by the SARB which, in the end, found that R2.7 billion had been misappropriated from the bank in a four-year spree from 2014 to 2018. "Fictitious credits" magically appeared in specified accounts, placed there by compromised bank executives, and just like that 53 individuals (at least) had spending money for Lacoste and Louis Vuitton.

Ho-hum.

For the ANC in the 2010s you might say this was just another day at the office, another minor news story. For the EFF, though, it was a problem, because it just so happened that one of those 53 individuals involved was Brian Shivambu, brother of Floyd. For the working man's EFF, this was serious, because it implicated the most senior party leaders as robbers of the poor. Sure enough, it was soon brought up by the ANC and the DA in Parliament. John Steenhuisen, then chief whip of the DA, had great fun riling up Julius Malema when he described the EFF as "the VBS bank looters".

Malema, to put it politely, completely mislaid his faeces.

Everything the EFF has done since needs to be understood in the context of VBS, its clear involvement in the theft, and its hugely embarrassing political consequences. Stealing from the rich may be defensible in the court of public opinion. But stealing from the poor... Thus VBS is the EFF's Arms Deal, their original sin.

There it is in a nutshell. Shivambu and friends are more than happy to put fire to racial tensions in the hope that the smoke might obscure the Range Rovers and Gucci trinkets bought with money stolen from the poor.

It hasn't worked.

Shivambu's other misdemeanours are small by comparison. He SMSed veteran reporter Carien du Plessis and called her a "white bitch". He physically attacked a journalist, which has attracted legal attention.

He has other interesting income streams that may well attract further legal attention in time. But that's all small beer stuff for an EFF goon.

VBS is the very large keg. More than 20,000 mainly poor and black people had kept their cash and their stokvels and their funeral policies with the bank. And now it is gone. Those small sums represent the fruits of a life of work by working-class black people. No money in this country was more deservedly earned or more responsibly saved, and if the treasury does refund some of it, as seems likely, then fair game. But where would the refund come from? You guessed it: the taxpayer.

The theft of this money illustrates the ethical vacuum that is the soul of the EFF. One can only hope, with grim irony, that Shivambu enjoys his Range Rover, built by a British company owned by an Indian family. The poor people of Limpopo will just have to struggle on.

Edwin Sodi

"Politically connected" CEO of Blackhead Consulting;
architect of the Free State "asbestos heist"; worst of the
tenderpreneurs; first of the charged tenderpreneurs;
living embodiment of vulgarity, entitlement and
disdain for his fellow human beings

Dishonourable mentions: Ace Magashule,
Ignatius Mpambani

IN VINO VERITAS, THEY SAY, but equally people tend to say what they really think when they're in a space they consider to be safe, be it a family braai or on a friendly WhatsApp group. When people feel safe, the embellishments and the real truths are likely to emerge.

It's funny, then, how Edwin Sodi, serial tenderpreneur and philanderer, felt so much at ease during his testimony at the Zondo commission, so much among his elite peers, that he was able to laughingly testify before the Deputy Chief Justice that "Chair, I know I like my holy waters." This in reply to a question of how he managed to run up a R600,000 alcohol debt to then director-general of the national department of Human Settlements, Thabane Zulu.

This explained the R600,000 deposit he paid for Zulu's Range Rover (once again with the Range Rovers). Because, you see, the director-general of the national department of Human Settlements, who owns a sports lounge more than 100 kilometres away from where you live, is the logical guy to be buying your premium alcohol from.

Sodi shot to national notoriety in 2020 when he was named as the man behind the "asbestos heist", a mid-decade tenderpreneurship joint venture that had fleeced the Free State government out of the bulk of a reported R230 million. (Almost enough to upgrade Nkandla!)

Asbestos is an incredible material, a brilliant insulator, and asbestos roofs were all the rage in the 1970s, being strong and cheap. The problem was, as we later learnt, that asbestos is also absolutely lethal. Exposure to it kills people, and mesothelioma – a cancer of the lung lining caused exclusively by the exposure to asbestos fibres – is an especially cruel way to die, essentially a painful six- or 12-month drowning. An asbestos roof is harmless if let alone, but 50 years after these apartheid-era roofs were installed, the people living under them are, as might be expected, breaking them down, fixing them up and generally fiddling with them.

Thus a valid need was established to audit the status of asbestos roofing on old state-built houses.

Sodi and partners, however, don't care about that kind of thing – they like their holy waters, after all. And, in illustrating the impact of corruption in this book, these asbestos roofs could easily be replaced by unbuilt schools and deteriorating educational outcomes *(see Mugwena Maluleke)*, sick people dying in filthy conditions *(see Qedani Mahlangu)*, the creeping water crisis in this country *(see Nomvula Mokonyane)* and the collapse of our energy infrastructure *(see Brian Molefe)*.

In these and other instances, it is crushingly depressing to think that an ANC government has made profoundly worse the circumstances of people living in accommodation provided by the apartheid government that explicitly hated them. The sheer wretched shame of it.

The R230 million Free State asbestos contract was by no means Sodi's only bonsela. His various firms have won more than a billion rand's worth of contracts from the state over the years. To give you some kind of sense of the scale of the gouging, Ori Group, the company that actually performed the Free State asbestos audit, under various layers of contractors and sub-contractors and political payoffs, did so for around R7 million. What's more, it came out at the Zondo commission that they seemed happy with their margin too – as well they might be, given that it apparently entailed counting houses on Google Earth and just two months of field work. Note, please, that there was no actual fixing or replacing of asbestos roofs. In the meantime, Blackhead Consulting evidently made nearly R200 million in profit from the deal. Nice work if you can get it.

On a now-famous spreadsheet found on Sodi's computer in his office was a column for "cost of business" – which you might read as "payoffs". One entry, for R10 million, was marked for the mystery character "AM", and the fact that the Free State premier's initials were "AM", we are asked to believe, is just happenstance.

Sodi denies creating the spreadsheet, saying his business partner in the Free State joint venture, Ignatius "Igo" Mpambani of Diamond Hill Trading 71, did so. Unfortunately for Zondo, Mpambani died in a hail of bullets in 2017 while transporting a million rand of cash in his Bentley, and dead men don't testify.

Sodi's obscene lifestyle came to the fore when the Asset Forfeiture Unit swooped in on his Bryanston mansion and Blackhead Consulting premises in Sandton in October 2020. The mansion had recently been

"Problem with govn procurement in a nutshell. Edwin Sodi, one half of the Blackhead/Diamond Hill JV, telling #ZondoCommission there's nothing wrong with making R100m profit on a R200m contract. Weep, taxpayer, weep."

Tweet by Pieter-Louis Myburgh, August 2020

listed for sale at R85 million, perhaps to pay his legal fees. The NPA, in its new-found media-savvy way, paraded Sodi's cars as they were attached – there was the Ferrari FF, there a Porsche Cayenne, there the Bentley Continental. A video clip then went viral of what was purported to be his extended fleet, including at least 14 luxury supercars.

Sodi doesn't, however, spend *all* his money on cars and champagne. He is, as all successful tenderpreneurs must be, a generous donor to the ANC and several of its high-profile members. The Zondo commission heard that he had paid R3.5 million for the purchase of T-shirts for ANC volunteers. It was also revealed that Health Minister Zweli Mkhize, Labour and Employment Minister Thulas Nxesi, ANC Treasurer-General Paul Mashatile and deputy ministers Pinky Kekana and Zizi Kodwa were all flagged as having received payment from Sodi. The degrees of legality and morality involved are yet, if ever, to be determined.

Sodi couldn't see the problem. "Because I grew up in the ANC," he testified, "the fact that there would have been some donations either from myself or my company, I do not see that as strange, fraudulent or corrupt unless someone convinces me otherwise. I do not say there is any crime in one supporting a political party of his choice."

As of this book's publication, Sodi had been arrested, along with several others, but not yet convicted. Thus we are obliged to note that he is not officially a criminal. Perhaps he will be one day, and for the pinprick of hope that this offers we felt we needed to include him here. Either way, he takes his place here as one of the worst of the tenderpreneurs. There are others who have been longer-running and at far greater cost to the country *(see Gavin Watson)*, but have any of them been more vulgar or given less of a damn about the people he might have been helping even while he turned healthy profits?

It's not that hard to make sense of the psychology behind the average tenderpreneur and the patronage network of Zuma acolytes. It's an angle – to riches and reward and a better life for you and your family – built on a sense of resentment and even entitlement. The past regime was corrupt in its own way; now it's our turn. Absolutely unethical and disgraceful, but there is a perverse logic to it.

But then you have an utter vulgarian like Sodi and you wonder, what madness drives this? Must the pillaging be so pronounced, the taking and hoarding of material goods so infantile, that you end up with 14 luxury cars tucked away in an underground garage in Bryanston?

What happens when impunity drifts into a different paradigm? Where up is down and buying off the politicians who award tenders is not corrupt, and the unshakeable faith that this is true means we just say it in front of the Deputy Chief Justice? Where a quarter-of-a-billion-rand government contract sees 10% being spent on the poorest citizens of the country and the bulk of it going into the pockets of a guy with a Ferrari and a Rolls and a Porsche and an AMG and a Bentley…

Wherever this strange, depraved place is, it's where we are.

And so, please, a moment's silence for a message from your humble public servants in the Free State. Bear your lung cancer stoically. Try to remember, between the guttural coughing attacks, that because of your suffering someone gets to have a Bentley. It is a worthy sacrifice. Please try to die quietly, lest you embarrass the movement. Thank you.

Iqbal Survé

b. 12 February 1963

"Mandela's doctor"; "Mandela's personal friend"; "Bafana Bafana mind doctor"; intimate associate of Prince Charles, Ahmed Kathrada, the Wizard of Oz, and the great and the good; quite possibly the vainest person in South Africa; clothes-less emperor of Independent Media

Dishonourable mention: Dan Matjila

RUPERT MURDOCH, CONRAD BLACK, MICHAEL BLOOMBERG, SILVIO BERLUSCONI AND JEFF BEZOS. What's this, then? A business meeting of the world's most influential media moguls? A dinner party where the close protection officers are outnumbered only by the helicopters? Or, perhaps, some kind of Bilderberg-esque meeting to direct the fate of the whole of humanity?

What fools we are to even consider this. How could it be any of these without Africa's greatest philanthropist, a son of the soil dedicated to the advancement of black businesses and the betterment of mankind, and not to mention Nelson Mandela's close friend and personal physician, Dr Iqbal Survé?

Murdoch, Bloomberg, Black and Berlusconi are all stinking-rich, and are the more obvious media entrepreneurs here. Murdoch may not be your cup of tea, and Bloomberg may not be your favourite bagel, and Conrad Black may indeed be a convicted fraudster, and Berlusconi's media background may be somewhat overshadowed by his more recent depredations in Italian politics and call girls – but they did all build media empires from scratch. And Bezos, our unlikely outsider, deliberately bought *The Washington Post* – not as an investment into a company, but because he wanted to own *The Washington Post*. Small man, big wallet; it's a thing they like to do. And, not incidentally here, it allows them to steer national conversations when they feel the need.

Which brings us to Iqbal Survé – close personal friend of Nelson Mandela, don't forget – who no doubt would consider himself in the Bezos mould, a man on a mission to build an "African unicorn", who invested in South Africa's largest English-language newspapers group to bring about a fairer and more just world…

In reality, Dr Survé bought a failing newspaper company already hollowed-out by its Irish owners, but still important to South Africa's democracy. He then, with all the grace you'd expect from such a guy, proceeded to savage to death its proud history and reputation in a matter of months.

The *Cape Times* was founded in 1876. Survé, through his Sekunjalo Group, bought Independent News & Media in 2013 with a billion-rand loan wangled from state workers' pensions via the Public Investment Corporation (PIC). By the end of that same year, the *Cape Times* had ceased to be a serious newspaper. Quite some work, to undo the culture and reputation of a journalistic institution built over 137 years in a matter of a hundred days or so. But that's the toxicity of Icky Iqbal for you.

It's hard to fully pin down Survé's motives. Money, for sure, and probably some desperate need for affirmation or acknowledgement that may be better explained by a psychiatrist than an author. Like many who do not understand newspapers, he seems to have thought that once you're the guy who "buys ink by the barrel", then you get to decide what the truth is. As Survé has found, it's not that simple, especially when the truth you seek to create and disseminate is so very obviously some kind of fever-dream fantasy scaffolding upon which you would like to build an imaginary monument to yourself.

If the journalist's job is to hold up a mirror to society, Survé seems to prefer holding one up to himself, and so Independent News & Media SA quickly became a parody of the strutting peacocking martinet who owned it. It was ably assisted in this cause by the hacks-turned-propagandists *(see Adri Senekal de Wet)* he hired to edit his newspapers when the real journalists were fired, chased out or just quit in despair.

Let's be clear about the scale of the complicity of these proselytising, praise-singing lickspittles. As laid out in *Paper Tiger: Iqbal Survé And The Downfall of Independent Newspapers*, the mind-bending account of the Survé-Independent train wreck authored by evicted editors Alide Dasnois and Chris Whitfield, this wasn't a matter of occasional acts of favourable editing or careful working around a Sekunjalo story.

"A quick count of mentions on the Independent Online website shows that over the next five years [2014-2019] Survé was to appear, often with photographs, at least 350 times in his newspapers: an average of 70 times a year, or about once every five days. Events in which he was involved, from the World Economic Forum to BRICS to the 'Saudi Arabia-South Africa Business Council', made the news, often on the front page.

"Survé's every step at the World Economic Forum was also faithfully recorded by his editors, who interviewed him time and time again on everything from the world economy to South

Africa's prospects to the successes of his various companies and the evil antics of his competitors.

"Sometimes the headlines seemed better suited to religious figures. Thus, on 13 February 2014, in a report co-authored by then *Business Report* editor Ellis Mnyandu, readers met 'The man who wants to change the world'. Readers of the *Cape Times* photo supplement 'Society' were regularly regaled with pictures of Survé and various members of his family out and about in town. By late 2018, the proliferation of photographs of Survé prompted CapeTalk radio host Kieno Kammies to hold a mock 'competition' between the *Cape Argus* and the *Cape Times* to see which title could post the most pictures of the owner."

Dasnois was removed from her job as editor of the *Cape Times* after she published the news that the Public Protector had found Tina Joemat-Pettersson, then minister of Agriculture, Forestry and Fisheries, guilty of "improper conduct and maladministration" in the awarding of an R800 million tender to Survé's Sekunjalo consortium. Numerous learned observers of the matter have suggested the timing was no coincidence, though Madiba's mate assured us it was for unrelated underperformance.

Like any newspaper editor worth her salt, Dasnois would have been intimately aware that in journalism your reputation is really all you

"Since the takeover, readers of the Independent's once-feisty titles, which include the *Cape Times* and *The Star*, have seen a distinct change in coverage. Besides displaying an odd predilection for puff pieces about Dr Survé, it has become markedly less critical of the government. Dozens of senior journalists and editors have left or been sacked. The group's executive editor, Karima Brown, was recently pictured at an ANC anniversary rally dressed in an ANC hat. With editors and owners like these, who needs censorship?"

The Economist, 2015

have, and that there is a long, flyblown and pitiless road between the abuse of a reader's trust and the hope of absolution. Darrel Bristow-Bovey, a gifted and sometimes magnificently irascible writer, took a full decade out of the public eye and issued an earnest *mea culpa* before daring to write again in his own name after plagiarising passages from Bill Bryson. Verashni Pillay published a bogus article while editor of *Huffington Post*, and had to resign.

This is as it should be, though Survé hasn't seemed able to take on board the learnings. And because he owns the building, he doesn't get kicked out onto the street for his reputation-ruining behaviour.

Inevitably, though, many of Survé's hagiographers have found themselves scrambling to find work as the absurdity of Independent Media's content drifts from incompetent agitprop to satire-by-accident – but of course their reputations precede them. That's their bed to lie in. Pity is reserved for the junior reporters too young and naive to see that they will long be stained by their association with Independent and Iqbal's imbongis.

Imagine working for a guy who exists in an almost-comedic fantasy. A world in which he has variously claimed he was:

- a close personal friend of Nelson Mandela, to whom he brought peace before he died;
- Mandela's private physician "on and off Robben Island", despite being a 19-year-old med student when Mandela was transferred from Robben Island to Pollsmoor Prison;
- the recipient of an award from Amnesty International as South Africa's "struggle doctor", though Mandela himself is the only South African to have received an award from Amnesty;
- mentored by Rivonia triallist Ahmed Kathrada – a claim to which Kathrada responded: "I don't know the man personally";
- a "Fellow of the Prince of Wales's Business and Sustainability Programme", and invited to tea at Highgrove by Prince Charles "many times", despite such a fellowship not existing;
- a "mind coach" who "miraculously turned Bafana Bafana around"

before they won the 1996 African Cup of Nations, and helped turn the Indian cricket team into "the best cricket team in history".

All of these claims, made in interviews and puff pieces, appear to be absolutely without basis in reality. So much so that one wonders whether Survé is mentally unwell and does, in fact, believe it all. But that's more work for the psychiatrist – or should it be the mind doctor?

Survé had what might be termed a friendly relationship with CEO of the PIC Dan Matjila, and it's a fact of history that Survé managed to persuade the PIC to invest R4.3 billion into his firm AYO Technology Solutions in 2017, a move described as "gross negligence" by the Mpati commission's investigation of activity at the PIC. It's a fact of history, also, that this money has found its way into Sekunjalo, his family firm, and that it has in turn been used to pay Independent staffers, raising a question: why did the PIC bankroll a deal to buy a stable of newspapers

"And then he told us, with eyes ablaze and Those Teeth – the ones cartoonists love to give emphasis, not that they need any – about how he and Madiba had been Like This, and how '(Mandela) said to me, just before he got ill, "Iqbal, are you still the same?" I said to him, "Tata, I am still the same." He said, "Now I can go.""
The sound of jaws dropping could be heard for several city blocks. Every journalist in the room looked down, shuffled their feet, glanced at one another. The sound of eyebrows raising could be heard in Muizenberg. The sound of muffled chortles disturbed the birds in the Company's Garden aviary."

Tony Jackman, former
Cape Times staffer

with readership in serious decline in the first place? Further facts of history are that Survé's buddy Matjila has been sent packing from the PIC, that it wrote down R1 billion of the original Independent loan in 2018, and that the new suits there want their investment back, with the threat of liquidation now hanging over Independent Media.

Survé's other suspect dealings and destructive behaviours are too numerous to go into detail here. That smelly fishing deal with his other buddy Tina Joemat-Pettersson; the allegations of share manipulation schemes as part of his outlandish fantasy to create an "African unicorn"; the inflation of newspaper circulation figures; the frequent use of racial outrage in his newspapers *(see Adri Senekal de Wet)* as a smokescreen for his behaviour, presumably, or to ingratiate himself to the powers that be.

For now, our focus is on the demise of Independent Media, and with it veritable institutions of the South African media landscape: *The Star*, *Pretoria News*, *The Mercury* and *Daily News*, the *Cape Argus*, the *Cape Times*. Crimes that are unforgivable, especially at a time when genuinely independent mainstream media is so vital for a healthy, functioning society.

If you're wondering just how low Independent Media has sunk, consider the role it played in the story of the decade, the Gupta Leaks investigation. Absolutely none. Where *Daily Maverick* collaborated with *amaBhungane* and *News24* to deliver the most important and influential investigative-reporting work in modern South African history, Independent Media was not trusted to be involved. How could they be, when Survé had followed the Guptas' very newspaper model – parroting the government narrative in return for favours – and even tried to go into business with them? The plan, nixed by the PIC in 2016, had been for them to buy half of Sekunjalo Group.

But even if Survé wasn't so politically compromised – a Zuma praise-singer from the early days and a committed advocate for Nkosazana Dlamini-Zuma to succeed him – no journalists who take themselves half-seriously would be able to partner with a company so utterly gutted of newsroom talent and riven with incompetence. Headline misspellings

> "Half the harm that is done in this world is due to people who want to feel important. They don't mean to do harm; but the harm does not interest them. Or they do not see it, or they justify it. Because they are absorbed in the endless struggle to think well of themselves."
>
> *TS Eliot*

and general copy-editing cockups were exemplified in 2015 in a short classifieds ad recruiting for two senior subeditors at the *Cape Argus*: it contained no fewer than six proofing errors. Clearly the subs were needed. But the ad was not as defining as the *Business Report* story that transcribed a spoken quote on a firm's "weighting in the DAX" stock market index as "waiting in the ducks". This spawned a short-lived but long-remembered "Ducks Waiting" Twitter account, which highlighted the many and glorious errors printed in the *Cape Times*.

It's a litany. The newspapers are on life support, propped up by suspect investments made for suspect reasons by the PIC in the Zuma era. Will Survé take Independent down with him when his fantasy world eventually collapses? Well, that's up to the kind of guy he is. What would Mandela's doctor do?

Des van Rooyen

b. 20 November 1968

"Weekend Special"; "2-Minute Noodle"; social media meme; arson attractor; Minister of Finance (2015-2015); face of Nenegate; R500 billion lesson in cause and effect; extreme outer limit of state capture

Dishonourable mentions: the Guptas, Jacob Zuma

IN A WAY, IT'S A PITY that Brenda Fassie's legendary B-side, *Weekend Special*, has been sullied by association with David Douglas "Des" van Rooyen, but online commentary in this country is seldom gentle. And the comparison is just so apt. The song captures not only the duration of Van Rooyen's tenure as minister of Finance, from 10 to 13 December 2015 – a long weekend, to be fair – but also the transactional role that Van Rooyen was there to play in the Gupta-Zuma constellation of state capture.

"Friday night, yes I know," you might imagine Minister Des singing in the shower before his Cabinet meetings in Saxonwold. "I know I must be ready for you, just be waiting for yooouuu – I'm your weekend, weekend special!"

For those who blinked and missed it, Van Rooyen was the idiot-pawn at the centre of the most brazen episode of state capture in the Guptas' long-running assault on South Africa and its citizens. The incumbent Minister of Finance, Nhlanhla Nene, was doing a decent job at the time, as President Zuma happily admitted to the nation on the day he let him go, but he wasn't as amenable to foreign persuasion as might have been hoped (Zuma didn't say that last bit out loud). As a result, he replaced Nene with Van Rooyen, an unknown backbencher, and the markets went haywire. The rand lost nearly 10% against the dollar in 48 hours, the market capitalisation of the JSE dropped by hundreds of billions of rand, and investors went running.

This was Nenegate, "a visible point in the state capture project", as Catherine MacLeod, economist at the National Treasury, put it to the Zondo commission in February 2019.

Des van Rooyen's history is murky, but he seems to have been an MK member in exile in the 1980s, and bolstered his activist credentials at the United Democratic Front, National Union of Mineworkers and elsewhere. The path took him to the dizzying heights of the mayorship of Merafong, a dusty local municipality among the West Rand's mines.

This did not go well.

The ANC plan to gerrymander some cross-border municipalities in its favour meant that Merafong would be incorporated into the broke

> "148,000 jobs were lost in terms of the model we ran. We saw a reduction of about R378 billion in the JSE markets capitalisation. We also costed the impact of at least 1.1% of GDP by the end of that year."
> *Treasury Director-General Dondo Mogajane,*
> *Zondo commission testimony, November 2018*

and even more corrupt North West. *(See Supra Mahumapelo.)* Van Rooyen ignored the howls of protest from Merafong's inhabitants and, like a good cadre, did nothing to stop it. He was thanked by the wider community for this sterling grassroots political activism by having his family home razed to the ground.

After his achievements in Merafong, Van Rooyen was redeployed to the National Assembly, where he served as ANC whip of the standing committee on Finance and of the Economic Transformation Cluster. These, to be clear, are political roles. After his shock promotion to the Finance ministry, veteran economist and South Africa-watcher Peter Attard Montalto explained the implications.

"Van Rooyen is a member of the portfolio standing committee on finance in Parliament. He has been a member of the committee since 2011 and so, while aware of fiscal and National Treasury issues, he has no central government experience, and no provincial government experience. From what we have seen, he has not been particularly vocal or independent from the ANC while on the committee or in the ANC. He does not appear to have had strong policy-making credentials within the ANC structures over the last 20 years in the way the previous three finance ministers did."

In the world of anodyne financial commentary, this is pretty savage stuff. Translated, it reads: "Van Rooyen doesn't know anything and just does as he's told." Ideal material, then, for the project of state capture – except when you do something as outrageous as putting a puppet into the most important ministry in Cabinet.

The appointment of Van Rooyen as finance minister represented the extreme limits of both Zuma's understanding of How Stuff Works and what the country, government and governing party would tolerate. Even the Guptas appeared to believe that something this outrageous was possible in South Africa. But with the markets in flames, senior ANC members took Zuma aside and his previously unquestionable authority was countermanded. Van Rooyen, having taken office on a Thursday, was gone by the Sunday, forever South Africa's Weekend Special. In his place, a Zupta nemesis, the legendarily honest Pravin Gordhan.

A country's economy is an infinitely complex thing, as Zuma wouldn't know or care, so the total damage of Nenegate is still not quantifiable, and may never be. General consensus is that it put a R500 billion hole in the economy back then and we're still feeling the effects today. The currency has never recovered, making us all the poorer. However you assess it, it was the most damaging single moment of state capture.

There's a mildly convincing conspiracy theory that certain people, knowing in advance of the announcement of Nene's firing and the market shock it would cause, positioned themselves to short the rand and make some serious money in the process. If true, it would have been a secondary crime. This wasn't a mere smash-and-grab incident; Zuma and the Guptas really assumed they could get away with the appointment of Van Rooyen, with all that might have meant for nuclear energy deals and SAA financing and all the rest.

As it turned out, Des van Rooyen was the limit of what we would take. Those in the know say it was, in fact, the moment Zuma, in the form of his ex-wife, lost the Nasrec 2017 vote. The sight of his weekend special being sworn in as finance minister, all puffed up and proud, is one of the most pathetic images of our recent political history. The man isn't fit to be a finance minister's jockstrap.

Gavin Watson

12 July 1948 – 26 August 2019

*CEO of Bosasa; evangelising lord of the tenderpreneurs;
seedy blur between morality and criminality; bad driver*

*Dishonourable mentions: Angelo Agrizzi, Gwede
Mantashe, Nomvula Mokonyane, Hlaudi Motsoeneng,
Dudu Myeni, Vincent Smith, Jacob Zuma*

IF YOU MANAGED TO TRACK DOWN A GUPTA BROTHER to his
R400 million pad in Dubai or his mountain eyrie in Uzbekistan or his
volcano lair in Japan, and you then managed to get him to speak on
record – and well done to you, Mr Bond – he would no doubt convey a
legally vetted version of, "Hey, we did nothing wrong." As an example
from 2017: "The family deny any wrongdoing or paying any amounts to
ministers or the president, and reserve its rights."

These guys will go to the ends of the world to insist they did nothing wrong; they were just hard-working businessmen trying to earn a living and have a nice wedding; it's all a big conspiracy. (That last one, learnt from their former friend, is a classic Zuma zinger.)

Those involved in the Watson family business, however, don't all appear to run with this approach. Just ask its COO Angelo Agrizzi. The Zondo commission did, and he was more than forthcoming.

Over the course of the past couple of years, Agrizzi has claimed under oath that Bosasa (now African Global Operations) was essentially a vampire squid patronage system that attached itself to influential members of the ANC, and funnelled money and gifts to the right places in exchange for a bounty of tenders. SAA-destroyer Dudu Myeni received R300,000 a month in a Louis Vuitton handbag, Agrizzi declared. SABC-destroyer Hlaudi Motsoeneng got more than R1 million for legal fees. ANC Secretary-General Gwede Mantashe scored a R300,000 security upgrade. ANC MP Vincent Smith got an upgrade too, along with cash. Nomvula Mokonyane was on a R50,000-a-month cash stipend, and Bosasa maintained her home, paid for a cousin's funeral and regularly bought her meat and high-end booze to keep her sweet.

The ANC got plenty of donations when the right people came knocking, and in return Bosasa earned lucrative security, catering, database-management and other tenders in the departments of Correctional Services, Justice and Home Affairs, and in the country's prison services, repatriation centres and airports.

Now here's the thing. Agrizzi is a Ferrari-loving fat cat with decent motivation for painting Gavin Watson as the head scumbag in this story. But there is clearly a lot of truth in what he's saying because many of those named happily conceded as much. Motsoeneng acknowledged the legal fees, but said it was in exchange for nothing. Mantashe acknowledged that part of his security system had indeed been installed by Bosasa and paid for by one of its directors, a family friend. And then there's Mokonyane, whose testimony at the Zondo commission in July 2020 in response to Agrizzi's was remarkable in its unwitting candour.

Mokonyane's political legacy is appalling in anyone's language. In her time in power she did little that was good and much that was bad, the exact details of which may or may not be ascertained in a court of law one day. *(See Nomvula Mokonyane.)* And as vehemently as Mokonyane denied the claims of actual bribery, she had no qualms in admitting that the ANC had awarded tenders to Bosasa because the company was a party funder. She went so far as to explain that they came "with no strings attached".

How might she reach this conclusion? Could she be so dim as not to realise the implications of what she'd said? Her 2017 quote that if the rand falls "we will pick it up" would suggest this may not be beyond the realm of possibility, and yet the overriding suspicion here is that this wasn't colossal stupidity or a slip of the tongue. This was simply her speaking her truth. Telling it the way she sees it. People donate to the ANC and the ANC rewards them with government tenders. Duh, Judge Zondo. The best lies being those that the liars believe themselves, this goes a long way to explaining the behaviour of the modern ANC.

According to Agrizzi, a lot of what Bosasa did was utterly corrupt and there are unquestionably crimes to be answered for. Vincent Smith's arrest in October 2020 is a good start. But much of their approach to securing tenders was technically not criminal, just unethical. Donate the money and, what do you know, your business flourishes. Jacob Zuma said as much in 2015: "I always say to business people that if you invest in the ANC, you are wise. If you don't invest in the ANC, your business is in danger."

Gavin Watson, Zuma's friend, was evidently wise.

Staunchly religious, Watson and his three brothers grew up in the Eastern Cape taking a proud moral stand in defying the apartheid laws of the 1970s to coach and play interracial rugby. The youngest, Cheeky, was picked for the Springboks but turned it down – clearly there was some real moral backbone in the family once upon a time. They joined the ANC, earned serious struggle credentials and, for the business-focused eldest brother looking to the future, potential government connections. Their Christian values appeared to underscore all their actions – they didn't drink or swear, and Gavin was fond of kicking off morning

> "There are no controls over campaign financing in South Africa, and so an operation like Bosasa can work on two levels: underground, through bribery, and above board, through making high-profile donations to the party, or running and staffing – as Bosasa did – huge campaign 'war rooms' for the ANC out of its head office."
>
> *Mark Gevisser*

business at Bosasa with fervent prayer sessions. The facade didn't convince everyone, though, and Adriaan Basson describes Watson in his book *Blessed By Bosasa* as a bully, racist, philanderer, manipulator and liar. He argues that Bosasa was a cult, with Gavin Watson as its leader.

In a lengthy piece for *The Guardian*, Mark Gevisser puts it more diplomatically, comparing the Watson brothers to the Shaiks: "The testimony before the state capture commission suggests a slippery slope: from comradely support into patronage and, in some cases, corruption."

Whatever it was, Bosasa raked in the cash – upwards of R12 billion before it went into liquidation in late 2019. And whatever the ultimate truth that Judge Zondo may divine from Angelo Agrizzi's testimony, the deeper insight here is into the ethical foundation on which our governing party has been run for decades now. As symbolised by Mokonyane's testimony, it's not only that the ANC refuses to self-correct; it's that deep down they don't even know the problem exists. It is a self-delusion of nation-destroying proportions.

And so we shouldn't be surprised to find, in the year of Covid, that our leaders' children are following this same logic. Mokonyane's daughter Katleho, Ace Magashule's sons Tshepiso and Thato, and yes, Cyril Ramaphosa's son Andile, have all been named as beneficiaries of multimillion-rand government contracts in response to the pandemic, from providing PPE to modifying taxis to comply with Covid regulations. Illegal? Possibly not. Unethical? Depends on your point of view, apparently.

In response to the enormous public outcry at Covid tender corruption, President Ramaphosa fired what appeared to be a first warning shot across the bows of all ANC members in August 2020, writing a letter addressed to them entitled "Let This Be A Turning Point In The Fight Against Corruption". It was as forceful a move as Ramaphosa makes, given the pains he has taken to lead by consensus. In it he spelled out some directives for the party: it should disassociate itself from anyone accused of being corrupt, members accused of corruption should account to the party or be suspended, leaders should declare financial interests and undergo lifestyle audits. And, finally, this imperative: "Develop a clear policy on ANC leaders and their family members doing business with the state. We must acknowledge that once one accepts a leadership position, a higher standard of behaviour applies."

Amazingly, 26 years into our democratic existence, more than two decades since Travelgate and the Arms Deal, a clear policy on doing business with the state does not exist. For much of that time, Gavin Watson and his congregation at Bosasa had been lapping it up.

* * *

In August 2019, Gavin Watson checked his BMW X5 in for repairs, and booked out a white company Toyota Corolla. Questions were later raised as to why he opted for a car with a manual gearbox, when he was apparently only comfortable driving an automatic. Early in the morning of 26 August, the car crashed into a bridge pillar near OR Tambo airport at high speed. The result was as mangled a wreck as you might see, the point of impact and extent of the damage permitting only one possible outcome for the driver.

It's quite something to think that we live in a time when one of the highest-profile potential criminal suspects in the country dies in an extraordinary car wreck in the strangest of circumstances, and then people kind of forget about it. In the mid-2000s, when the white-collar gangster Brett Kebble was killed in his car, it caused international headlines, *skok* and *skandaal*. Today, more than a year after Gavin Watson's death, the high priest of Bosasa is gone – but his life and career still swirl behind a veil of mystery and corruption.

Xi Jinping

b. 15 June 1953

President of the People's Republic of China (2013-);
Covid-19 accelerant; 2020 economy killer;
21st-century neo-coloniser; debt-trap diplomat

Dishonourable mention: Vladimir Putin

THE UNCENSORED INTERNET REALLY FREAKS OUT CHINA, and this comes right from the top. Xi Jinping, leader of the Communist Party and the People's Republic (*snigger*) of China, is really super-sensitive about the memes that liken him to Winnie the Pooh. This, evidently, is why a picture of a Winnie the Pooh toy was the most censored picture in China in 2015, and why the bear of very little brain has continued to bother the Chinese censors ever since. (*South Park*, for one, has gone to town on this.)

China is especially touchy about its overseas image. You'd think, then, that they would behave less appallingly.

There is no need to believe that China intentionally created the novel coronavirus SARS-CoV-2 to understand that the country behaved badly once they recognised what was going on. Unsanitary practices at a notorious "wet market" in Wuhan, the Huanan Seafood Wholesale Market, seem to be the likely source of the Covid-19 outbreak. There, you could find the usual market produce, from shellfish to freshly butchered chicken, and if you required something a little more interesting, there was a delectable selection of beavers, snakes, crocodiles, porcupines and bats. The earliest cases appear to have emerged in November 2019, and certainly by late December an alarming cluster had been identified by local government. By 7 January scientists had isolated the new virus. Human-to-human transmission was confirmed soon after.

What did China do? Warn the world? Shut down international flights to prevent it going global? Send out a mayday to scientists and doctors who might help China understand the virus more quickly?

No, the opposite.

The censorship instinct kicked in. Doctors who tried to raise the alarm in December were reprimanded and gagged, their interviews scrubbed from the internet. (The original whistle-blower, Dr Li Wenliang, an ophthalmologist in Wuhan, died of Covid-19 in February.) By late January, Beijing was putting pressure on the World Health Organization (WHO) not to make a big deal of things – "divergent views", it was called. Soon 50 million people in 15 cities across Hubei province were locked down and domestic flights were being heavily curtailed, and yet international flights from China were encouraged to continue merrily out into the world. When Italy, which would see horrific scenes in the following months, identified its first cases and dared to close travel between the countries, it was dressed down by China's vice-minister of foreign affairs.

Meanwhile, as authorities were doing what they could to hide the raging outbreak, the call went out to consulates, embassies and Chinese diaspora organisations around the world to source as much personal protective equipment (PPE) as was possible at the best possible prices. In the six weeks from mid-January, Chinese government data showed that 2.5 billion items of PPE were imported into the country, while exports were greatly reduced. Now, this could have been a practical necessity to protect the motherland – and that's how the state-controlled Chinese media have played it. However, what actually happened is that once the virus had circled the globe and people were starting to die in large numbers, China sold the PPE back to foreign countries at prices often inflated by a factor of 20 or 30.

It took until mid-March before China would concede that, actually, yes, Covid-19 was a thing, the world had best start preparing and perhaps they'd like to buy some PPE. To cut a long story short, the country responsible for a global pandemic profited massively off it instead of doing its best to help.

China is not very nice.

And it wasn't done yet. As the clear global leader at unleashing viruses onto the world, China then duped the world into adopting what became the widely accepted way to handle it: lockdown. This, if we're being generous, was less intentional. Within months, the purpose of lockdowns seems to have been completely forgotten. To quote the WHO's Dr David Nabarro, commenting with the benefit of much hindsight in October

> "What we can be certain of is that the type of hard lockdown imposed in March will only inflict further, perhaps fatal, damage to an economy which was on the ropes before the pandemic – and which the hard lockdown rendered moribund. It will also significantly undermine any chance of an economic recovery, without achieving any meaningful net health impact."
>
> *The Scientists Collective, including Professor Shabir Madhi,*
> *Professor Glenda Gray, Professor François Venter,*
> *Professor Marc Mendelson, Dr Lucille Blumberg and Dr Aslam Dasoo*

2020, "The only time we believe a lockdown is justified is to buy you time to reorganise, regroup, rebalance your resources, protect your health workers who are exhausted, but by and large, we'd rather not do it."

What's more, "Lockdowns just have one consequence that you must never, ever belittle, and that is making poor people an awful lot poorer." But here we were, along with much of the rest of the world, misunderstanding the purpose of a lockdown and using it as some kind of rolling relentless ongoing totalitarian national regulatory disinfectant. These things tend to only work in actual totalitarian societies who've been practising them for some time – something to bear in mind when you listen to experts counting the economic costs of 2020 in the years to come. As it stands, the Chinese economy was forecast to have fully recovered and even grown 2% by the end of 2020, while the US would drop 5%, the Eurozone 8% and South Africa 8.5%.

If life is relative, then it turns out Covid-19 has worked out pretty well for China.

Now, bear this in mind when you consider that it's been 11 long years since China overtook the US as Africa's largest trading partner. In the decade and a half to 2015, China loaned the continent almost $100 billion. According to the Centre for Global Development, eight African countries are highly vulnerable to debt distress as a result.

Benedict Peters, founder of Nigeria's largest domestic oil-producing firm, is one of those who have recognised it as the "new colonialism", an accusation China is as sensitive about as Winnie the Pooh pics.

What's in it for China? Well, we have what they want, which is to say, a third of China's oil, half the world's manganese, more than half the world's cobalt and more than half the world's carbonatites, the

---

"In Africa, it is clear that China's campaign of foreign investment is a new form of colonialism. The continent, where I live and work, is ground zero."

Benedict Peters, New African

source of rare earth metals. If this is sounding familiar, that's because what we're seeing is history starting to repeat itself. Like the British, French, Belgians and others before them, China appears to be creating a giant extractive machine in Africa, built by Chinese companies and often Chinese labour, using Chinese machines, all on a mountain of unsustainable debt owed to – you know it – China.

Let's look at Sri Lanka as a model of what might lie in store. In 2010 Sri Lanka agreed to pay a Chinese state-owned corporation $1.5 billion to build Hambantota port on its south coast. In 2017, struggling to make repayments on $8 billion of loans for this and other projects, the government agreed to lease the port and a huge area of land around it to the same Chinese company for 99 years.

Interestingly, this is not dissimilar to the modus operandi Victorian-era Britain used to extract a 99-year lease of Hong Kong from the Qing rulers at the time. China, they say, has a long memory, and in using the British-Hong Kong blueprint, they would appear to have learnt from the best.

China now has a port in the Indian Ocean.

Let's look at Angola as a model closer to home. The former Portuguese colony was gifted $4 billion of cheap loans in the 2000s to build infrastructure – by Chinese companies, naturally – and this

"China is now Africa's biggest trade partner, with Sino-African trade topping $200 billion per year. According to McKinsey, more than 10,000 Chinese-owned firms are currently operating throughout the African continent, and the value of Chinese business there since 2005 amounts to more than $2 trillion, with $300 billion in investment currently on the table. Africa has also eclipsed Asia as the largest market for China's overseas construction contracts… expect Africa to continue swaying to the east as economic ties with China become more numerous and robust."

Forbes, 2019

was leveraged into multiple oil exploration rights. According to the Brookings Institute, oil and gas enterprise "Sinopec's acquisition of rights coincided with the announcement of a new $2 billion loan from China Eximbank to the Angolan government".

In 2008, the China Railway Group used a similar model to secure mining rights in the Democratic Republic of the Congo's copper and cobalt mines.

All well and good, but who lends the capital and harvests the interest? Whose company builds the infrastructure? Where do the workers and the engineers come from? Where does the construction equipment come from? And to the point: who's getting rich here? Because it sure doesn't look to be ordinary Sri Lankans, Angolans and Congolese.

Back home in South Africa, doing what is right for South Africans is not necessarily the business of our government, as you will have read elsewhere in this book, so you have only one guess as to who our biggest trading partner is. In 2013, Xi Jinping launched his massively ambitious Belt and Road Initiative, a global infrastructure project to "~~colonise developing world economies~~" "enhance regional connectivity and embrace a brighter future". In 2015 he boldly declared that "The programmes of development will be open and inclusive, not exclusive." We really should not have been surprised, though, that when President Ramaphosa took R196 billion of Chinese loans in 2018, variously for Eskom and other SOEs, it came with a raft of secret terms and conditions. Not so "open and inclusive", then.

Public debt, public terms, you might have thought. But not with China, especially when the guy in charge has actively built a cult of personality around him, reversed much of the gradual liberalisation of his country that we had witnessed before his arrival, and is now the closest thing to Mao we've seen since Mao.

He is the leader who shalt not be known as Winnie the Pooh and, while he may look quite cuddly, Xi Jinping is categorically not our friend. Covid-19 proved it. By the time Africa's debt trap with China is clear for all to see, it will be far too late – and once again, this will be a situation that ends well for China and far less well for us.

We should be as wary of Xi as we are of Russian nuclear energy deals proposed by Vladimir Putin. The likelihood of our government heeding the lessons of 2020 are, however, about the same as a cadre turning down a PPE tender (probably imported from China).

Xi Jinping is a latter-day Cecil John Rhodes, and he cares as much for the average African as he does for a Uighur Muslim.

Helen Zille

b. 9 March 1951

*Leader of the DA (2007-2015); GodZille; once one
of the very few world-class politicians in South Africa;
egomaniac; control freak; social media disaster*

HELEN ZILLE IS A GOOD SPORT, and she might have guessed she would appear in this book. Someone from the DA had to, and she has repeatedly shown us that, since she rose to lead in 2007, she pretty much *is* the DA. Even when she's "retired". We might have added Mmusi Maimane here, too, come to think of it – for reversing the party's electoral growth in 2019 and so cutting the ANC some slack when the country really, really didn't need it cut. And we could have added one of the lower-profile higher-powered white guys in the federal executive, whose lurking presence behind the scenes seems to be the real reason the DA has hit its glass ceiling a little lower than it might have.

But no, one is enough. Given the calibre of plunderers and scoundrels they're up against in this book, the addition of any boys in blue would simply be overplaying our quest for equal-opportunities ideology bashing. Because let's not forget that, through all the simmering resentment at the success of the DA across so much of mainstream and social media, it remains the lone political party in South Africa to show consistent accountability over time and produce world-class standards of governance where it retains power. Unqualified audits, reliable services, an effective Covid-19 response – imagine an entire country run along those lines. The square-in-round-hole moral equating of the opposition party with the governing party, observable online on an almost daily basis, is so often absolute rubbish. It's almost as if it's regarded as a fresh manifestation of the National Party, even though that particular hangover of the apartheid era was, if anyone's forgotten, absorbed into the ANC.

This is not to suggest that the DA can, or should, ever become the governing party in South Africa. There are a couple of damn good reasons why the majority of the population repeatedly vote in the ANC despite its glaringly abusive track record after 26 years of "freedom", and conversely why they don't vote in the DA. The principal understanding here, as frustrating as it is for some commentators to accept, is a fairly rudimentary psychological one: people don't just get over 350 years of colonial and apartheid rule, and the DA's popularity among the white population is an understandable cause for mistrust. (For those still struggling with this slow pace of change, it is perhaps worth re-reading the Adam Catzavelos entry.)

Meanwhile, Helen Zille has, after a stellar decade in the 2000s, made some repeated royal stuff-ups in the 2010s. Again, the principal understanding here is a fairly rudimentary psychological one: she's got a great big ego and she just can't help herself.

We're talking about the Twitter stuff.

Back in the 1970s, Helen Zille was a young reporter at the *Rand Daily Mail*, where she had undergone classic, hands-on journalism training in the age before Google. In her own words, "We had to learn to take accurate notes, and hear that every story has two sides. Both had to be reflected, succinctly but accurately. We also learnt that there was rarely 'moral equivalence' between two arguments: one side is usually closer to the truth than the other. We had to learn to evaluate this without letting our personal prejudices enter the picture."

It was this training that she applied in her investigation into the death in detention of Steve Biko in September 1977. Following a tip-off, she flew to Port Elizabeth, chased witnesses, deduced facts and compiled enough evidence for her editor, Allister Sparks, to publish the story that would reveal to the world that Biko had been murdered by the apartheid state. It was classic rational journalism that reported an important objective truth, and Zille was the young epitome of such a journalist.

Decades later, she found Twitter.

While many news editors see Twitter as a modern-day wire service – to the detriment of all humanity *(see Jack Dorsey)* – there is nothing journalistic about the thing. It is the absolute inverse of important objective truth; rather, it's where truth goes to die and subjective lunacy reigns supreme. Aunty Helen, however, thinks she's got it waxed. She thinks she can play the game and she's justified in doing so because it allows her to connect with her followers. Ultimately, she feels, her continued active presence on Twitter is a net positive for her and the DA.

The first problem is that people on Twitter aren't real. Astoundingly often, this is true at face value. In January 2020, Zille revealed that she had discovered that some 600,000 of her 1.4 million followers were bots. They literally were not real people. But even the users who aren't bots and sock puppets aren't real either, in the sense of being representative of real people in the street. The ones doing all the replying and liking and retweeting are the attention-seekers and the trolls, the bullies and the deranged. Swimming in bad faith, they are, to paraphrase Ricky Gervais, the type of people who write on toilet walls.

And yet there they are, blowing things up, including Zille's reputation and, by immediate association, the DA's. All the while, everyone else in the bubble looks on slack-jawed thinking this is the crux of our political narrative, and then the news editors make it so by reporting on it.

In 2012, Zille was assailed for using the word "refugees" in a tweet in a disparaging way. In 2014, she had a meltdown on journalist Carien du Plessis. In 2015, Eusebius McKaiser had a meltdown on her. In 2017, she caused a furore for tweeting about the positive aspects of colonialism. In 2018, having been suspended for the previous debacle, she again tweeted about colonialism.

What was the full context of all these tweets? Who cares? Certainly not those furiously commenting and retweeting and reworking the narrative to their own ends and painting her as "an unrepentant racist".

In February 2020, the penny finally dropped. Following a string of appalling comments in response to a picture she had tweeted of her adopted black grandchild, Zille made the call to quit Twitter for good. The fact that she had placed a picture of her grandchild on Twitter in the first place is an indication of just how tenuous her grasp on the workings of social media is. But the message had now come in loud and clear. She tweeted as much.

> "Twitter has degenerated into a platform for irrationality and mob-lynching. Everything that can be distorted and twisted for a hate-filled agenda, is used for the purpose of manufacturing outrage and inflicting maximum damage."

> "For a long time I have sought to promote Twitter as a platform for rational and civil debate, but it clearly is not possible. It has degenerated into a space of distortion, de-contextualisation, demonisation, de-legitimation and double standards."

> "Instead of democratising debate, it has severely curtailed freedom of speech and discussion. It emboldens your enemies and silences your friends."

Finally, she'd worked it out. The basics of Twitter as they had been for a decade or so. And so she was gone… until she came back. Because, like a cadre at a tenderpreneur's buffet, she just couldn't help herself.

> "If we have to spend time explaining, contextualising and defending comments on social media, we are losing ground in our real fight."
>
> *John Steenhuisen, June 2020*

By June she was in hot water again, this time for comparing the number of racist laws today versus during apartheid (what could possibly go wrong?). Yet again her party was distracted from doing real work, and yet again fuel could be added to the DA-as-racist fire.

Whatever your take on the DA – whether your love it, hate it or are genuinely neutral – it is critical for a functioning democracy to have a real opposition. Indeed, there is no such thing as a functioning democracy without a real opposition. *(See David Mabuza.)* Helen Zille was the politician who did more than any to make this a viable reality at the 2009 and 2014 elections. Now, every time she tweets, her party quivers.

Quite amazingly, this intelligent and once-brilliantly effective politician *still* hasn't worked out that old-school journalistic values of rational discussion and objective truth do not apply online, let alone on Twitter. Her obsession with tweeting adheres worryingly closely to that famous definition of insanity – doing the same thing over and over and expecting a different result. How do we explain it? Certainly, it appears to manifest as an addiction, a compulsive fascination with a medium that defies her best attempts to master it. A metaphor for obsessive control, perhaps?

Zille's argument for being on Twitter might be something like a teenager justifying her joyriding in her parents' car. *I'm a good driver,* she would say, *I didn't crash – the bad driver crashed into me!* But, Helen, if you weren't joyriding in the first place, there wouldn't have been an accident. And if you didn't *keep* joyriding, there wouldn't be more accidents that keep getting you and your team into ever more trouble. Because that's what it is, isn't it – joyriding? Taking your ego out for a spin?

Helen, step out of the car, put the phone away and, please, get back to the *real* and *important* politics.

Jacob Zuma

b. 12 April 1942

"JZ"; "Number One"; "Baba"; "uBaba ka Duduzane";
"Msholozi"; "Butternut Head"; "Teflon President";
"one who laughs while causing you harm"

Dishonourable mentions: everyone else in this book

PROFESSOR HENRY PEARSON, the first director of Kirstenbosch Botanical
Gardens (1913-1916), is buried beside an Atlas cedar in the gardens on
the eastern slopes of Table Mountain. The epitaph on his gravestone reads:

"If ye seek his monument, look around you."

This is a localised take on a more famous inscription, on the tomb
of Christopher Wren, the polymath architect who designed St Paul's
Cathedral and many of the other great churches of London, and is

buried in one of the corners of St Paul's crypt. His epitaph, translated from Latin, reads:

> "Here in its foundations lies the architect of this church and city, Christopher Wren, who lived beyond ninety years, not for his own profit but for the good of the public. Reader, if you seek his monument, look around you."

It's sort of exhausting, in the penultimate chapter of this book, to find ourselves facing the *Meneer* himself, the Big Daddy of State Capture, the Godfather of Graft, Number One, Jacob Zuma. To suggest that his legacy is the contents of this book is not untrue, but let's be honest. This book is but a wafer-thin mint in Mr Zuma's buffet of malfeasance. And we're full.

So, if you seek his monument, look around.

Zuma has utterly trashed his own legacy, which was there for the taking – a courageous man who did a ten-year stretch on Robben Island and then went straight back into the ANC and the MK in South Africa, Mozambique and Zambia. It's a genuinely interesting story, which we wrote about a decade back in *50 People Who Stuffed Up South Africa* – but in the light of what was to come, it is not unreasonable to wonder what it was he struggled for.

Zuma has committed great and lasting crimes against the people of this country. On his watch, and with overt and shameless intent, he oversaw the sale of the state to malicious actors. He set out to do this from the beginning not through some great plan, because Zuma never had a plan beyond surviving, getting rich and looking after those close to him. So it just happened. He was simply unconcerned about it happening, and about who would get hurt. He deliberately and nonchalantly created the circumstance in which corruption would flourish, utterly uninterested in what that actually meant.

Well, now we have some idea.

Zuma will always take shelter in the fact that the scale of his crimes is unknowable. If he ever goes to jail, it will be for a trifling detail resulting from some long-distant, comparatively minor crime – the Arms Deal, what a lark! – and we will simply have to take solace from his incarceration, if not in the detail of his conviction. And the man is, at the time of writing in November 2020, 18 months from his 80th birthday, so justice in the earthly realm is still far from certain. Then again, Mugabe got to 95.

How much opprobrium do we heap onto his shameful epitaph? The consequences of the appalling violence of corruption are not just ongoing deprivation, but worsening deprivation, and the theft of millions of people's opportunity to attain some level of dignity in life? How is this to be quantified? If not in court, then in our national memory, ought he not to be held accountable for all the deprivation caused by all the crimes of corruption committed in all the departments of the state in all his nine years as president?

It's not as if we can count the corpses – God knows how many can be attributed to his catastrophic degradation of education, health, transport and policing in this country, not to mention the years of living lost by keeping people poor. In any case, the Zuma corpses will continue to pile up, because South Africa will live with the consequences of this time for decades, possibly many decades.

Too much hyperbole? We don't think so. Under his watch, unemployment soared and the national debt ballooned to more than 55% of GDP (now more than 90% of GDP on the back of Covid-19) – which would be less horrendous if the borrowed cash wasn't simply looted offshore the moment it landed. Today, in late 2020, South Africa sits with debt of R4 trillion. Let's write this so that even Jacob Zuma can say it: that's four-thousand-billion rand. This will, the treasury says, rise to five-thousand-five-hundred-billion rand by 2024.

The general estimates – for estimates are all we will ever get – now reckon that something like R1.5 trillion was lost to state capture. In isiZuma, that's one-thousand-five-hundred-thousand-million-zillion rand. And in reality, as we've noted to some degree already, it really is an unknowable number. How do you make sense of the destruction of potential, the absence of what might have been?

What do we have for this debt? Well, some people in Dubai are very happy. Luxury car sales went along at a clip during the Zuma Years, though they have rather collapsed since. We've got some trains that don't fit on our rails and we've got Medupi, which might have been the world's biggest coal-fired power station but which, those in the know say, will never work at full capacity because it is so poorly built.

The currency has tanked, the debt is junk and growth is dead. The institutions are gutted, the municipalities are bankrupt, the roads are ruined, the railways destroyed, the airliners grounded, the energy infrastructure in tatters. Our hospitals are death factories, schools produce illiterate and innumerate citizens, and the police are overwhelmed. We are one dry year from a genuinely frightening water crisis in Johannesburg and Pretoria that would make Cape Town's travails look like a picnic.

We could go on. But we have already – take your pick from almost any page in the book.

Most tragically, these manifestations of the workings of the state capture machine impose a worse life on the people Zuma was elected to help, people already dealing with the festering intergenerational wounds of colonialism and apartheid.

Thus Jacob Zuma's garden, his cathedral, is the countless unknowable indignities, suffering and pain he has imposed on his fellow citizens.

Mosebenzi Zwane

Minister of Mineral Resources (2015-2018);
Gupta appointee; state capture pawn; cautionary tale

Dishonourable mentions: the Guptas, Ace Magashule,
Duduzane Zuma, Jacob Zuma

BUT WAIT! THERE'S ONE MORE.

Jacob Zuma is not the final entry in this book, as he was in *50 People Who Stuffed Up South Africa*, because we point-blank refuse to give the last word to a guy who so royally shafted our country in his time in charge. As a nation, we are still psychologically and economically processing the traumatic extended clusterfuck that was the Zuma Years, and we will be for a long time to come. For there to be any hope of a recovery, any chance for us to "fix our shit", as Nando's would put it, we need to be able to see a hopeful future. And for that we can consider, in brief, the trajectory of our former Minister of Mineral Resources Mosebenzi Zwane.

Having navigated the oceans of capture and corruption to arrive at these late pages, we are less interested in the twisting rivers of Zwane's misdeeds than what his future may hold. A quick summary, then.

As Free State MEC for Agriculture in 2012, Zwane was involved in the cynical machinations of the Vrede/Estina dairy project, which the Gupta Leaks have exposed as a front for laundering money from the provincial government to offshore Gupta companies. This was the cash-cow dairy farm without actual cows that paid for a R30 million wedding in Sun City in 2013. *(See The Guptas.)* Zwane was thanked for his efforts with a misspelt invite to the wedding in question and a promotion to minister of Mineral Resources in 2015, despite having no actual experience in the mining sector and having been made a member of the National Assembly a mere three weeks before getting that particular job. When people talk of Gupta-appointed Cabinet ministers, there is no clearer case – before it happened, his CV was sent to Tony Gupta and from Big Tony to Duduzane Zuma. We don't feel the need to call in Gerrie Nel to connect the dots. Zwane did what he was there to do, most notably in pushing through the sale of the Optimum coal mine from Glencorp to Tegeta, a company majority-owned by the Guptas and Duduzane Zuma. Tegeta went on to receive "non-competitive contracts with inflated rates" from Eskom to the value of R11.7 billion. *(See Brian Molefe.)* There were many other shenanigans.

Zwane subsequently claimed in Parliament that he had not met the Guptas or any of their associates since becoming a Cabinet member, a lie that was thoroughly debunked by the Gupta Leaks. Turns out they had put him up in the Oberoi hotel in Dubai – their glitzy international hotel of choice for impressing impressionable South African politicians – for a debriefing after his trip to Switzerland to negotiate the Optimum sale.

As with all the higher-profile Gupta accomplices, their own lives took a dramatic turn for the worse in December 2017 when, to their collective horror, their patron Jacob Zuma lost his grip on power. Zwane was one of the first ministers to go, booted from Cabinet the following February, within two weeks of Cyril Ramaphosa assuming the presidency.

Even before then, the case against Zwane was so evident that the Organisation Undoing Tax Abuse (OUTA) saw fit to lay charges of treason against him in July 2017, calling for a minimum sentence of ten years. Perhaps of more concern for Zwane, though, was the news in August 2020 that he had been named as one of 12 individuals who have had a civil suit launched against them by Eskom and the Special Investigating Unit for the recovery of R3.8 billion related to the purchase of the Optimum coal mine.

Now, as the NPA ever-so-slowly starts picking off the beneficiaries of state capture, one wonders what Zwane thinks of his arrangement with the Guptas and Duduzane Zuma and those who ran with them during the heady years of Saxonwold visits and staying in five-star hotels and feeling like a mover and a shaker as they sold out the country. As of writing Zwane was, amazingly – or not-so-amazingly, really, as we have worked out by now – still a member of the all-powerful ANC National Executive Committee. And yet, one imagines that his collar is feeling rather tight these days.

The first entry of this book included mention of Shamila Batohi, head of the NPA under the new and supposedly self-correcting regime of Cyril Ramaphosa. This last entry ends with Zwane, a corruption case gifted on a plate for any prosecutor looking to make a difference. Will Batohi take it? And, if she does, and Mosebenzi Zwane (along with his friends) comes to serve as a cautionary tale for those politicians considering selling out their fellow citizens for a quick buck, what effect might that have on our future? As a cathartic measure of justice served to South African citizens recovering from the hammering we've taken in the 2010s, might this be the tonic we need for a brighter decade ahead? Might we have a real chance at fixing our shit?

Bibliography

BOOKS

Animal Farm by George Orwell (Penguin, 2013) • *Blessed By Bosasa* by Adriaan Basson (Jonathan Ball, 2019) • *Fighting For The Dream* by RW Johnson (Jonathan Ball, 2019) • *Gangster State* by Pieter-Louis Myburg (Penguin, 2019) • *Is It Just Me Or Is Everything Kak? The Zuma Years* by Tim Richman (Two Dogs, 2016) • *Not Without A Fight: The Autobiography* by Helen Zille (Penguin, 2016) • *Paper Tiger: Iqbal Survé And The Downfall of Independent Newspapers* by Alide Dasnois and Chris Whitfield (NB Publishers, 2019) • *Ramaphosa's Turn: Can Cyril Save South Africa?* by Ralph Mathekga (Tafelberg, 2018) • *SA Politics Unspun* by Stephen Grootes (Two Dogs, 2013) • *So, For The Record: Behind The Headlines In An Era of State Capture* by Anton Harber (Jonathan Ball, 2020) • *The A-Z of South African Politics: People, Parties & Players* by Kashiefa Ajam, Kevin Ritchie, Lebogang Seale, Janet Smith and Thabiso Thakali (Jacana, 2019) • *The President's Keepers: Those Keeping Zuma In Power And Out of Prison* by Jacques Pauw (Tafelberg, 2017) • *The Rise Or Fall of South Africa* by Frans Cronje (Tafelberg, 2020) • *We Have A Game Changer: A Decade of Daily Maverick* by Francesca Beighton, Tudor Caradoc-Davies and Tiara Walters (Maverick 451, 2019) • *We Have Now Begun Our Descent* by Justice Malala (Jonathan Ball, 2015)

REPORTS

"Commission of Inquiry Into Tax Administration and Governance by SARS Final Report" (Judge R Nugent, 2018) • "Money Down the Drain: Corruption in South Africa's Water Sector" by Mike Muller (Corruption Watch and the Water Integrity Network, March 2020) • "Race Relations in South Africa: Reasons for Hope 2019" (The South African Institute of Race Relations, 2019) • "Radio and Listenership Report: Commercial and PBS" (Broadcast Research Council of South Africa, March 2020) • "Report of the Ministerial Task Team Appointed by Minister Angie Motshekga to Investigate Allegations Into the Selling of Posts of Educators by Members of Teachers Unions and Departmental Officials in Provincial Education Departments" (18 May 2016) • "Secure in Comfort: A Report of the Public Protector" (2014) • "State Capture: An Entirely New Type of Corruption" by Judith February (The Institute for Security Studies, September 2019) • "The Corporations and Economic Crime Report Volume 2: The Auditors" (Open Secrets, 2020)

PODCASTS & FILMS

Influence, directed by Diana Neille and Richard Poplak (2020) • *The Social Dilemma*, directed by Jeff Orlowski (Netflix, 2020) • *Welcome To The Cult Factory: A Conversation With Tristan Harris* (September 2020, Sam Harris podcast with Tristan Harris)

WEBSITES

act.represent.us/sign/electoral-college • amabhungane.org • brcsa.org.za • businesslive.co.za • cgdev.org • citizen.co.za • dailymaverick.co.za • economictimes.indiatimes.com • ewn.co.za • fastcompany.com • forensicsforjustice.org • gsb.uct.ac.za • gupta-leaks.com • htxt.co.za • iol.co.za • irr.org.za • latestnewssouthafrica.com • mg.co.za • mybroadband.co.za • news24.com • nicspaull.com • nytimes.com • politicsweb.co.za • polity.org.za • reuters.com • sahistory.org.za • salon.com • savetherhino.org • section27.org.za • spectator.co.uk • statista.com • talkwalker.com • theguardian.com • thesouthafrican.com • timeslive.co.za • twitter.com • youtube.com

Acknowledgements

We've included them in the content itself, but heartfelt acknowledgement goes to the journalists whose digging, dot-connecting and defying of the odds allows us to write a book like this from the comfort of our desks. We've mentioned some by name (from p23), but thank you to all who have bravely searched for and reported on the truth, especially in the last ten years.

Many people have provided invaluable assistance in the writing of our book in the latter months of a crazy, complicated year. To all of you, we offer our deep gratitude, more so given the circumstances. The end result is that much better for your input. The mistakes that remain are ours alone, for which we apologise.

To those involved in putting it all together, thank you for your brilliant, efficient, warm-hearted work.

Of course, to Jonathan, thank you as ever. And to Eleanora, you are the greatest pleasure to work with.

Finally, to our long-suffering families – did we mention what a crazy and complicated year it's been? – thank you for standing by us as we rattled along towards the finish line late of a night and early in the morning. We will be better in the decade ahead, promise.

ALSO AVAILABLE

PRAISE FOR THE FRANCHISE